Comparative Evaluation of Long-term Care Policies for the Elderly in the EU

European University Studies

Europäische Hochschulschriften

Publications Universitaires Européennes

Series XXXI

Political Science

Reihe XXXI Série XXXI

Politikwissenschaft

Sciences politiques

Vol./Bd. 476

PETER LANG

Frankfurt am Main · Berlin · Bern · Bruxelles · New York · Oxford · Wien

Jürgen Holdenrieder

Comparative Evaluation of Long-term Care Policies for the Elderly in the EU

PETER LANG
Europäischer Verlag der Wissenschaften

Bibliographic Information published by Die Deutsche Bibliothek

Die Deutsche Bibliothek lists this publication in the Deutsche Nationalbibliografie; detailed bibliographic data is available in the internet at <http://dnb.ddb.de>.

ISSN 0721-3654
ISBN 3-631-51597-9
US-ISBN 0-8204-6514-3

www.peterlang.de

For my Granddad

Contents

List of Figures and Tables

List of Abbreviations

AA	Attendance Allowance
ABRAPA	Association Bas-Rhinoise d`Aide aux Personnes Âgées
ACOSS	Agence Centrale des Organismes de Sécurité Sociale
ACTP	Allocation Compensatrice pour Tierce Personne
ADL	Activity of Daily Life
ADMR	Association du Service à Domicile
AGGIR	Autonomie, Gérontologie, Groupe Iso-Ressources
AOK	Allgemeine Ortskrankenkasse
APA	Allocation Personnalisée d`Autonomie
AWBZ	Law on Special Medical Expenses
BKK	Betriebskrankenkasse
BSHG	Federal Social Assistance Law
CAF	Caisses Locales d`Allocation Familiales
CCAS	Centre Communaux d`Action Sociale
CLIC	Centre Locale Information Conseil
CNAMTS	Caisse Nationale d`Assurance Maladie des Travailleurs Salariés
CNAF	Caisse Nationale d`Allocations Familiales
CNAV	Caisse Nationale d`Assurance vieillesse des Travailleurs Salariés
CPAM	Caisses Primaires d`Assurance Maladie
CRAM	Caisses Régionales d`Assurance Maladie
CRIMS	Conseil Regional des Institutions de Soins Médicaux et Sociaux
CSG	Contribution Sociale Généralisée
DDASS	Direction Départmentale de l`Assurance Sanitaire et Sociale
DM	German Marks
DSS	Department of Social Security
EC	European Commission
EEC	European Economic Community
EU	European Union
Eurostat	Statistical Office of the European Communities
FR	French Francs
GDP	Gross Domestic Product
GIR	Groupe-Iso-Ressource
GP	General Practitioner
ICA	Invalid Care Allowance
I-ADL	Instrumental Activity of Daily Life
NHS	National Health Service
NI	National Insurance
OECD	Organisation for Economic Co-operation and Development
P-ADL	Personal Activity of Daily Life
PED	Prestation Expérimentale Dépandance
PSD	Prestation Spécifique Dépendance

SERPS	State Earnings Related Pension Scheme
SGB	Social Welfare Legislation
SGB XI	Care Insurance Act
SSD	Social Service Departments
UK	United Kingdom
URSSAF	Union Locales de Recouvrement des Cotisations de Sécurité Sociale et d`Allocations Familiales
WHO	World Health Organisation
ZFW	Law on Mutual Health Insurance
€	Euro
£	British Pounds

Acknowledgements

There have been a number of people throughout the duration of the study (which was submitted in a similar form to the University of Ulster in the UK for the degree of Doctor of Philosophy) who have provided support, encouragement and guidance. I owe a particular word of thanks to the following:

Professor Denise McAlister and Professor Colin Knox, my PhD supervisors, whose continuing guidance, advice and patience have been both helpful and encouraging. Their prompt and detailed comments on the preliminary chapters and general expertise in the field of research have all contributed to the completion of the final draft of this study.

Professor Albrecht Eschermann from the University of Applied Sciences in Augsburg for encouraging and supporting me in undertaking this research.

The European Union for providing financial support for this research.

The experts from different EU countries who have participated in the empirical investigations of my study, for their time and very constructive comments with which they have significantly contributed to the success of this research.

Mr. Maurice Hallworth for his valuable linguistic recommendations throughout the duration of my graduate studies.

My colleagues at the AWO Ulm for their help, support and understanding.

My family and friends for their continued support, patience and encouragement always and especially throughout this research.

Finally, I would like to thank Susanne for her invaluable support, motivation, love and understanding.

Abstract

A combination of demographic, social and macro-economic developments have put long-term care schemes in nearly all EU countries under severe pressure they were not intended to cope with. Adopting a cross-national comparative approach and combining existing literature with empirical findings, this exploratory study provides standardised information on the organisation and financing of long-term care for the elderly in the Union, and evaluates the respective merits of selected schemes (i.e. France, Germany and the UK) in meeting emerging pressures. It discusses the advantages and disadvantages of individual schemes using 'equity' and efficiency' criteria as an evaluation framework. Based on this evaluation, it offers reflections that may serve as a starting-point for policy strategies.

The information presented is drawn largely from semi-structured telephone interviews and documents. Qualitative data collected from key French, German and UK stakeholders provides the main basis for detailed country-specific research and cross-national comparisons.

With regard to the institutions responsible for the administration of long-term care the study found that in countries with a tradition of tax-funded health care provision, the creation of partnership arrangements between health- and long-term care administrations, or even better, the integration of different services from the two are likely to promote co-ordination and efficiency. In countries with an insurance tradition, the introduction of separate long-term care insurance is likely to promote co-ordination and efficiency. In relation to provision in terms of equity and efficiency, it seems advisable that the services are provided by a mix of private, voluntary, non-profit and public bodies. In terms of access, it appears both efficient and equitable to use a fixed set of standardised eligibility criteria on a national basis (including a standardised means test which excludes no one completely, simply on the ground of income and capital) and to provide a well-balanced number of clearly fixed and limited long-term care benefits and services, the funding of which should be spread across the whole population by some sort of national public scheme that works on a 'pay-as-you-go' basis.

Part I

1 Introduction

The main aims of this study on long-term care for elderly people in the European Union countries are:

- To provide standardised information on the financing of long-term care for the elderly and on the organisational structures within which care is provided in the EU;
- To analyse in detail how selected EU countries intend to provide domiciliary long-term care for elderly people within a context of increasing pressures on the demand for and the supply of long-term care. In this context, existing differences and similarities are brought to light;
- To provide an empirically-based assessment of each country's scheme, including possible options for dealing with the difficulties that have revealed themselves within the schemes;
- To explore a range of policy strategies for the future provision of long-term care, analysing and synthesizing evidence from the countries empirically studied and combining these findings with the extremely limited amount of scientific literature published; and
- To examine the relationship between the current individual schemes and welfare state models.

To introduce the rest of the work, this introductory Chapter first of all offers an overview of the complex issues currently confronting long-term care policy-makers in the EU. A definition of terms is provided together with a study-specific delimitation of the different institutional and human resources that provide relevant services for those in need. Following from these considerations, the purpose and structure of Part I of the study is outlined.

1.1 The public policy issue

In general, all EU countries are experiencing similar problems with regard to the future: As a result of a decline in the population, i.e. diminishing birth-rates, societies are growing older. Due to this, the proportion of the elderly age group is increasing. In relation to this an improvement of life expectancy at birth is also taking place (See, for example, Eisen, 1995; European Commission, 2001). Over the period 2000 to 2045, the EU average rate of growth in the proportions of total populations aged 65 or older will be approximately 73.5% (Eurostat data bank 2002a and 2002b).

As the elderly constitute the majority of disabled people in need of care (See, for example, Wiener, Illston and Hanley, 1994; Edvartsen, 1996), we can imagine that these population trends will lead to an increase in the levels of national expenditure for long-term care services. There are a number of diseases that can cause disability in the elderly. According to an international recognised study by Wiener and his colleagues, "Alzheimer's disease, osteoporosis, heart disease, multiple sclerosis and strokes are just a few of many. Long-term care is the help needed to cope, and sometimes to survive, when physical or mental disabilities impair the capacity to perform the basic tasks of everyday life, such as eating, bathing, dressing, and housekeeping" (Wiener, Illston and Hanley, 1994, p. 1). A study carried out for the European Commission (1999) stated that about 15% per cent of people aged 65 and over in the EU as a whole are in need of long-term care.

These above-mentioned demographic developments could be described as the demand side of long-term care. Besides, there are difficult trends on the supply side that aggravate the circumstances (Compare Eisen, 1995). Over recent decades, long-term care for the elderly in need has been predominantly a family task in most EU countries (Rostgaard and Fridberg, 1998) and, at the turn of the millennium, the informal sector still is the largest provider. Nevertheless, caring for the disabled within the family, so-called informal care, is on the decline and is no longer adequate (See, for example, Wittenberg and Sandhu and Knapp, 2002). Due to the increasing tendency towards small or one-generation families, more women are entering the work force and there is a growing number of elderly people who live alone. For example, it is expected that by the year 2010, about one-third of people aged 65 and over will be living in single households (European Commission, 2001). For more details see Chapter 2 of this study.

In addition to the difficulties arising from the diminishing supply of informal care, there are also new and difficult developments in the nature of the supply. The content of the care provided is also changing (Hutten and Kerkstra, 1996). For example, the enormous technological development over the recent decades has generated new care treatments for conditions for which previously there was no treatment. Additionally some existing forms of treatment have been replaced or supplemented systems (Saltman and Figueras, 1997). As a consequence, the range of the forms of treatment currently available, and the quality of services provided, have also increased in many EU countries. These factors are very positive developments. However they have also contributed to the current pressure on long-term care schemes (Saltman and Figueras, 1997).

Another notable reason for the increasing difficulties where government financing is concerned, is the fact that only a small fraction of long-term care is paid for by private insurance (Garber, 1995). Apart from that, public policy intervention is also necessary in the private insurance market. It is, for example, necessary to counter certain policy tendencies of insurance companies, such as accepting only mainly healthy individuals or those who have other characteristics predictive of long life, as policy-holders (OECD, 1994a). This view is also represented by an earlier study on economics of care for the elderly by Pacolet and Wilderom (1991). The study points out, however, that "no private insurer is willing to guarantee a certain level of services. Also private insurers exclude applicants likely to need long-term care and impose certain conditions on the type of care that will be provided. In addition, premiums are very high. The private sector approach is not affordable for the majority of the elderly" (p. 15). That the increasing need for care has to be mainly covered by public financing has also been shown by different recent studies on the long-term care for the disabled elderly (See, for example, Royal Commission on Long-term Care, 1999; Wittenberg, Sandhu and Knapp, 2002).

The above illustrated changes in the demand for and supply of long-term care and other social protection services seem to have strongly contributed to the paradox condition that in spite of the fact that EU economies are wealthier than ever before and real income, apart from brief interruptions, has continued to grow, the demands on systems of social protection, maybe in particular the dependency on public expenditure for the disabled elderly, has risen even more rapidly. Moreover, as this increasing need has occurred in an extremely difficult context in which, in most parts of the Union, Governments actually have given priority to limiting the growth of expenditure and consolidating public finances, pressure has been exerted on the individual systems they were usually not designed to cope with (See, for example, European Commission, 1998). Besides the fact that most EU countries have cut back their public spending in order to reduce their budget deficit to the required level for the adoption of the new European currency (Euro) (Kokot, 1997), these proceedings have become necessary because of macro-economic difficulties in most EU countries (See, for example, Saltman, Figueras and Sakellarides, 1998). The greatest of these difficulties is the fact that unemployment has increased markedly above that experienced in the earlier post-war years, which means that a significant proportion of people of working age have been unable to pay social protection contributions, tax income is steadily declining and the need for unemployment benefit or social assistance is growing (European Commission, 1998). In 2000, unemployment was extremely high in most EU countries, the highest rate being recorded in Spain with 14.1%. Compared to the average (8.2%) for the EU, a relatively low level of unemployment was recorded for Luxembourg (2.4%) and the Netherlands (3.0%) (Eurostat data bank, 2002c). In addition to these difficulties, another problem is that the ageing of the population is also resulting in the fact that the demand for such services as long-term care is likely to increase. The condition that the population above the official age of retirement (65 in most countries) has increased in relation to the number of people of working-age, and will rise even more dramatically in the years to come, is at the same time contributing to significant changes in the relation between the numbers of those who are predominantly paying for and the number of those receiving pensions, care services or the like (European Commission, 1998).

As a consequence of this combination of demographic, social and macro-economic developments, which have imposed pressure on the existing long-term care schemes they were not designed to deal with, the challenging question in nearly all countries is how to adapt the individual schemes to the existing circumstances, how best to provide sustainable long-term care funding for good quality care of the elderly and how costs should be shared between the working population (taxpayers) and the individual in need of care. However, while the underlying problems and challenges tend to be similar, the development of necessary reforms in the individual countries is, apart from the above-mentioned macro-economic factor, also strongly influenced by a mix of other contextual factors from outside the schemes itself that usually vary from country to country across the Union (See, for example, Héritier, 1996). The range and number of such factors that influence what governments do or, for that matter, what they choose not to do is very long. Long-term care (social) policy may be influenced by further circumstances, such as a country's history, societal values, legislative basis, type of government and the relative power of stakeholders. Cross-national influences or even cultural and religious values also play a part (Saltman and Figueras, 1997; Saltman, Figueras and Sakellarides, 1998).

Because of the situation outlined above, many governments in the EU have effectively planned or initiated reforms of their own, organising and financing schemes for ensuring the provision of long-term care (OECD, 1996a). In the 1990s, some countries, such as Germany and Austria have formally chosen comprehensive reform programmes: Germany has introduced a new branch of social insurance to cover long-term care (Clasen, 1997) and Austria has implemented an attendance allowance for those in need of care (Plute, 1996). Elsewhere, for instance in Denmark and Sweden, limited reform strategies have been implemented to deal with specific difficulties (OECD, 1996a). However, for all the contextual differences between the individual countries, certain features of the reforms introduced in a particular country have nevertheless been transferred across national borders. For instance, the reform of the long-term care scheme in Germany, based on a social insurance model, has in turn influenced the content of discussions concerning long-term care reforms in other EU countries with insurance-based health schemes, e.g. France and Luxembourg (See, for example, Luxembourg Ministry of Social

Security, 1995; OECD, 1996a). To date, there is little empirical evidence concerning the effectiveness of many reform policies, not just in those countries on the receiving end, but also in countries championing such strategies (Saltman and Figueras, 1997; Österle 1999). The evidence presented in this study may increase the readers' knowledge of the merits of particular long-term care schemes in dealing with future challenges.

1.2 The conceptual framework

An important problem that should be clarified before examining such a global topic as long-term care for the elderly in the EU is finding some operational definitions of the essential terms that will be used. This is necessary because of the non-uniformity of national definitions in the field of research, making it difficult to provide standardised information. In doing this, one main difficulty lies in selecting the central areas upon which to focus attention and, on this basis, establishing criteria that justify excluding all of those areas, which have to be left out. In addressing these problems, at least conceptually, this part of the study concentrates upon four areas of definition that might be of particular importance. First of all, it attempts to provide a definition for 'the elderly' which accords with the aims of this study. Then it looks at possible meanings of the term 'disability'. In a further step, the different 'sectors of long-term care provision' will be discussed and finally, definitions with regard to the services provided as 'long-term care' will be considered.

1.2.1 Ageing defined

At the outset, it is useful to define what is meant by 'the elderly', as there exist a variety of meanings over the years and in different countries. For example, within the framework of the long-term care scheme in the United Kingdom, disability is only classified as age-related, if it occurs at the age of 65 or later for the first time (Fieber, 1997). Such an age-clause does not, for instance, exist in the German scheme (German Ministry of Social Affairs, 1996).

However, the focus in this study is on disabled people aged 65 and over. Those parts of the different long-term care schemes that provide benefits for people under the age of 65 (also children) are not considered. The main motivation for the selection of this age group is that securing the provision of long-term care has become a widely recognised problem because of the demographic changes that have taken place (See, for example, Wiener, Illston and Hanley, 1994; Edvartsen, 1996). Owing to these rising demographic pressures, a decreasing number of the working population has to provide long-term benefits and services for an increasing number of elderly people (OECD, 1996b). Primarily because of the progress in medicine, the older age group also has, and will continue to have, a longer life expectancy. Therefore, the age limit of 65 is, in particular, of interest because it is the most commonly used age criteria where retirement from full-time paid employment in EU countries is concerned. Also the vast majority of people in this age group become eligible for some form of pension on the basis of age alone (Johnson and Falkingham, 1992).

An alternative possibility would be to determine a study-specific measure concerning 'the elderly' not mainly based on the usual age of entry into retirement but from the known incidence of the relationship between increasing age and increases in the levels of chronic disability. In this case, the over-75 group might be most suitable, since after about age 75, the proportion of the population in need of long-term care starts to grow rapidly. Furthermore, there could be plausible grounds for focusing on people aged 80 and over. In this group, additional age-related phenotypes should be identified that may cause disability (Hugman, 1994). As we will see in more detail in Chapter 2, the age of 80 would, moreover, be of interest since it is frequently mentioned in connection with a second demographic change that is under way, the so-called 'secondary ageing process' (OECD, 1996a). This means, that the percentage of the population aged 80 and over will rapidly increase in the next few decades in most EU countries (Eurostat data bank, 2002a).

To summarise, it can be emphasised that any attempts to strictly demarcate 'the elderly' would seem to be quite difficult. However, the focus in this study is on the organisational structures and on the financing of long-term care schemes. Therefore, a definition of 'the elderly' according with the generally common retirement age of 65 in the EU countries, having in mind the change this involves from a potential payer of a social system to a possible receiver, appears sensible to the author, since in particular the financing of a long-term care scheme is strongly dependent on the ratio between the people aged under 65 (working population) and those aged 65 or over. At the same time, the age group to which this study refers is used as a standard in several scientific works. The reports by the Organisation for Economic Co-operation and Development (See, for example, OECD 1996a) and the surveys carried out for the World Health Organisation are examples (See, for example, Saltman and Figueras, 1997). They contain useful information that the present survey might be able to fall back on.

1.2.2 Disability defined

For the purposes of making comparisons between EU countries, it would be beneficial to have a consistent definition of 'disability', that is, the eligibility criteria for benefits and services. The main problem is that there are differences of interpretation in various countries (European Commission, 1999).

The preconditions for the provision of long-term care may, in some countries, be very stringent, while in others there are more flexible legal definitions of 'disability'. This can give rise to a situation where a group of elderly people, who are defined as 'disabled' in one country, may not be legally defined as 'disabled' in another. There is also no uniform agreement on how long one has to be ill before being classified as a 'disabled' person (Kratz and Simpson, 1980; European Commission, 1999). In general it can be said that the conditions for receiving long-term care provision in EU countries are largely based on the physical and on mental condition of the person concerned. In addition, for some long-term care benefits and services, the financial need of the disabled person (or his or her relatives) and the social environment in which he or she lives are likewise decisive factors (European Commission, 1999).

It is worthy of notice that in contrast to several other EU long-term care arrangements, the schemes in Scandinavian countries usually include no standardised assessment procedure for establishing an elderly persons need for long-term care provision (Compare, Gabanyi, May and Schneider, 1992; European Commission, 1999). For example, in Denmark provision is mainly allocated on the basis of an assessment of individual needs, whereby the main criteria for allocation are the inability to perform items of personal care and a need for home-making assistance. In general, the more incapacity there is, the more provision is granted (Lund Pedersen, 1998). In Sweden, there is likewise no specific definition applying to disabled elderly people. The view is taken that as a result of age-related physical and mental changes, the elderly human being simply has needs different from those of younger people and there is a duty to offer public long-term care services of such a kind as to ensure that the individual receives services according to his or her needs and wishes (European Commission, 1999).

In contrast to the Scandinavian approach, Austria, for example, since 1993 has used a standardised definition of 'disability', including fixed sub-divisions. There, 'disability' is said to exist if, because of a physical, mental or psychic handicap or a sensory disorder, the need for regular care and help will or would continue for approximately six months at least. Sub-division into seven degrees of 'disability' is made according to the respective time spent in caring for a patient and is not dependent on medical criteria. As can be seen in the following table, people who are, for instance, in need of care for more than 50 hours a month are classified as being in the first degree of 'disability'. For people who are in practice unable to move, or whose 'disability' is comparable, and are in need of care for more than 180 hours a month are classified as being in the seventh degree of 'disability' (Austrian Federal Ministry of Labour and Social Affairs, 1995; European Commission, 2000).

Table 1 Levels of need for assistance

Degree of disability	Monthly extent of need for care
Level 1	More than 50 hours
Level 2	More than 75 hours
Level 3	More than 120 hours
Level 4	More than 180 hours
Level 5	More than 180 hours, need for an unusually high level of care
Level 6	More than 180 hours, necessity for permanent supervision
Level 7	More than 180 hours, practical immobility or comparable condition

Source: Austrian Federal Ministry of Labour and Social Affairs, 1995

A special 'ADL'-scheme ('De aangepaste Katz-schaal') has been used since 1991 in Belgium for those benefits which are provided within the framework of the health care scheme. 'ADL' stands for 'Activity of Daily Life'. This scheme is a modified form of the one put forward initially by the Australian doctor Katz and his colleagues in deciding who qualifies for benefits of a long-term care scheme (Katz, Ford, Moskowitz, Jackson and Jaffe, 1963). The Belgium scheme that is illustrated below in Table 4 (See p. 9) consists of six questions about physical criteria, two items about mental problems and three about social circumstances. For provisions of domiciliary care, only the physical criteria are taken into account.

Table 2 'De aangepaste Katz-schaal' as criterion of disability

Level	Category	1	2	3	4
N	Bathing	Without help	With some help for lower body parts	With some help for lower and upper body parts	Absolute help for lower and upper body parts
N	Dressing	Without help for dressing and undressing	With some help for lower body parts	With some help for lower and upper body parts	Absolute help for lower and upper body parts
A	Moving	Getting up without mechanical aid or help from a third party	Getting up and sitting down with mechanical aid, crutches for locomotion	Absolute help for getting up and for locomotion	Bedridden or absolutely dependent on a wheelchair for locomotion
A	Toileting	Without help	With some help	Absolute help	Not possible
B	Continence	Continent at urinating and bowel movements	Occasional incontinent at urinating and bowel movements (incl. catheter)	Absolute incontinent at urinating (incl. catheter)	Absolute incontinence at urinating and bowel movements
B	Eating	Without help	With some help for meal preparation	With some help	Only possible with help

Source: Belge Assurance des Mututalités Chrétiennes, 1992

For the determination of the degree of 'disability', the physical disorders are divided into three levels. The first level (N) consists of bathing and dressing, the second level (A), moving and toileting, and the third level (B), continence and eating. The minimum qualification for the benefits and services of the Belgium long-term care scheme is a handicap in both bathing and dressing within the third or fourth categories (level N). Level A requires 'disability' at

Level N and additionally at least one handicap from the third or fourth category of moving and toileting. The same procedure is used for the third level (B), requiring the first (N) and second (A) levels and also at least one handicap from the third or fourth category regarding continence and eating. For 'disabled' people to be accommodated in a nursing home or a similar institution, an examination of their orientation in time and place (Gabanyi, May and Schneider, 1992), and also of their social circumstances is required in addition to meeting the above criteria[1].

In France, for the establishment of the degree and seriousness of a 'disability', the decision-makers at regional level have to orientate themselves towards a scale which mainly focuses on the need an elderly person has in performing different 'ADLs', comprising 'Personal Activities of Daily Life' ('P-ADLs') (e.g. washing, dressing, eating, using the toilet and general mobility) and 'Instrumental Activities of Daily Life' ('I-ADLs') (e.g. shopping and housework). Based on this, it is possible to classify elderly people into one of six degrees of disability (Appendix II, French Decree No. 97-426, 2000; Para. 2 French Law No. 97-60, 2000). With regard to the most important cash benefit ('Attendance Allowance' - 'AA') in the UK which is granted on a national basis to those elderly people who have a frequent and continuing need of a certain amount of help with 'ADLs' (e.g. washing and bathing, preparing food for easy consumption, using the toilet, getting in and out of bed, outdoor walking, dressing, walking, standing and using stairs) or help in avoiding substantial danger (e.g. from falls or due to mental illness or learning disability) (UK Department of Social Security, 1997a).

In addition to the methods outlined to define 'disability' one may consider the frequency in which help for the 'ADLs' is needed (Compare Edvartsen, 1996). This is, for instance, the case in Germany in long-term care insurance. Introduced in 1995, a disabled person is defined as 'an elderly human being that is permanently unable to perform a special number of 'P-ADLs' and 'I-ADLs' due to physical, mental or psychic illness or disability. The degree of 'disability' is defined by the frequency in which help for these activities is needed (German Ministry of Labour and Social Affairs, 1996).

In a synopsis of EU long-term care schemes, one could argue that the most common method in assessing the degree of 'disability', and the eligibility for benefits and services, would be to use inability to perform the 'ADLs' ('P-ADLs' and 'I-ADLs'). 'ADL' criteria, for instance, can be found in the schemes of Belgium, France, Germany and the UK. Although the use of

---

[1] The three levels of the physical disorders from the domiciliary care sector keep their validity for disabled persons who live in a nursing home or a similar institution.

'ADLs' is a positive development, policies in the EU do not use a standard set of such criteria, nor do they generally describe how 'ADLs' are assessed. These differences in defining and measuring 'ADLs' results in large variations in the proportion of elderly people who qualify for services and benefits in the countries concerned.

The growing tendency in some public long-term care schemes in the EU, to assess 'disability' by using measures of 'P-ADLs' and 'I-ADLs' can also be seen in the scientific literature. Unfortunately even in the literature, the establishing of 'ADL' elements are quite broad. An essential difficulty might be to choose such 'ADL' elements, which allow first to include a complete as possible area of the different phenomena of 'disability' and second to put them into different levels. It is beyond the scope of this thesis to review the several 'ADL' measures of the scientific literature or even to make an evaluation. However, the two oldest and best known 'ADL' scales were developed by Katz, Ford, Moskowitz, Jackson and Jaffe (1963) as well as Mahoney and Barthel (1965). Each is considered to address 'P-ADLs', such as bathing, dressing, and toileting. Through the supplementary inclusion of 'I-ADLs', such as shopping and house cleaning, a bridge between 'P-ADLs' and measures of social functioning is represented (McDowell and Newell, 1987).

On the basis of those two 'ADL' scales, for example, essential parts of an international recognised study of the 1990s by Wiener, Illston and Hanley (1994) were constructed. Wiener and his colleagues have analysed the major options for reforming the way long-term care is financed in the United States of America. 'Disabled' individuals are defined as persons who need help, for a health-related reason in performing at least one 'I-ADL' (that is, doing heavy work, doing light work, preparing meals, shopping for groceries or other personal items, getting around inside, walking outside, managing money, and using the telephone), or who need help with at least one of the five 'P-ADLs', for a period of at least ninety days (that is, bathing, dressing, eating, getting in and out of bed, and toileting). Additionally Wiener proposes a division of elderly persons into four degrees of disability.

Of interest is also the definition of 'disability' by the OECD (OECD, 1996a, p. 4), which is partly in agreement with some already offered within this chapter. The disabled are defined as "elderly people whose overall level of functioning is substantially reduced, so that they are likely to require from a third party, or from appliances or the like, in order to carry out the 'Activities of Daily Life'". Not only a number of other studies, but also several public and private long-term care insurance schemes, use similar criteria in determining eligibility for benefits and services (See, for example, Cologne Reinsurance Company, 1995).

To summarise, this discussion has shown that it is not an easy exercise to present a clear and uniform definition of 'disability'. In the author's view, it is even inappropriate to search for a specific meaning within the framework of a cross-national investigation. Too many essential elements of the individual long-term care schemes would be left out if this was done. However, the above section has also indicated that the most widely method of defining 'disability', that is, to lay down the eligibility criteria for long-term care benefits and services, is to use some 'ADL' ('P-ADL' and 'I-ADL') criteria. This seems to be true regarding the individual EU long-term care schemes and scientific literature as well as in the case of private insurance institutions. For these reasons, this study seeks to focus on 'ADL' criteria, wherever this seems to be possible and of benefit. The conclusions presented in the empirical part of this thesis may help in arriving at an accurate definition of 'disability'.

1.2.3 Sectors of long-term care provision

1.2.3.1 Overview

In most EU countries, long-term care benefits and services for disabled elderly people are a very complex policy field in which various providers need to be co-ordinated. In order to reduce this complexity, at least conceptually, it might be useful to distinguish between 'domiciliary care' and 'residential care'. Additionally one should refer to the part played by so-called 'protected dwellings and specialised accommodation units'. The following figure (p. 13) may illustrate this possible classification.

Figure 1 Sectors of long-term care provision

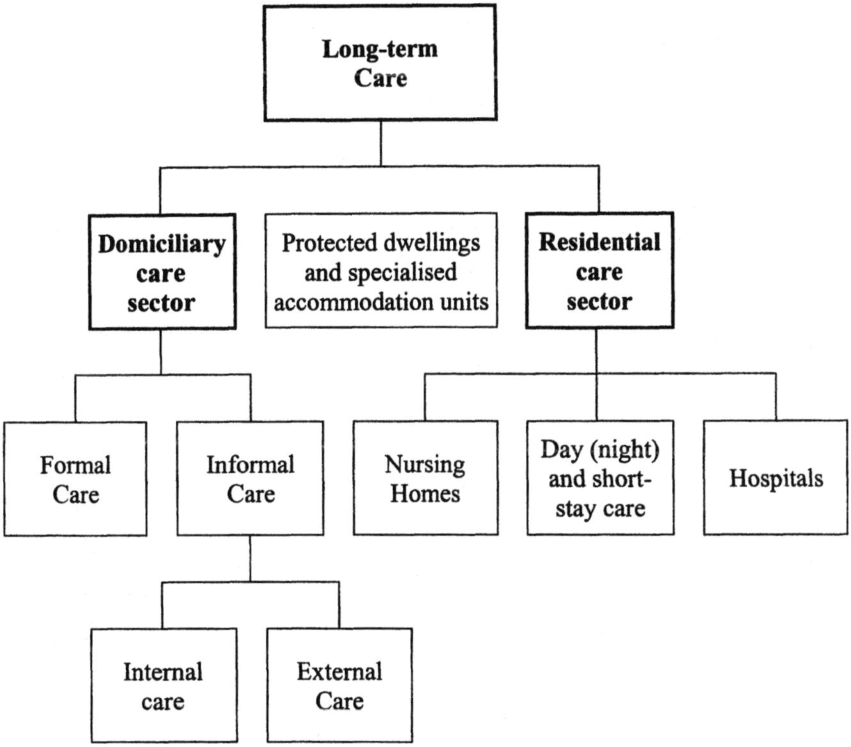

Source: Modification of Garg, 1995

1.2.2.2 Domiciliary care sector

The sector of 'domiciliary care' in recent times, has in most EU countries become even more prominent. The official policy aim is to help disabled elderly people to stay in their own home as long as possible. The reason behind these developments in policy orientation is not very clear (Alber, 1993). Several cross-country investigations on the field of long-term care have noted that recent policy shifts have been driven by rationalisation of governmental expenditures (See, for example, Gabanyi, May and Schneider 1992; Walker, 1993). Although there is little data available to determine the cost-efficiency of various forms of services, different governments appear to be of the opinion that an enlargement of the 'domiciliary care' sector is a favourable opportunity to reduce the increasing number of disabled persons in the sector of residential care and with it the consequential expenditure in the public health service (See, for example, OECD, 1996a). While these financial aspects are far from being clarified, several surveys verify that the majority of those in need of care prefer to stay at home as long as possible (See, for example, Jamieson, 1991; European Commission, 1999).

The field of 'informal domiciliary care' can be sub-divided into internal and external providers of long-term care services. The traditional element of 'informal domiciliary care' is the field of internal care, which is particularly widespread in Southern European countries. Here, the providers of care are those who live with the disabled elderly person in the same household. In the past, these were mostly wives and daughters (OECD, 1994b). The external provision of informal care is met by relatives (who do not live in the same household as the person in need of care), friends, neighbours or networks on a kinship, voluntary or charity basis.

In addition to the field of 'informal domiciliary care' there exists the field of 'formal domiciliary care'. The relevant providers of such care are mainly public, private and voluntary, non-profit organisations (usually contracted by public authorities). These offer partly nursing care (e.g. taking blood pressure, exchanging catheters, giving injections) in addition to personal care and home-making (e.g. bodily cleaning activities, nourishment-related activities, mobility-related activities, home-management related activities and communication) (Jamieson, 1991).

1.2.3.3 Residential care sector

There are number of possibilities which can result in 'residential care' becoming necessary. In most cases the extent of the disability is the decisive factor whether care in a nursing home or a similar institution is necessary or if 'domiciliary care' is adequate. Also the age and the personal circumstances are important elements in the determination of the appropriate type of care. Elderly people can often find themselves alone. This is mainly the case, if the partner is already deceased and possible children are unable or unwilling to take care of their mother or father. Finally the provision of 'domiciliary care' can become difficult because of the patient's domestic surroundings. This might, for example, be the case if, for care that meets the demands of the disabled elderly person, certain building measures are necessary but the house owner will not allow these to be carried out. Thus, 'residential care' becomes necessary.

In the sector of 'residential care' institutions in the EU countries, nursing homes play a prominent role. These are not only the traditional types of nursing homes which provide care for persons with a long-term care illness or disability, but also general homes for the aged which can include a long-term care section. Additionally there exist mixed institutions that offer a combination of both types of accommodation.

The field of short-stay care includes residential care institutions, which offer limited care on a temporary basis. This is primarily considered for short-term needs and crisis situations. For instance this is the case after treatment in a hospital or when the necessary care is not available from the informal provider of care arising from, for example, illness or vacation. Institutions providing day and night care are intended for those disabled persons who cannot be looked after at home for a part of the day or during the night.

The field of hospitals includes those institutions with beds for long-term care. At best these have geriatric sections, which are designed for chronically ill and other elderly persons in need of long-term care (Jani-Le Bris, 1994). Frequently however, disabled persons are accommodated in general medicine departments, which are often unable to provide the necessary specialised care.

1.2.3.4 Protected dwellings and specialised accommodation units

These are different types of 'protected dwellings', which have been introduced in many member states as alternatives to the 'domiciliary' and 'residential' long-term care facilities. They can often be ordinary state-subsidised dwellings, which are renovated and equipped in such a manner that they are suitable for the disabled elderly. For instance, many have an alarm system whether connected to a person who is in charge of the disabled person or to an institution, which can provide assistance in a case of emergency.

There are also several forms of 'specialised accommodation units' in the EU countries. One of which are collective flats, where disabled and non-disabled elderly people live together in a flat. Here the care is based on mutual help. There also exists a scheme where disabled elderly people can live together (up to ten) in so-called minihomes within a community or village, where the care is provided by professional care providers and people within the community.

1.2.3.5 A study specific delimitation

There is a high level of agreement among the EU countries as to the overall objective of relevant policy-makers where long-term care is concerned. This is that disabled elderly people, should, wherever possible, be cared for in their own homes. "This social objective - which has been termed 'Ageing in Place' - " (OECD, 1994a, p. 37) might be the most widespread wish of elderly people themselves as well (See, for example, Scharf and Wenger, 1995). Consequently, governmental long-term policies are more and more focused on 'domiciliary care' instead of 'residential care' (Hutten and Kerkstra, 1996).

Since this study *inter alia* intends to draw some conclusions regarding future developments based on experience with recent implementations in the individual schemes, the above objective needs to be taken into account. Therefore, this study concentrates on 'domiciliary care'. Within the sector of 'domiciliary care', the main focus will be on the field of formal 'domiciliary care'. This weighting appears useful because of the fact that the supply of informal care has markedly decreased over recent years, a process which is expected to continue in the future (Compare, for more details, Chapter 2) and, therefore, may lead to an increasing need for formal 'domiciliary care'. This situation may make new organisational structures and methods of finance necessary.

Since an EU-wide investigation of the sector of 'domiciliary care' alone is a very complex issue, a very detailed analysis of other sectors will have to be left out of consideration. However, for instance, the demand for 'domiciliary care' is frequently influenced by the availability of and accessibility to the 'residential care' sector. Therefore it would not make sense to consider 'domiciliary care' in complete isolation from other services used by disabled elderly people. Thus, the sector of 'residential care' and also so-called 'protected dwellings or specialised accommodation units' will be included in this study, whenever this seems necessary in order to complete the information.

1.2.4 Long-term care defined

After considering possible definitions of 'the elderly' and 'disability' and then having decided to focus on 'domiciliary care', it is necessary as well to define 'long-term care'. There exist, of course, divergence between the EU countries in the services provided as 'long-term care' (Hutten and Kerkstra, 1996). Moreover, in many countries, there are services, which are not described as 'long-term care', although they may perform similar tasks (Jamieson, 1991). In this connection, the areas of responsibility of 'long-term care' providers may in several schemes overlap with those of other services provided in a variety of ways (See, for example, OECD, 1994a). Frequently, one and the same provider makes a range of different services available (Jamieson, 1991). In the light of these difficulties, within the framework of an international comparison, it seems to be insufficient to focus on the specific and different kinds of aid described as 'long-term care' in the individual EU countries.

However, following from the above brief overview of the main difficulties, it is clear that this study has to use a provisionally specific definition, with the consequent restrictions, regarding the kind of aid provided. In order to reduce the complexity described, at least conceptually, it might be useful to classify the different components of 'long-term care' provision into pre-defined categories. Therefore, the following consideration of services is divided into three major fields of aid and is based on a mixture of recent studies by Jamieson (1991) and the OECD (OECD, 1996a):

- Nursing care (i.e., tasks that everywhere are seen as the domain of a qualified nurse, including tasks such as taking blood pressure, exchanging catheters, giving injections, etc.);
- Personal care (i.e., assistance with the 'P-ADLs', including getting into and out of bed, bathing, dressing, eating and toileting); and
- Home-making (i.e., assistance with the 'I-ADLs', including help with shopping, cooking, cleaning, laundry, heating the accommodation, administrative tasks, etc.).

Certain further activities, generally regarded to be part of 'normal life', such as socialising or going for a stroll, should also be seen as part of the field of home-making, even though they are not instrumental activities such as those mentioned above. They are, nevertheless, significant and regarded by several providers as one part of their service (Jamieson, 1991 and OECD, 1996a). Other specific services, for example those provided by general practitioners, physiotherapists, etc., are beyond the scope of this study. Also domestic services exclusively concerned with such assistance as meals-on-wheels are excluded.

Accordingly, in the present study, the above fields of aid are adopted wherever possible. 'Long-term care' will refer to personal care and home-making, although in some schemes this means the study refers to more than one service. Since the main goal of this study concerns help with activities of daily life, nursing care at home will be discussed mainly in so far as it affects the provision and supply of 'long-term care' services (Jamieson, 1991).

An essential point that should additionally be considered within the definition of 'long-term care' is that, because the theme of this study is public policy responses to the 'long-term care' needs of the elderly, purely commercial services should not be included in the definition of 'long-term care services' (personal care and home-making). Ideally, 'long-term care services' are universal services available to all citizens. However, commercial services cannot be entirely excluded from 'long-term care services' because in many countries 'long-term care services' are financed by public authorities even though provided by private companies. What the present study can accept as a criterion is that 'long-term care services' must be controlled and subsidised by state authorities (Compare Antonnen and Sipilä, 1996).

1.3 Summary and format of Part I of this study

This chapter has given a brief overview of the complex issues currently confronting EU long-term care schemes and the consequent difficulties in making necessary policy interventions, to ensure a provision of benefits and services that meet the needs of the disabled elderly and which can be financed. It has been emphasised that there is a steady and nearly EU-wide increase of the proportion of elderly people in the populations of the EU countries. This situation is a dominant feature of the growing pressure on long-term care related expenditure, since it might lead to a rise in the demand for formal long-term care, reinforced by the fact that the role of informal carers, such as relatives and friends, is decreasing in many countries. Besides, various other factors, such as the increasing availability of new and frequently expensive care treatments, or macro-economic difficulties, have contributed to these complicated circumstances.

In order to delimit the complex research area, some operational definitions of the essential terms that are used in this study are discussed in the next part of this introductory Chapter. In this connection, it was first of all decided to focus on persons aged over 65. Following this, consideration was given to how the word 'disability' should be defined. Here it turned out that there is no uniform definition of disability among EU countries and no uniform eligibility criteria for benefits and services in the long-term care schemes. Nevertheless, the investigation has also shown that the most widely used method for defining disability is to use some 'ADL' elements. Consequently, this study will focus on these elements, wherever it seems to be possible and of use. In a subsequent part, the institutional and personnel applications of long-term care services for elderly people have been reviewed in some detail. Thereby it was decided to concentrate on domiciliary care, since it is an objective largely shared by the appropriate EU policy-makers, that elderly people in need of long-term care should be enabled to stay in their own homes, wherever this is possible. Finally, the services provided as long-term care have been examined in some detail. Here it was decided that for the purposes of this study, long-term care would be taken to refer to personal care (i.e., assistance with the 'P-ADLs', including getting in and out of bed, bathing, dressing, eating and using the toilet) and home-making (i.e., assistance with the 'I-ADLs', including help with shopping, cooking, cleaning, laundry, heating the accommodation, administrative tasks, etc.), and that the care services must be controlled and subsidised by state authorities, wherever it is possible for the individual countries to do this.

The subsequent chapters of Part I of the study are organised in the following manner:

The next Chapter offers a more detailed explanation of the main reasons for the increasing needs in the long-term care schemes themselves. Firstly, demographic changes are reviewed, as they affect the current and future generations of elderly people who consequently represent a very important factor in the demand for long-term care. Since there is no automatic link between the demography of a country and the demand for long-term care, it requires knowledge of the state of health of elderly people in general, and this is examined later. In addition, difficult trends on the supply side of long-term care, particularly the reasons for the decreasing ability of the family to care for the disabled - so-called informal care - is analysed within this part of the study.

As was already partly illustrated in the introductory chapter, EU countries differ in the structure of their long-term services and in their policies with regard to support needed by their elderly people. This is not only based on the complex context surrounding the demand for and supply of individual long-term care schemes. Instead, it might also be based on the fact that the characteristics of the schemes are also the result of a mix of contextual factors from outside the schemes itself that vary considerably throughout the Union. Therefore it is important to be aware of further elements, which have determined the nature of the existing long-term care schemes. Chapter 3 deals with those two factors that have been shown to define in particular the environmental context in which the development of the EU long-term care schemes is being pursued: the reality of macro-economics and political circumstances.

Chapter 4 puts the discussion on a broader theoretical foundation that takes into consideration that the individual long-term-care schemes are usually embedded in a country's social protection system. It first of all reviews basic principles (relating to the public sector, the market, and the family) in the provision of social protection. The way a country applies such basic principles indicates what type of welfare state it is. This point is taken into account in the second part of this chapter, by means of illustrating two models of welfare state: the classification put forward by Esping-Anderson (1990) and the division of welfare states of the Bismarck and Beveridge type. As a next step, the section that follows gives an overview on how domiciliary long-term care schemes in EU countries are organised and funded in practice. Based on this overview, the individual schemes are classified by reference to pre-defined categories. The final section of Chapter 4 looks at the current relationship between the EU domiciliary long-term care schemes and the models of state welfare regimes dealt with in the second part of the Chapter.

2 The growing need for long-term care

2.1 Introduction

As briefly illustrated in the introductory Chapter of this study, there is a growing recognition of the increasing needs of disabled elderly people in the European Union and to meet these, many countries have, out of necessity, put policies for long-term care into the front line of policy discussion (See, for example, OECD, 1996a). However, when searching for alternative public policy responses, an essential prerequisite for examining any certain policy area is an awareness of the relative magnitude of the problem being considered. Therefore, this Chapter analyses the main reasons for the growing need, looking at the factors that influence both the demand for and the supply of long-term care.

In doing this, one factor that appears to play an important role where the demand for care is concerned is the ageing of EU populations over recent decades. Although the use of long-term care services differs from country to country, governments are concerned that a continually increasing number of elderly people will need more long-term care services, and that overall spending rates will increase (See, for example, European Commission, 1998).

Regarding future trends, the percentage of people aged 65 and over, in particular the very old (people aged 80 and over) will continue to rise in most EU countries (Eurostat data bank, 2002a and 2002b). This might lead one to conclude that there will be a comparable growth in the demand for long-term care services (Eisen and Sloan, 1996). However, hardly any reliable data exists on the question, whether an increase in life expectancy will mean that people not only live longer but also simultaneously experience less disabling conditions or whether, on the contrary, a higher life expectancy will mean a longer life in constant need of long-term care (OECD, 1994a). Considering this element of uncertainty, a second key factor affecting the demand for long-term care might be the state of health of the EU population aged 65 and over. In this connection it would appear useful both to review evidence on the current state of health of the elderly and to try to identify some indicators of possible changes in the future.

In addition to these developments in the demand for care, circumstances are aggravated by some unfortunate trends in the supply of long-term care. This is mainly because of the fact that the availability of traditional informal care by relatives, friends, neighbours, etc. is on the decline in most EU countries (See, for example, Wittenberg and Sandhu and Knapp, 2002). Instead, more and more disabled elderly are compelled to enlist formal long-term care services.

In view of the above, this chapter firstly considers changes in the absolute numbers and relative size of the elderly EU population; secondly it seeks to analyse the state of health of elderly people and the way in which they use available services, as well as the ways in which these two factors might change; and thirdly, it examines social changes that are relevant to the supply of long-term care. However, the following sections have to be limited and, therefore do not claim to be exhaustive. This is necessary, since the investigation of the three fields referred to above has already taken up considerable space. Consequently, the development of further factors, such as the income position of the elderly, prices of services and difficult developments in the supply of care (Hutten and Kerkstra, 1996), e.g. the generation of new and expensive care treatments (Saltman and Figueras, 1997), is not dealt with. In addition, it might make sense to refrain from dealing with such additional factors in some detail, since compared to the three main indicators mentioned with regard to the need for long-term care, they are of lesser importance.

2.2 Demographic component

One of the major factors associated with the demand for services by the disabled elderly is that of demographic change. As the Organisation for Economic Co-Operation and Development has argued, "the backdrop, against which many key debates in long-term care policy have been conducted in recent times, has been that of a rapidly ageing population" (OECD, 1988, p.12). There are many elements that have contributed to these changes. In particular, on the one hand, changes in cultural attitudes have taken place, such as the acceptance of contraception, a growth in the number of couples who do not wish to have children and the postponement of childbirth, that have led to a decline in birth rates and, on the other hand, there has been an improvement in general health and nutrition (Nijkamp, Pacolet, Spinnewyn, Vollering, Wilderom and Winters, 1991) (For example, the average life expectancy at birth for women in the EU as a whole rose from 72.7 years in 1960 to 80.8 years in 1997 and for men from 67.5 years to 74.5 years (Eurostat data bank, 1998)). In EU countries this has led to a considerable increase of the elderly population both in absolute numbers and in proportion to the total population (See, for example, Centre for Policy on Ageing, 1993; Eurostat data bank, 2002a).

Where planning services for the elderly are concerned, their absolute number in the individual EU countries appears to be very important. As illustrated in Table 3 (p. 23), there is, of course, national diversity. This is largely based on the fact that this absolute number of elderly people in a specific country depends, in general, on the number of its inhabitants.

Table 3 Absolute numbers of people aged 65 and over, EU countries, 1970, 1985, and 2000

Countries	65 and over 1970	65 and over 1985	65 and over 2000	Total population 2000
Austria	1,044,133	1,071,317	1,254,861	8,102,557
Belgium	1,288,936	1,350,103	1,715,093	10,239,085
Denmark	597,738	766,054	790,402	5,330,020
Finland	415,500	606,270	767,168	5,171,302
France	6,473,612	7,051,929	9,422,797	59,225,683
Germany	10,585,440	11,247,112	13,351,252	82,163,475
Greece	976,971	1,322,900	1,819,338	10,542,808
Rep. of Ireland	327,800	384,384	423,491	3,776,577
Italy	5,782,000	7,293,727	10,370,488	57,679,895
Luxembourg	42,195	48,423	62,204	435,700
Netherlands	1,310,975	1,729,746	2,152,442	15,863,950
Portugal	799,990	1,175,050	1,533,840	9,997,590
Spain	3,200,856	4,573,545	6,589,898	39,441,679
Sweden	1,085,576	1,424,615	1,532,555	8,861,426
United Kingdom	(1972) 7,470,657	8,497,592	9,301,719	59,623,406
EU 15	41,402,379	48.542.767	61.087.548	376.455.153

Source: Eurostat data bank, 2002a

For instance the total population in the EU countries varied in 2000 from 435,700 in Luxembourg to 82,163,475 in Germany. Similarly, in the same year, the absolute number of elderly people in these two countries varied from 62,204 (Luxembourg) to 13,351,252 (Germany). Noticeable differences also exist with regard to the level of increase over the past three decades. In Spain, the number of people reaching 65 years of age increased from 3,200,856 in 1970 to 6,589,898 in 2000. This represents a rise of over 100 % and, followed by Portugal, Greece, Finland and Italy, is the biggest in the EU countries. However, overall, there was a significant growth in the absolute number of elderly people in the European Union as a whole between 1970 and 2000, namely from 41,402,379 to 61,087,548 (Eurostat data bank, 2002a).

The above-noted trend in the absolute numbers of the EU population aged 65 and over has obvious relevance for policy makers in the field of long-term care. Nevertheless, as described by Allen and Perkins (1995, p. 2), "for many purposes it is the relative size (% of total population) of the elderly population which is most important, as this will influence the priority attached to elderly people by policy makers and the capacity of a population to provide for the needs of its older members". At the EU level as a whole, there was a significant growth in the relative size of the proportion of elderly people between 1970 and 2000 (Eurostat data bank, 2002a). As a result of differences in terms of fertility, mortality, and migration rates in the individual countries, some variations exist across the Union (Centre for Policy on Ageing, 1993). However, notwithstanding these minor discrepancies, Table 4 (p. 25) shows the clear general tendency that, over recent years, nearly all EU countries have experienced significant changes in their population structure. In 2000, Italy had the highest proportion of older people with 18.0%, followed by Greece and Sweden (17.3%), Belgium (16.8%) and Spain (16.7%). Of the fifteen EU countries, the Republic of Ireland, with 11.2% of the population aged 65 and over, had the lowest proportion of elderly people in 2000.

Table 4 Percentages of total population aged 65 and over, EU countries, 1970, 1985, and 2000

Countries	65 and over 1970	65 and over 1985	65 and over 2000
Austria	14.0	14.1	15.5
Belgium	13.3	13.7	16.8
Denmark	12.2	15.0	14.8
Finland	9.0	12.4	14.8
France	12.8	12.8	15.9
Germany	13.5	14.5	16.2
Greece	11.1	13.3	17.3
Rep. of Ireland	11.1	10.8	11.2
Italy	10.7	12.9	18.0
Luxembourg	12.5	13.2	14.3
Netherlands	10.1	12.0	13.6
Portugal	9.2	11.7	15.3
Spain	9.5	11.9	16.7
Sweden	13.6	17.1	17.3
United Kingdom	(1972) 13.3	15.0	15.6

Source: Eurostat data bank, 2002a

All the signs are that this trend will continue in the future. For the clarification of the extent of this ageing process, one can review the data of several statistical investigations carried out by international agencies in this field (e.g., the EC, the OECD, and the WHO). As an example, the statistical inquiry from the Statistical Office of the European Communities (Eurostat) is presented in the following table.

Table 5 Predicted percentages of total population aged 65 and over EU countries, 2015, 2030, and 2045

Countries	2015	2030	2045
Austria	18.8	24.9	29.2
Belgium	19.2	24.9	26.8
Denmark	18.4	22.1	24.0
Finland	19.8	25.3	25.7
France	18.6	24.0	26.4
Germany	20.4	26.1	28.9
Greece	20.2	24.1	29.4
Rep. of Ireland	13.1	17.7	22.4
Italy	22.2	27.6	33.7
Luxembourg	17.0	22.2	23.8
Netherlands	17.3	23.1	25.0
Portugal	17.0	20.5	25.6
Spain	19.1	24.5	32.2
Sweden	20.6	23.6	25.1
United Kingdom	17.8	22.4	25.0

Source: Eurostat data bank, 2002b

The above table shows the predicted percentages of the total populations aged over 65 years in the EU countries. Figures are projected for the years 2015,

2030 and 2045. Here it can be seen that there will be a rapid growth in the proportion of people aged over 65 in the future. In several EU countries, the percentage of this age group will increase by more than half from the year 2015 to 2045. The highest proportions of elderly people out of the whole EU in the year 2045 are expected in Italy (33.7%), Spain (32.2%), Greece (29.4%), Austria (29.2%), and Germany (28.9%). Compared to the rest of the European Union, the Republic of Ireland will still have a lower percentage of its total population aged 65 and over in the year 2045 (22.4%) (Eurostat data bank, 2002b).

What is particularly noticeable in all EU countries among those of the population aged 65 and over is the growth in the numbers of the very oldest, commonly defined as people aged 80 and over (See, for example, Knauth, 1993). This secondary ageing process, often called the ageing of the aged is already having a significant influence on public discussions about policies for elderly people (OECD, 1994a). According to a study by the OECD, the reason for this is that "the prevalence of disabling conditions increases sharply after the age of 75, and the consequent loss of independence in daily activities leads to a corresponding increase in the need for care" (OECD, 1994a, p. 37).

However, despite the fact that the number of people in the Union aged 80 and over continues to be small in relative terms, its increase is greater than the growth of the EU population as a whole and greater than that of the population aged 65 and over (OECD, 1996a). As shown below in Table 6 (p. 28), all EU countries have experienced a growth of at least 68.6% in the numbers of those aged 80 or over between 1970 and 2000, rising to over threefold in Finland. This increase is likely to continue in the future and will have wide implications on the development and costs of the provision of long-term care services for the elderly. Even if, for example, the organisational structure and composition of service provision varies widely among the EU countries as a whole, the issues involved in the need for care for the elderly population are similar (King, 1993). If, for instance, we combine the estimates regarding the elderly EU population from the Tables (3 to 6) with the data in Table 8, page 31, on the concentration of total expenditures on elderly people, one can foresee that there will be an even more urgent problem to deal with in the future.

Table 6 Absolute numbers of people aged 80 and over, EU countries 1970, 1985, and 2000

Countries	80 and over 1970	80 and over 1985	80 and over 2000	Total population 2000
Austria	157.890	236.070	280.372	8.102.557
Belgium	204.719	308.968	356.498	10.239.085
Denmark	99.245	164.385	208.837	5.330.020
Finland	50.799	108.996	171.055	5.171.302
France	1.157.253	1.784.888	2.131.310	59.225.683
Germany	1.502.632	2.457.365	2.934.830	82.163.475
Greece	173.924	265.100	373.299	10.542.808
Rep. of Ireland	57.100	69.098	96.289	3.776.577
Italy	941.500	1.397.147	2.265.183	57.679.895
Luxembourg	5.884	9.477	13.426	435.700
Netherlands	221.743	370.708	500.339	15.863.950
Portugal	110.950	194.950	282.520	9.997.590
Spain	497.528	895.318	1.452.649	39.441.679
Sweden	183.567	304.115	436.482	8.861.426
United Kingdom	1.260.657	1.774.993	2.357.395	59.623.406
EU 15	6.625.391	10.341.578	13.860.484	376.455.153

Source: Eurostat data bank, 2002a

To summarise, all the demographic trends in the EU countries reviewed here - the increase in both the absolute numbers of elderly people and in their proportional relationship to the numbers in other sections of populations, as well as the growth in the numbers of the very oldest - are likely to have far-reaching consequences. Regarding the subject of the present study, they might well lead one to expect a proportionate increase in the demand for long-term care services used by elderly people. Since a judgement about this, of course, greatly depends on the state of health of the elderly population, this needs to be further explored.

2.3 Health status of the elderly

A factor of prime importance in the demand for long-term care is the state of health of the elderly population. In this connection, nothing would be more misleading than to think of elderly people as being predominantly disabled. Instead, overall, there has been an increase in the life expectancy of the elderly in the EU countries (See, for example, Saltman and Figueras, 1997) and, most of the people aged 65 and over in the EU countries are able to live for a long time on their own (Alber, 1993). This longer average life span alone may lead some optimists to suggest that the health of elderly citizens is getting better. However, in 2000, as is shown below in Table 7 (p. 30), life expectancy at the age of 65 for women was highest in France (20.9 years) and lowest in the Republic of Ireland (17.7). For men it was highest in Sweden (16.7 years) and lowest in the Republic of Ireland (14.6 years).

Undoubtedly the trend towards an increasing life expectancy is interesting and might give the reader a general feeling that the state of health of the elderly is improving gradually. However, it is important to note that the health of the elderly population is not necessarily reflected by life expectancy (Williams, 1989). Therefore, it appears extremely questionable to refer to a longer span of life as an indicator of the state of health of the elderly EU population, as may have been possible in the past. This is mainly based on the proven fact that patterns of disease have changed over recent decades and that a large number of diseases prevalent today, for instance arthritis, do now not immediately result in death but presumably increase the demands made on long-term care services (Allen and Perkins, 1995). On the contrary, many chronically ill elderly people have some years of life ahead of them mainly, of course, as a result of the progress in medicine. This is a process, which is expected to continue in the future.

Table 7 Female and male life expectancy at age 65 in EU countries, 2000

Countries	Female life expectancy at age 65 (in years)	Male life expectancy at age 65 (in years)
Austria	19.6	16.2
Belgium	19.5	15.5
Denmark	18.3	15.2
Finland	19.3	15.5
France	(1999) 20.9	(1999) 16.5
Germany	(1999) 19.2	(1999) 15.5
Greece	(1999) 18.7	(1999) 16.3
Rep. of Ireland	17.7	14.6
Italy	(1996) 19.8	(1996) 16.0
Luxembourg	19.8	15.6
Netherlands	19.2	15.3
Portugal	18.3	14.7
Spain	(1999) 20.1	(1999) 16.1
Sweden	20.0	16.7
United Kingdom	18.9	15.6

Source: Eurostat data bank, 2002d

When one considers pathological symptoms among older people in the EU, as noted in a study by Alber (1993), cardiovascular disease is the most prominent illness among elderly people in several countries (e.g. Denmark, Germany, Italy, and Portugal). In addition, the survey draws attention to the rising rate of mental disorders among the very old in the EU countries (people aged 80 and over). In making a rough assessment of the extent of this syndrome, Alber suggested that, in some countries, up to about one half of those aged 80 and over suffered from such mental disturbances. Of these mental diseases, dementia is one of the most serious. Several studies (See, for example, Saltman and Figueras, 1997) project a further growth of dementia in the immediate future (apart from the expectation of a general increase in heart disease, cerebrovascular disease, cancer, and fractures).

However, even if the inevitability of the association between ageing and an increasing demand for health services might well be overstated (or, more likely, understated in the light of the general increase in life expectancy) the evidence that this association exists is, of course, incontestable (Chapman and Johnson, 1995). This has, for example, been clearly shown by an earlier survey by the OECD (OECD, 1996b), which has collated data on public health expenditure according to age in selected EU countries. Table 8 gives an overview.

Table 8 Concentration of total public health expenditure on elderly people, 1993

Countries	Age group 0-64		Age group 65+		Age group 75+	
	Population (in %)	Expenditures (in %)	Population (in %)	Expenditures (in %)	Population (in %)	Expenditures (in %)
Finland	86.2	61.5	13.8	38.5	5.7	22.1
France[1]	80.4	58.6	19.6	41.4	----	----
Germany	84.9	67.7	15.1	32.3	6.5	16.5
Netherlands	86.9	60.1	13.1	39.9	----	----
Portugal	86.3	64.1	13.7	35.9	5.4	18.7
Sweden	82.5	62.2	17.5	37.8	8.1	21.4
United Kingdom[2]	84.4	58.0	15.6	42.0	6.8	27.1

Source: OECD, 1996b

[1] France: 0-59, 60+, 70+.
[2] United Kingdom: England only.

As can be seen, the overall share of expenditure on the health of people aged 65 and over is usually 2-3 times higher than the proportion of the population they represent and in the age group of 75 and over are as much as 3-4 times higher. The survey further suggests that age-related increases in health expenditure are particularly significant in the sector of residential care (e.g. in hospitals and nursing homes). The rising costs at a further stage of life would to a smaller extent be influenced by, for example, consultations with doctors, medicine and medical appliances. With the costs of dentistry there is an early peak around the age of 60, with steady decreases beyond this age (OECD, 1996b).

Besides the variations among age groups, Table 8 shows differences, in part significant, between individual countries. Thus, for example, in the Netherlands, elderly people account for 15.6% of the total population, but for 42.0% of all health expenditure. In Germany, 15.1% of the total population are older than 65 years but account for 32.3% of all health expenditure. This particular difference might mainly be due to the fact that in the year the data were collected, only small parts of long-term care provision for the elderly were included in the German public health insurance scheme (Meier, 1995) whilst, on the other hand, the Netherlands already had a public policy that covered the whole population against the risk of age-related disability (Schrijvers, 1997). Regarding the meaningfulness of the above, where long-term care as a whole is concerned, in the other countries where figures are available, it is necessary to view the data with some caution since public expenditure in the sector of residential care and (domiciliary) nursing care are actually part of the expenditure on health care schemes and therefore the respective expenditure is probably included in the above figures. This is, however, virtually not the case (except the Netherlands) for the sector of domiciliary long-term care selected for this study (personal care and home-making assistance) as it was administered by the social services and therefore may not be included in the above table (Hutten and Kerkstra, 1996).

However, in addition to the study, referred to here in some detail, by the OECD (OECD, 1996b), several other investigations have clearly demonstrated that expenditure on health, and especially long-term care, in the EU countries is heavily concentrated among elderly people, particularly among the very old (See, for example, Chapman and Johnson, 1995; Edvartsen, 1996). Of these different investigations, a very interesting one seems to be a recent work by Alber (1993), particularly, since it offers information on the demand by elderly people in the EU as a whole (subdivided into three different age groups) for assistance in the 'Activities of Daily Life' ('ADLs') (except Austria, Finland, and Sweden). Alber suggested that the average proportion of chronic disability among the EU population for the 60 - 69 age group still is below 5%, it sharply increases about five to six fold to about 30% among the age group 80 and over. The significant rise of disability among the very old in the EU (people aged 80 and over) might again point to the difficulties that arise with the second ageing process mentioned above. Clearly, as discussed in earlier sections, current statistical data from such a cross-national analysis may only be indicative of the relationship between age and disability and single values from the individual countries involved may show much variation. In particular therefore, since international surveys are usually based on country-specific definitions or typologies, an EU-wide standard of what is, for instance, 'disabled', does not exist (Compare, for more details, Chapter 1, pages 5-18). However, such standards are a significant research topic by themselves.

Considering future developments in the state of health of elderly people, as the OECD has argued, "there is a very lively scientific debate as to whether, as people live longer in old age, very elderly people will experience less illness and disability (this has been termed 'the compression of morbidity' theory, or whether, on the contrary, more years of old age will mean more years of living in some state of dependency" (OECD, 1994a, p. 37). Following 'the compression of morbidity' theory, a very optimistic view about the future of morbidity development is that originally put forward by Fries (1980), which has attracted noticeable attention and is based on a fixed biological restriction of life expectancy. Fries suggests that, in the near future, mainly due to changes towards healthier life styles, the onset of morbidity will be delayed, while life expectancy will remain the same. This will lead, as a result, to a compression of morbidity at the end of life. In other words, this means that most elderly people will enjoy a sufficiently healthy life until around the age of 85 and then will be in need of care for a very short period immediately before death. If this theory comes true it will mean, in terms of planning services for the elderly, that the average duration of age-related disability and the consequent need for long-term care will probably go down. Other previous studies, for example Gruenberg (1977), have also projected changes in the association between life expectancy and morbidity. Their view, however, is more pessimistic than that of Fries (1980). Gruenberg puts forward the theory that a decrease in mortality among old people is the result of medical treatment that postpones the fatal consequences of chronic disease, rather than indicating a reduction in the incidence of degenerative conditions or a slowing down of their progression. Another view of future developments, occasionally called 'dynamic equilibrium' approach, has been put forward by Manton (1982). He also argued that there would be a rising number of elderly people with chronic disability, but not due to the postponement of fatal consequences. Manton suggested that the effect of medical treatment and other health-related changes had been to slow down the rate of progression of certain degenerating illnesses. In short, elderly people might be suffering impairments to their health for longer than was the case in years past, but the accompanying disability was not so grave.

Hopefully, these three alternative scenarios have illustrated the ranges of uncertainty surrounding the projection of demand for long-term care provision. Unfortunately, these differing views of possible changes in the state of health of the elderly have not been reconciled, partly as a result of significant problems connected with data and its interpretation. One important factor to take account of, for example, is the different health legacy of different groups. Attempts to elucidate the relationship between ageing and health are made more difficult by the fact that the very old are an exceptional group of survivors.

Evidence provided by some studies concerning trends where different indicators of health are concerned does not seem encouraging at first glance. Investigations based on data from different countries, such as France, the Netherlands, and the UK, concluded that there exists a discernible growth in reported age-related disability (Allen and Perkins, 1995). As noted earlier, such national figures conceal considerable diversity (See, for example, Edvartsen, 1996), for instance, because of the lack of a precise EU standard of what constitutes 'disability'. A further element of uncertainty exists due to the fact that such investigations frequently fall back upon information from household surveys, where the elderly person himself or herself has described his current state of health and possible limitations in the 'ADLs'. Therefore, it might not be surprising to learn that the answers to questions of this kind vary considerably from one group to another and over periods of time and it could be that changes in personal expectations where health is concerned and in the recognition of illness, rather than any real change in health explain these findings. However, since health expectations have an influence on the extent to which services are used, even this explanation points to an increase in the demand for services by the disabled elderly (Allen and Perkins, 1995).

To summarise, clearer evidence about future trends on the relationship between states of health and ageing is necessary. Such evidence would facilitate more accurate estimates of the demand for care for the elderly. However, until we better understand these trends, it would seem rash to assume that improvements in the state of health of the elderly people are likely to result in a reduced need for long-term care services in the near future.

2.4 Social component

The preceding sections have examined the current demand for long-term care and explored how it might develop in the future. The following section moves away from this point of view to examine essential developments on the supply of long-term.

In the past, long-term care for the elderly was predominantly a family task (so-called informal care). Looking at the EU as a whole, the state played a relatively minor role either as a direct provider or as a source of funds (Alber, 1993). This has meant that in most EU societies the greatest burden of long-term care has been carried by females who were usually living in the same household as the disabled relative (Knauth, 1993; Rostgaard and Fridberg, 1998). However, far-reaching social changes have led to the fact that caring for the disabled within the family is on a decline in many countries (See, for example, Wittenberg and Sandhu and Knapp, 2002). There might be two main reasons for this development and these will be examined below.

First of all, there has been a significant growth in the proportion of elderly people living alone over recent decades. The so-called extended family, where three or more generations lived together in one house has become very rare. This 'social institution' often resulted in the middle generation of the household looking after the parents when they had become elderly and disabled (Alber, 1993). There exists, however, a variation in estimates of the proportion of elderly people living alone. This is mainly because of differences in definition of what 'living alone' means among various surveys and censuses that have made it difficult to get accurate figures. Nevertheless, the tendency towards a growing number of 'elderly-single-households' is marked (Compare European Commission, 2001). For instance, a publication by Eurostat (2002e) provides details of the number of elderly people aged 65 and over and living alone as a proportion of the total population aged 65 and over. These findings are shown below in Table 9 (See p. 36).

As can be seen in the table, in 1998, more than half of the women aged 65 and over were living alone in Denmark (57%), Belgium, Germany, the Netherlands and Sweden (all 53%) and the UK (52%). In the case of men, figures are highest in Sweden (27%), Denmark (25%), the UK (24%), the Republic of Ireland (22%), Belgium, the Netherlands and Finland (all 21%). The proportion of women aged 65 and over living alone in 1998 was lower compared with the EU average of 44% in Spain (24%), Portugal (29%), Greece and the Republic of Ireland (both 37%). For men, the share was below the EU average (16%) in Spain (8%), Portugal and Italy (both 12%), Greece and Germany (both 14%). In each EU country, however, the percentage of elderly women living alone is much higher than that of men (Eurostat, 2002e). This is mainly because of the differences in life expectancy and in marital status between women and men (Compare Knauth, 1993).

Table 9 Percentage of elderly females and males aged 65 and over, living alone, 1998

Countries	Females aged 65 living alone (%)	Males aged 65 living alone (%)
Austria	47	16
Belgium	53	21
Denmark	57	25
Finland	50	21
France	46	18
Germany	53	14
Greece	37	14
Rep. Of Ireland	37	22
Italy	39	12
Luxembourg	----	----
Netherlands	53	21
Portugal	29	12
Spain	24	8
Sweden	53	27
United Kingdom	52	24
EU 15	44	16

Source: Eurostat data bank, 2002e

It is worth emphasising that although living alone has become more common, it does not imply that there exists a simultaneous decline in contacts between elderly people and their relatives. Instead, a number of studies have shown that most elderly people have regular contact with their offspring. For example, according to an earlier Eurobarometer survey for the Commission of the EC in 1993, in Italy 92.2% of elderly people saw a member of their family at least once a week on average, followed by Spain (83.6%), the Republic of Ireland (83.5%) and Greece (80.3%). The lowest figure was found in Denmark, where, nevertheless, 65.2% of the elderly had at least weekly contact with a member of their family (Centre for Policy on Ageing, 1993).

However, apart from the fact that most elderly people in the EU countries have regular contact with their relatives (including those living alone), as a study by the OECD (OECD, 1994b, p. 22) notes, "it remains a fact that independence may mean isolation for some elderly people, even if less frequently than generally believed. At any rate, the provision of care is more problematic under these changed circumstances", in particular, since the amount of time devoted to informal care is largely influenced by whether or not the care provider lives in the same household as the disabled elderly person (Parker 1992). Alber (1993) points out that changes in the structure and size of households and the lessened ability with which generations are able to look after each other will inevitably lead to an increasing demand for either residential long-term care or help from formal domiciliary care services to enable the elderly continue living in their own homes.

In addition to the above, it is well known that informal care in private households is widely provided by one person and mostly by a woman, for example, a wife, mother or (married) daughter or daughter-in-law (OECD, 1996a). Several estimates (See, for example, Knauth, 1993) have shown that this informal care potential has clearly diminished over recent years and will become even smaller in the future. The reason for this is first of all the reduced proportion of middle-aged people in relation to the elderly (OECD, 1996a), mainly because of falling birth rates, and the increase in life expectancy (Centre for Policy on Ageing, 1993).

Another important reason for the decline in the availability and provision of informal care might be the increasing number of women who are in paid employment and therefore not able to stay at home to take term care of the disabled elderly over a protracted period (See, for example, Wittenberg and Sandhu and Knapp, 2002). This tendency is, for instance, illustrated in 10 EU countries between 1985 and 2000 by an investigation of Eurostat (Eurostat, 2002f) (See Table 10, p. 38). The data have been recorded for two different age groups (15-44, 45-64). It shows that a very clear growth of participation in the labour market by women between 15 and 64 is discernible in most EU countries. For example, between 1985 and 2000, the total number of women aged between 15 and 44 in paid employment grew from 261,000 to 515,000 in the Republic of Ireland, from 1,411,000 to 2,449,200 in the Netherlands and from 6,957,000 to 10,463,200 in Germany. This increase in the number of women in paid employment must clearly influence the informal care potential, since it is associated with a reduction of the overall time such women have available for the care of disabled elderly relatives (Compare OECD, 1996a).

Table 10 Absolute numbers of women of working age who are in paid employment by age group (15 - 44 / 45 - 64) in EU countries, 1985 and 2000

Countries	**1985**		**2000**	
	15-44	**45-64**	**15-44**	**45-64**
Belgium	969,000	256,000	1,276,500	454,100
Denmark	820,000	306,000	819,300	439,100
France	6,274,000	2,510,000	6,887,800	3,562,600
Germany	6,957,000	3,129,000	10,463,200	5,325,500
Greece	751,000	424,000	980,500	479,200
Rep. of Ireland	261,000	62,000	515,500	159,100
Italy	4,706,000	1,828,000	5,430,500	2,197,400
Luxembourg	40,000	10,000	52,800	18,000
Netherlands	1,411,000	331,000	2,449,200	901,800
United Kingdom	6,926,000	3,040,000	8,108,100	4,139,000

Source: Eurostat data bank, 2002f

To summarise, this decline in the ability of the family unit to look after elderly relatives, in addition to the difficulties arising from the increase in the proportion of elderly people living alone, clearly demonstrates that the traditional forms of support for elderly people are no longer sufficient. In order to compensate for the shrinking availability of informal care, a growing supply of formal services will probably be necessary in the future.

2.5 Summary

This Chapter has given an overview of the major reasons for the increasing need for services used by the disabled elderly EU population over recent decades and has tried to offer some indications with regard to future developments. In this overview, the demographic component and the state of health of elderly people have been considered as the most relevant factors where changes in the demand for long-term care are concerned. Trends leading to difficulties in the supply of long-term care have been studied mainly by analysing the diminution of informal services for the disabled elderly.

Considering the demand for long-term care, three specific demographic shifts with regard to elderly people in the EU countries may have contributed to an increasing need: a growth in the absolute number of elderly people, an increase in their proportional relationship to the total population and a rise in the proportion of the very old (people aged 80 and over) within the group of people aged 65 and over (the so-called 'double ageing' process). Although there have been variations among the individual countries in recent times, the broad phenomenon of an ageing population was to be found throughout the whole EU.

It is obvious that the indicated demographic trends have contributed to an increased proportion of the national income being devoted to services for the disabled elderly over recent decades. However, prospects regarding future developments appear much more uncertain. This is particularly due to the fact that there is no clear research evidence available, which shows how the state of health of the elderly will develop. One optimistic view suggests that the EU will have an older, but also a much healthier society in the future. On the other hand, three facts suggest that the need for public provision in the field of long-term care will continue to grow: first, the proportion of elderly and very old people is expected to rise in the twenty-first century, second, the demand for care sharply increases with age and, third, the self-help potential in the family system is continuing to a decline. In the light of these factors, it would seem unwise to expect that possible improvements in the state of health of the elderly EU population will lead to a general reduction in the need for long-term care.

In addition to the difficulties arising from the developments on the demand side, significant social changes over recent times have influenced the supply side of long-term care services for the disabled elderly. More and more elderly people are living alone and under such conditions the provision of long-term care is often very difficult. In addition, the overall informal care potential has clearly diminished over recent years, mainly due to the fact that more and more women are in paid employment and therefore are not staying at home to care for the elderly. These developments suggest that the traditional forms of support (informal care) for disabled elderly people are no longer sufficient.

As we have also seen in this Chapter, the underlying problems that have led to an increasing need for long-term care tend to be very similar in the EU countries. In consequence, before studying long-term care throughout the EU, one might conclude that countries have adopted similar schemes to deal with these difficulties. As we know, this is clearly not the case. In particular therefore, since - in addition to the problems arising from increasing needs in the long-term care schemes themselves - a variety of contextual factors have played an important role in the formulation of long-term care policies. For example, country-specific economic growth and decay, political situations, and ideological values have influenced the processes of reform. Having knowledge of these different pressures from outside the individual schemes, one may understand the development of the variations between the EU countries in the financing of long-term care for their elderly population and in the organisational structures within which that care is provided. Such contextual factors will be further explored in the following Chapter 3.

3 Contextual factors with influence on long-term care scheme

3.1 Introduction

The nature of the funding and organisational structures within which care is provided in the European Union is more marked by diversity than by uniformity. In addition to the differences in needs within the long-term care schemes themselves, this diversity is mainly based on the fact that the characteristics of long-term care schemes are the result of a mix of contextual factors from outside the scheme itself. These factors vary considerable throughout the Union (See, for example Héritier, 1996). There is, in fact, no end to the diversity and number of such factors that have influenced what governments have done or elected not to do. Public policy (e.g. in the sector of long-term care) may be influenced by a country's history, economic circumstances, legislative basis, violent events, cross-national influences, type of government and the relative influence of stakeholders or even cultural and religious values. Almost anything could have led to government action or inaction. These contextual factors are, of course, also having a decisive influence on possible reforms, since the solutions considered in individual countries frequently reflect the specific local concerns and circumstances (Hugman, 1994; Saltman and Figueras, 1997; Saltman, Figueras and Sakellaridis, 1998).

However, when studying long-term care schemes from a cross-national perspective, it is necessary to understand the contextual factors that lead to country-specific policies and services for the disabled elderly population and based on this, it is useful to take into consideration the possibilities of change as well as the limitations to such possibilities (Jamieson, 1991). In other words, one of the key factors for the success of long-term care policies is an understanding of the context in which they are to be implemented (Scharf, 1995).

It is not possible to consider all contextual factors that influence public policy throughout the EU, particularly policy with regard to long-term care. The aim of this Chapter is to focus briefly on the two contextual factors that have been shown to be particularly effective in the process of arriving at policy decisions: the reality of macro-economics and the political background against which decisions have been or are made (See, for example Jamieson, 1991; OECD, 1996a). It is clear that two factors alone are not sufficient to explain precisely the development of the different ways of dealing with the problems of long-term care in the EU countries. However, they should be useful for demonstrating how such country-specific contextual circumstances affect policies in general, special attention being paid to policies in the field of long-term care.

The author is aware that collating and examining the available evidence is an important step in trying to understand the influence of the two contextual factors on government policy. Therefore, two broad categories (i.e. 'situational' and 'structural') will be used in considering the two factors. Following similar definitions from earlier studies (See, for example, Alford, 1969; Leichter, 1979) the study defines the two categories as follows: A situational factor is a condition or event of short duration, or a special circumstance, that has an impact on policy making, although the fact should not be overlooked that a condition or event of apparently short duration may have a relatively lasting effect. Typical situational factors are violent events, economic cycles or changes of government. Structural factors are the relatively unchanging features of a society and the system of government. Structural factors include the more permanent features of a system, such as the basis of its economy or its political institutions. However, it is clear that a situational factor, such as a change in political regime, can become a structural factor. The study is primarily concerned with considering the relatively immediate impact of a transient event or condition on public policy. It is impossible to say when a transient event becomes institutionalised and, therefore, part of country's economic or political structure.

3.2 Economic context

A good deal has been written in the last few years about the relationship between the economy of a society and its government's policies. For example, as the Organisation for Economic Co-Operation and Development has pointed out, the continuing financial viability of any long-term care scheme is greatly influenced by the relative health of the national economy and by its ability to stimulate growth, employment and incomes (OECD, 1996a).

3.2.1 Structural economic factors

The economic wealth or income of a country, usually measured in terms of its gross domestic product (GDP), has a clear impact on public policy. In general, the extent to which a country's policy makers are able to provide social services depends on the degree of economic well being of the country. From a worldwide view, the EU, seen as a whole, is an economically advanced region with highly developed industries and comparatively high levels of GDP. Nevertheless, there are still substantial differences between the 15 individual member countries. As shown in the following Table 11 (p. 43), countries vary substantially in terms of GDP, GDP per head and social protection expenditure per head.

Table 11 Some structural macro-economic characteristics of EU countries for the year 2000

Countries	GDP[1]	GDP per head[2]	Social protection expenditure per head[3] (1998)
Austria	204,843	24,570	6,654
Belgium	248,338	25,130	6,040
Denmark	176,490	27,140	8,784
Finland	131,670	23,200	6,092
France	1,404,775	22,250	6,696
Germany	2,025,534	23,540	6,865
Greece	122,986	15,460	2,516
Rep. of Ireland	103,470	26,800	3,339
Italy	1,165,677	22,890	4,664
Luxembourg	20,934	43,750	9,395
Netherlands	401,089	26,310	6,371
Portugal	115,255	16,770	2,239
Spain	608,787	18,110	2,707
Sweden	246,619	22,960	7,980
United Kingdom	1,547,903	23,560	5,717

Source: Eurostat data bank, 2002g and 2002h

1 Nominal gross domestic product at current market prices and in millions of Euro.
2 Gross domestic product at current market prices per head of population (purchasing power parity) in Euro.
3 Social protection expenditure per head of population in Euro.

In 2000, GDP in Germany was 2,025,534 million Euro, while that of Luxembourg was 20,934 million Euro. The main reason for such an enormous difference is, of course, the difference in the size of population. Much more important is the difference between EU countries in terms of the GDP per head, which is highest in Luxembourg (43,750 Euro), with others lagging well behind (Denmark 27,140 Euro, the Republic of Ireland 26,800 Euro, and the Netherlands 26,310 Euro). In 2000, three Southern EU countries, Greece (15,460 Euro), Portugal (16,770 Euro) and Spain (18,110 Euro) had the lowest GDP per head. The final column in the table below shows social protection spending per head of the population whereby great disparities are revealed. In 1998, Luxembourg had the highest level of expenditure on social protection per head with 9,395 Euro, followed by Denmark, Sweden, Germany, France, Austria, the Netherlands, Finland and Belgium, all of which had expenditure of over 6,000 Euro per head. At the other end of the scale, Portugal (2,239 Euro), Greece (2,516 Euro) and Spain (2,707 Euro) spent the least per head on social protection. However, as the above figures reveal, there are substantial differences between the EU countries. These differences would be more emphatic if the analyses also took account of the structure of the economies, government total expenditure, government net lending or borrowing and the like (Compare, for more details, European Commission, 1997).

If a comparison is made between the two above-mentioned macro-economic characteristics 'social protection expenditure per head' and 'gross domestic product per head' of a country, a more unified and very interesting picture emerges. This is shown in the figure below (p. 45).

As can be seen, there is a correlation between social protection expenditure per head and the gross domestic product per head (this reflecting the stage of economic development of a country). This can be seen as a confirmation of the tendency for the financial resources available in the field of social protection to be invariably exhausted and again, of course, also of the fact that the provision of services, such as long-term care for the elderly (which might come to a considerable share of the total social protection expenditure, in particular for those aged 65 and over) (Compare OECD, 1996b), is probably strongly influenced by the macro-economic situation of a country.

Figure 2 Social protection expenditure per head in Euro and gross domestic product per head in Euro, 1998

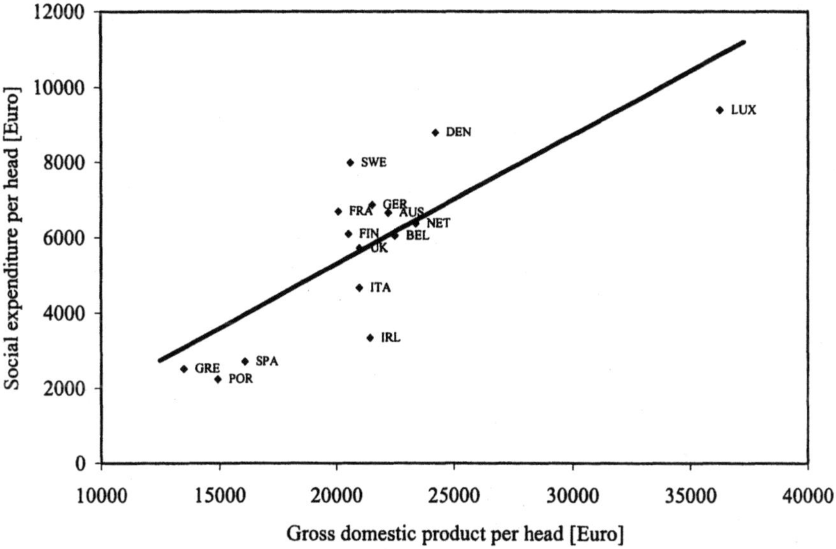

Source: Eurostat data bank, 2002g and 2002h

In addition, however, the above graph could lead us to conclude that the necessity of a higher level of public social protection provision becomes more pronounced as a country's macro-economic position improves, since traditional services, such as the provision of long-term care by relatives and neighbours or others, becomes weaker because, as a country becomes economically stronger an increasing number of people are in paid employment and there is usually a resulting higher degree of job-related mobility which makes families less able to offer domiciliary care (Kokot, 1997). Taking this conclusion further, one might argue that the development of schemes of social service, such as one covering the risk of age-related disability, is an important contribution to the positive development of the macro-economy of a country in the long-term.

It is recognised that despite the above-noted structural economic issues, there are, of course, further structural economic factors that influence public policy, such as the ´complexity of economic organisation` (modern or traditional economy) and the ´type of economic system`. It is impossible to deal with all these structural economic factors within the framework of the present study. The same can be said to apply to the following sections of this chapter. However, this limitation would seem reasonable, as the majority of other structural economic factors not dealt with within the framework of this chapter, seem to be quite similar within the Union. Consequently they may have not in the same way contributed to the country-specific differences within the Union, such as difference in the GDP, where public policy (long-term care for the elderly) is concerned. Nevertheless, in order to show even more clearly the possible effects on public policy arising from possible differences in structural economic factors, the study briefly looks at least at the type of economic base - a factor that may indeed be largely responsible for differences in public policy.

When considering the different types of economic base, it has often been said that it is very useful to distinguish between industrialised and agrarian societies. The EU countries all belong to the former. Considering, for example, the nature of the issues and, therefore, the policy decisions needed, there exist large differences between the two types of economic structures. In an industrialised society, for example, the economy becomes increasingly complex. As large corporations and industrial enterprises develop, some basic public services of a remedial nature may be provided but there are still some countries where no great emphasis is placed on industrial pollution, unemployment or long-term care insurance. In addition, a nation's economic structure influences not only the content of public policy but also its administration. Industrialised economies are more highly organised and concentrated than agrarian economies and it is, therefore, easier to provide social protection, such as long-term care services for the elderly (Leichter, 1979).

3.2.2 Situational economic factors

Despite the above-noted structural economic factors (GDP, GDP per head, social protection expenditure per head), which vary from country to country, a range of countries in the EU currently face the same situational macro-economic difficulties, such as an increase in the number of families with a low income, inequality of opportunity and the persistent level of high unemployment (the last being probably the greatest of these difficulties) (See, for example, European Commission, 1998).

For instance, in the Union as a whole, the average unemployment rate was consistently below 3% of the labour force throughout the 1950s, 1960s and early 1970s, whereas it has been persistently above 8% since 1982 - except in 1990 (European Commission, 1998). The unemployment rates from 1998 to 2000 are illustrated in Table 12 (p. 47).

Table 12 Unemployment figures (%) in July, EU countries, 1998, 1999, 2000

Countries	1998	1999	2000
Austria	4.5	3.9	3.7
Belgium	9.5	8.8	7.0
Denmark	5.2	5.2	4.7
Finland	11.4	10.2	9.8
France	11.8	11.2	9.5
Germany	9.3	8.6	7.9
Greece	10.9	11.6	11.1
Rep. of Ireland	7.5	5.6	4.2
Italy	11.8	11.3	10.5
Luxembourg	2.7	2.4	2.4
Netherlands	4.0	3.4	3.0
Portugal	5.2	4.5	4.1
Spain	18.8	15.9	14.1
Sweden	8.3	7.2	5.9
United Kingdom	6.3	6.1	5.5
EU 15	9.9	9.1	8.2

Source: Eurostat data bank, 2002c

As the table shows, the average unemployment figures went down slightly for the EU countries as a whole, from 9.9 to 8.2% between 1998 and 2000. However, in several countries, the proportion of the population without work is still extremely high. The highest unemployed figures in 2000 are reported for

Spain (14.1%), Greece (11.1%) and Italy (10.5%). Compared to the rest of the EU countries, figures are lower in Luxembourg (2.4%) and the Netherlands (3.0%). As a result, a significant proportion of the people of working age have, therefore, been unable to obtain a job and thus contribute to the generation of income required to support those elderly people in retirement or in need of long-term care and have instead added to the need for unemployment benefit or social assistance.

Demographic developments are another major feature leading to macro-economic difficulties. The ageing of the population is not only resulting in the fact that the demand for services such as long-term care is likely to increase. The condition that the population above the official age of retirement (65 in most countries) has increased in relation to the number of people of working-age and will very probably rise even more dramatically in the years to come is at the same time contributing to significant changes in the relation between the numbers of those who are predominantly paying for and the number of those receiving pensions, care services or the like. In 1986, for every person aged 65 and over in the Union (the present 15 Member states), there were five people aged 15 to 64. By 1996, the increase in the number of persons of 65 and over meant that for every one person in this age group, there were a little in excess of 4 people of working age. By 2020, according to the prognostications, the figure of 4 will have gone down to 3. At the same time, the number of men aged between 55 and 64 no longer earning has increased markedly, from 43% in 1986 to almost 50% in 1996 (the proportion of women remaining about the same), largely because of the slow rate of economic growth and the inadequate rate in the creation of new jobs. If this trend continues, it will add to the pressure, in particular, on pension schemes (but also on long-term care schemes) in the future as the increase in the relative number of people aged 65 and over accelerates (European Commission, 1998).

In addition to the above, for those EU member states that have given up their own currency and adopted the new European currency, the relevant admission ('Maastricht') criteria have also been having a strong influence on economic policies. In order to achieve the necessary economic stability, the control of inflation, a drastic reduction of financial deficits and government debt have been and are prime considerations. These concerns have led policy makers to cut back their public spending, particularly on social services such as long-term care for the elderly (Saltman, Figueras and Sakellarides, 1998).

A social policy study of the OECD has argued that, as a consequence of this general economic crisis, "those countries which had recognised a need for change, but had not formulated specific reforms, were hardly encouraged to push a new and potentially expensive issue to the head of the agenda.

Even countries which had hitherto managed to accommodate greater needs for long-term care by gradual adoption of existing schemes found themselves pushed to make sharper decisions about priorities and faced with more difficult choices about public costs" (OECD, 1996a, p. 13).

Over recent years, tendencies to take steps to counter increasing costs in the field of long-term care have already become obvious in several countries. Such measures bring with them the danger that less and less attention is paid to the quality of the care supplied. For example, as Jamieson has said in an earlier study, while the notion of domiciliary care appeals to people who really care about the welfare of older people, it is certain that the justified awareness that domiciliary care costs less than residential care has also led to its ready acceptance by decision makers, whatever their political colour (Jamieson, 1991). As briefly noted in Chapter 1 of this study (pages 13 and 14), most governments appear to be of the opinion that an enlargement of the domiciliary care sector is a good way of reducing the rising number of disabled elderly who need residential care and, therefore, public health service costs, although there is little data available to determine the cost-efficiency of various forms of long-term care services (See, for example, OECD, 1996a). Another example of political measures being adopted as a reaction to financial pressures can be seen in connection with the fact that it has become increasingly obvious that families, neighbours, etc. (informal carers) in most EU countries have provided the main bulk of long-term care for elderly people over recent decades, and that the current decline in informal care potential has costly service implications. This has increasingly led to emphasis being placed on the support - with cash or services - of such informal carers. This development can be seen, for example, in Germany, where since the introduction of a separate long-term care insurance scheme, that came into force in 1995, informal carers, for example, who have to care for another person, perhaps a family member, can now have their pension insurance contributions paid for them (Para. 3 German Pension Insurance Act, 2000; Para. 19 German Care Insurance Act, 2000).

3.3 Political context

At the end of the day, all public policy requirements, whether they are concerned with social change, economic circumstances, or outbreaks of violence, must be dealt with by the political system. The political environment within which decisions are made then influences the course taken by and the content of such policy decisions.

3.3.1 Structural political factors

Political structures and institutional settings can have a major impact on the current state of a long-term care scheme in a specific country and on the ability to attain reform. Federalist and centralist structures, local and national traditions, the varying preferences of people or organisations involved and changing priorities with regard to the relative importance of individual cases as guiding principles for the implementation of long-term care policies, determine the extent and availability of care services for the disabled elderly (Schulze and Wirth, 1996). As a direct consequence, the emphasis where long-term care reform is concerned will vary from country to country. Sometimes the government of the country concerned is responsible as it is in the Netherlands (Vollering, 1991) and France (French Ministry of Labour and Solidarity, 1998). In some countries, national and local authorities are jointly responsible, as the case is in Denmark (Danish Ministry of Social Affairs, 1995). In other countries, the authority to reform the provision of long-term care may be a joint product of national and regional government as in Germany (OECD, 1996a). In each case, a different degree of importance is attached to the reform process and each country approaches long-term care reform individually (Saltman and Figueras, 1997).

The institutional framework varies from country to country and makes the introduction of reforms in long-term care far from straightforward. Denmark is an example of a country that has, in the last few years, shown itself capable of making several structural reforms. In Denmark, particularly important steps that have been taken over recent years where services for disabled elderly people are concerned include, for example, the obligation on local authorities to provide a domiciliary-help-service, the prohibition of the building of further nursing homes on the residential pattern and, the support of specialised housing schemes for the elderly in need (OECD, 1996a). In contrast to what Denmark has done, discussions for many years about the implementation of a new compulsory insurance scheme for long-term care in Germany well illustrates the difficulties which arise from complex institutional settings, despite the generally recognised pressure to solve the problems involved (Gabanyi, 1995). As Saltman and Figueras (1997) have argued, in countries where the political system tends to lead to governments formed by the coalition of two or more political parties (e.g. the Netherlands) or where a second legislative body has a voice in the proceedings (e.g. the Bundesrat in Germany), all reforms to be instituted by the government must be negotiated by the parties in the coalition concerned, this typically leading to slower, step-by-step reform. What we think of the different schemes in various countries is naturally influenced by what degree of importance we attach to radical measures as opposed to the more cautious approach of supplementing already existing care arrangements.

3.3.2 Situational political factors

In addition to the structure of a country's political institutions as illustrated above, the political ideology, determination and leadership of a government are significant factors affecting policy implementation where long-term care is concerned (Saltman and Figueras, 1997). Concurring with this approach, Jamieson (1991) argues that policies are always the consequence of political decisions. The study points out, however, that welfare traditions, economic factors and, the structure of the political system all impose restrictions upon the degree to which politicians can influence events. But within the limits of these restrictions, the options chosen reflect the interests and beliefs of governments (Jamieson, 1991).

Whether a long-term care scheme, for example, includes inducements that increase willingness to provide care within the family or, on the other hand, includes features that make it easier for the disabled elderly to live independently away from their relatives by providing a wide range of public services, depends beside the existing welfare regime, to a large extent on political ideologies dominant at the time. There is a high level of agreement among the guiding principles in the countries of the EU that the elderly should, as far as possible, be enabled to continue living in their own homes (See, for example, OECD, 1994a). Nevertheless, one can see divergence when looking more closely at this policy objective within the individual EU countries. In Germany, as in different other EU countries, priority is attached to the support of domiciliary care services. Similarly, the willingness of relatives or neighbours (informal carers) to provide care is encouraged by cash benefits (German Ministry of Labour and Social Affairs, 1996). In Denmark, on the other hand, the political aim is to ensure that elderly people are able to cope without support from their families (Danish National Institute of Social Research, 1994).

Another noticeable factor affecting long-term care reforms is the existence of governments, which are a coalition of different political groups as, for example, in Italy, where the differing objectives of each party frequently lead to complications and to a delay in the reform process. Furthermore, some of the difficulties experienced in introducing long-term care scheme reform in many EU countries can be seen to arise from a lack of sufficient political will and stability. Many governments have been short-lived and a succession of different, sometimes conflicting, reform proposals have been put forward. Lack of political leadership can be a further complication. Some political leaders have only a general idea of their objectives, and may as a result introduce inadequately worked-out policies. In a political vacuum, different organisations will seek to promote reform towards changes that are more acceptable to themselves. The conflict of a variety of attitudes to policy formulation can lead to inaction. On the other hand, reform may reflect the partisan interests of a wide range of interested parties, such as members of the professions, experts in particular fields, etc. Therefore, the necessary pre-condition to the successful implementation of reform might well be to rally as much political support as possible by establishing alliances of groups of people, and organisations which are in favour of the proposed changes (Saltman and Figueras, 1997).

Finally, it is likely, if not certain, that various types of political change affect public policy. This is particularly true if the party in power is replaced by another. The type and extent of the policy changes that are then likely to be made will reflect the ideological differences between the two parties. The important policy changes that were made in the UK in 1945 after the Labour Party's victory over the Conservatives are an example of this. Among these changes were the relinquishment of the UK's colonial empire, the nationalisation of the coal, railway, iron, steel, and domestic airlines industries and a comprehensive social welfare programme. The nationalisation of the British iron and steel industries by the Labour government in 1946 is a very good example of the impact of party change on public policy. This policy decision was reversed by the Conservatives when they regained power, but in 1967 when Labour again returned to power, they nationalised the steel industry again (Leichter, 1979).

3.4 Summary

This Chapter has discussed contextual factors that affect EU long-term care schemes, in particular the realities of macro-economics and the political circumstances, which have been illustrated by using two categories: situational and structural factors. Some differences and some similarities have been highlighted and a brief attempt has been made to show how these factors may affect policies in the field of long-term care. Although the impact of these factors has been discussed as if their influence could be seen in isolation, it must be remembered that there is an interplay between them and many other factors.

The outlined diversity between the contextual factors in the various countries may help to explain why, on the one hand, national long-term care schemes in the EU, for a long time, have developed differently with regard to their main sources of financing and the predominance of particular providers, as we will we see in Chapter 4 and, on the other hand, why reform strategies that work in one country, currently cannot be carried over into other countries without substantial adaptation in most cases. However, despite the differences referred to, this chapter has shown that there are unmistakable similarities between the various countries, particularly where the situational factors illustrated are concerned (e.g. persistent level of high unemployment). It remains to be seen if these similarities will sooner or later result in comparable reform strategies in the field of long-term care among the EU countries.

4 Theoretical framework

4.1 Introduction

As Edvartsen (1996) has said, comparing the public long-term care schemes for the elderly in different European Union countries requires a detailed knowledge of each national scheme. Moreover, owing to the fact that the individual schemes are usually an integral part of a country's social protection system, it is an important objective of this study to base the discussion on a broader theoretical foundation that takes this fact into account. This would help to increase our understanding of the ways in which individual countries provide service for their disabled elderly inhabitants. According to Richard M. Titmuss[1] (1964), social protection systems "relate to transactions by Government (or agencies approved by Government) which increase individual money in certain specific circumstances of income loss or need for income protection" (p. 173). Old-age pensions are, by a considerable margin, the largest item of social protection expenditure in the Union, and amounted to about 42.5% of the total in 1995, followed by health care, accounting for some 22%, benefits paid to the unemployed amounting to about 8% of the total and others like widowhood, needs of children and the increasing sector of (domiciliary) long-term care for the elderly (European Commission, 1998).

In order to fulfil the objective outlined above, the first part of this chapter seeks to illustrate basic principles in the provision of social protection. In doing this, an attempt is made to orientate the discussion principally towards the topic of this study, namely, long-term (domiciliary) care for the elderly. Here the intention is to indicate the basic principles underlying a country's provision of social services for its inhabitants.

The way a country applies these basic principles, normally in combination, indicates what type of welfare state it is. Within the framework of scientific discussions in which welfare states are compared there is often reference to a range of models, of which the classification illustrated by Esping-Anderson ('The Three Worlds of Welfare Capitalism', 1990) and the division into welfare states of the 'Bismarck' and 'Beveridge' type (See, for example, Saltman and Figueras, 1997) are probably the most important ones. These two classifications have become established as a major contribution to the literature

---

[1] Philosopher, social critic and adviser to governments at home and overseas, Richard Titmuss enjoyed a worldwide reputation for his contribution to the discipline of social administration. Through a range of challenging studies - 'Essays on the Welfare State' (1958), 'Commitment to Welfare' (1964), and 'The Gift Relationship' (1970) - he dominated a whole generation of social thought (Abel-Smith and Titmuss, 1987).

on comparative welfare states (See, for example, Kemeny, 1995; Bräutigam and Schmid, 1996). This fact is taken into account in the second part of the present chapter, in the form of an illustration of these two models, in some detail. By using particular countries as examples, an attempt is additionally made to show how these different types of welfare state had an effect on the development of the social protection system in countries belonging to the Union, with particular reference to the scheme of domiciliary long-term care for the elderly.

In the third part of this Chapter, the domiciliary long-term care arrangements made within the Union in practice are illustrated. By using national based country information as well as cross-national literature and, focusing on common aspects, i.e. in particular the providers (the operation of domiciliary long-term care organisations, and the employment of long-term care personnel) responsible for long-term care services and the major source of funding it should be possible to reduce the existing diversity among the individual schemes. Based on the information from the available data, a further step is to classify the domiciliary long-term care schemes in the EU countries according to pre-defined categories which have emerged from the discussion.

In the fourth section of the present Chapter the aim is to look at the current relationship between the domiciliary long-term care schemes illustrated in the third section of the Chapter and the type of state welfare regimes dealt with in the second part. This particularly includes the question whether the welfare state classification of Esping-Anderson and the division into welfare states of the Bismarck and Beveridge types still cover the various forms that a long-term care scheme could take at the present time, as appeared formerly to be the case.

4.2 Fundamental principles applying to systems of social protection

Evers (1990) has developed an analytical model, following two earlier studies by Gershuny (1983) and Rose (1985), which allows in simply theoretical form, the identification of three basic principles theoretically underlying the provision of social protection services (including those for domiciliary long-term care), and these are illustrated in the figure below (p. 57).

Figure 3 The 'welfare triangle'

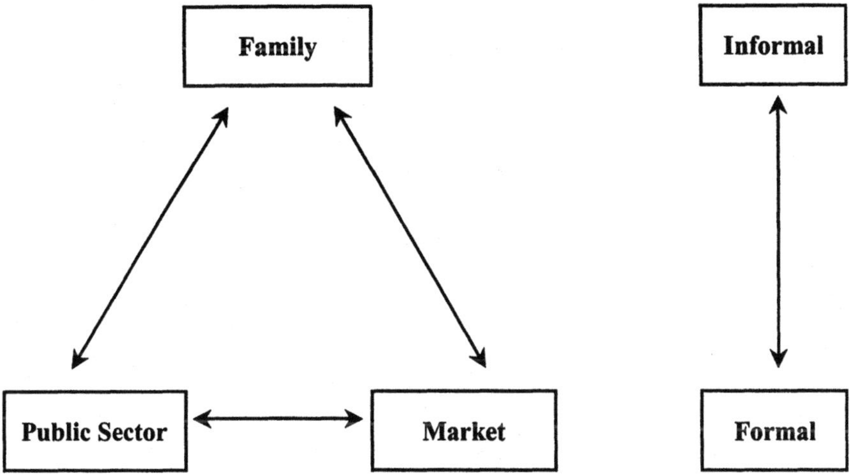

Source: Modification of Evers, 1990

They relate to the public sector, the market, and the family. There is no country in the EU where only one of these principles is applied to the social protection services. All systems include a mix of the principles, but differences in a country's history, demography, social and economic circumstances, ideological influences, legislative basis, cross-national influences, type of government and the relative influence of stakeholders or even cultural and religious values (See, for example, Saltman, Figueras and Sakellaridis, 1998 and compare, for more details, Chapters 2 and 3 of this study) mean that the mix tends to gravitate towards one dominating principle. What mix is chosen and what principle tends to dominate the choice of mix, plus the tendency to place emphasis on one of the principles, establishes the prerequisites for the individual to make decisions himself with regard to his economic security and access to services. It also defines the conditions for ensuring that the systems are just and equitable (possibly including various degrees of a planned, free market or mixed economy). Another feature in the mix of principles can be responsibility split between those who organise the individual services and those responsible for financing (Leichter, 1979; Swedish National Board of Health and Welfare, 1993). In the section that follows, mainly based on information from studies by Richard M. Titmuss (1958; 1964) and a survey carried out for the Swedish National Board of Health and Welfare (1993), the three principles are briefly illustrated independently of one another.

4.2.1 Family-based systems

Social protection was first aimed at the family. Based on the family, or other close personal relationships, it was the only way the problem could be tackled in the primarily agricultural communities in EU countries in those early days. The situation is still the same in primitive societies and in rural or deprived areas of developing countries. The family, organisations based on a family relationship and voluntary or religious bodies meet the individual's need for social protection.

Family-based systems tend to provide only limited assistance and are not particularly formal. They are part of an informal economic structure and assistance is usually given in kind and not in cash. Another feature of such systems is that they do not give the individual much freedom to make decisions for himself. Social justice and equity have effect only within the group concerned and are limited by what the group decides or is able to pay for. In addition, there is usually no external, independent system that supervises or ensures the quality of the service provided, except perhaps what arises from general legislation or, for instance, from charitable organisations.

Systems based on the family, or other informal systems, will still be vitally important for social protection in the future. However, as Salvage (1995) has argued within the framework of a study carried out for the European Foundation for the Improvement of Living and Working Conditions, "smaller families, increases in the number of young people who live together rather than marrying, increased divorce and re-marriage rates and geographical mobility are considered to reduce the potential availability of family members to care for frail elderly people" (p. 4). In addition, she said "the increasing entry of women into the labour force in Europe raises questions concerning the likely availability of women (who represent the majority of the informal caring population) to care for elderly relatives" (p. 4). This means that although family systems cannot be dispensed with, they are not enough to fulfil the growing needs among the EU countries.

Another aspect is that different studies have demonstrated that most elderly people are unable to pay the often huge and unforeseeable costs of long-term care (See, for example, Royal Commission on Long-term Care, 1999). Consequently, what we need are more comprehensive systems, developed by the market or the public sector, which meet these needs.

4.2.2 Market-sourced systems

Differing from informal systems that are based on the family or personal relationships, market-sourced systems do not involve a personal relationship. A free market economy is the foundation for such systems. A regular contribution to some kind of insurance institution is the way in which the individual's rights are safeguarded and the market services he/she thus has access to guarantee that he/she does not need to rely exclusively on more informal support such as the family.

Market-based systems, like the kind of informal support provided by the family or personal relationships, are not all embracing, in that they provide only for individuals who are accepted in the system or who are able to become members of a particular group. Moreover, in a market-based system, bodies responsible for providing the financial resources are normally separate from the bodies, which organise the services, and this, in turn, may make independent government regulation necessary. As Arvidson observed (1995), such regulation is necessary for at least the following three reasons: "First, one function of regulation is to stabilize systems which are principle self-regulated (e.g. families and commercial markets). Such regulation enacted and enforced by legislation, means the creation of 'rules of the game` and codes of behaviour. The second type of regulation is used for sanctioning direct intervention in such systems, for example price controls. The third type is used for controlling the use of public resources (e.g. public investment and consumption, or for transferring payments to private entities)" (p. 66).

An alternative to government regulation is self-regulation, by which the private insurance organisations place restrictions on themselves, for example initiated by an industry association (Arvidson, 1995). However, despite the possibility of regulation in different market systems, this option of service provision in the sector of long-term care seems to have met with some criticism within in cross-national literature in the field. For example, as 'The Economist` (1998) has noted, "private insurance for unlimited long-term care, like health insurance for the elderly, is expensive because of the uncertainty about costs" (p. 17). A comparative overview on payments for care by Evers, Pijl and Ungerson (1994) has pointed out even more clearly that "the market sector is only accessible to those who have money to buy private care" (p. 5).

4.2.3 Public sector systems

The prime characteristic of systems based on the public sector is that they are virtually general, that is, they cover everyone, even individuals who may have no, or only a tenuous connection to the labour market. The community as a whole assumes responsibility for ensuring that social protection is unconditionally available to everybody and on equitable grounds. Public systems also often include the pronounced desire to redistribute income and wealth. The powers that be in such systems regard egalitarianism as being a fundamental principle.

Just as with systems based on the market, the financing and organising of services can be performed by different bodies. Services that are publicly financed may be in the hands of private or voluntary, non-profit organisations. Public authorities, in the form of local or central government agencies or health insurance associations, then usually oversee and ensure the quality of such services, the financing, and often the organisation, of which involves a considerable degree of planned economy (Richard M. Titmuss, 1958; Richard M. Titmuss, 1964; Swedish National Board of Health and Welfare, 1993).

4.3 Models of state welfare in the EU countries

The fifteen EU countries have in their historical development selected different combinations of the three basic principles discussed above. As mentioned earlier, the (historical) development of state welfare was influenced by a range of factors, maybe in particular influenced by a country's political environment and economic circumstances (See, for example OECD, 1996a). Although there exists more or less significant differences, there are nevertheless countries among the Union that have selected similar combinations between public, market and family in view of the finance and organisation mechanisms of their social protection systems. Common grounds that as well can be find themselves within the framework of different models.

Within the framework of scientific discussions in which welfare states are compared there is often reference to a range of such models (Bräutigam and Schmid, 1996), of which the probably most important might be the classification illustrated by Esping-Anderson (1990) ('The Three Worlds of Welfare Capitalism') and the division in welfare states between the 'Bismarck' and 'Beveridge' types. Both have become established as major contributions to the literature on comparative welfare states (See, for example, Kemeny, 1995; Bräutigam and Schmid, 1996) and will therefore be illustrated below.

4.3.1 Esping Anderson's 'Three Worlds of Welfare Capitalism'

Esping-Anderson, argues that when comparing cross-national variations in social rights and welfare state stratification, there are different arrangements between the state, the market, and the family, depending on the type of welfare state concerned. The existing welfare state variations are therefore not linearly distributed, but clustered according to regime types. He distinguishes between different welfare regimes which he refers to as 'liberal', 'conservative' and 'social-democratic' schemes (Esping Andersen, 1990). These three types are described below.

First, we have the 'liberal' welfare state, in which means-tested assistance, modest universal transfers, or modest social-insurance plans play a leading part. Benefits are provided mostly for people of low income, usually working-class, who are dependent on state assistance. In such a welfare state, entitlement is assessed according to strict regulations, is often associated with stigma and benefits awarded are usually low. In turn, the state encourages the market, either passively - by guaranteeing only a minimum - or actively - by subsidising private welfare schemes. The consequence is that this type of regime minimises de-commodification effects, effectively contains the area of social rights, and institutes a stratification within society that combines relative equality of poverty among state-welfare recipients, with a class-political dualism of the two. This kind of welfare regime is, for example, found in Australia and the United States of America. Countries which come close to the 'liberal' regime are, e.g. Switzerland and the UK.

The second type of regime is the 'conservative' or 'corporatist' welfare state. In this type of regime, the liberal preoccupation with market efficiency and commodification was never in the foreground and the granting of social rights was an issue about which there was scarcely any dispute. Status differentials were all-important and; rights continued to be attached to class and status. This corporatism was subservient to a state ready to replace the market as a provider of welfare; thus, private insurance and occupational fringe benefits only play a marginal role. On the other hand, the state's emphasis on maintaining differences in status means that virtually no redistribution takes place. But the church also has a shaping role in such 'corporatist' regimes, and great stress is laid on the preservation of the traditional family unit. Social insurance usually excludes non-working wives, and family benefits encourage motherhood. Day care, and similar family services, are noticeably under-developed; the principle of 'subsidiarity' serving to emphasise that the state will only interfere when the family is no longer able to look after its members. For instance, France and Germany are countries, which have a welfare regime of this type.

Thirdly, there is a regime that can be called 'social democratic', since in nations where this type is predominant, the concept of social democracy was obviously the driving force behind social reform. Rather than tolerate a balance between state and market or between working class and middle class, the social democrats sought to set up a welfare state that would promote equality in terms of the highest possible standards and not in terms of minimum requirements, as was the case in other countries. This meant, first, that the quality of services and benefits were to be upgraded to levels on a par with even the most discriminating tastes of the new middle classes; and, second, that equality was to be achieved by ensuring that workers fully participated in the same kind of rights enjoyed by those better-off than themselves. A practical application of this policy takes the form of a mixture of highly de-commodifying and universal programmes that are, nevertheless designed to meet a variety of expectations. Thus, all levels are linked together in one universal insurance system, while benefits are graduated according to accustomed earnings. This system disposes of the market, and fosters a universal solidarity in favour of the welfare state. Everyone benefits, everyone is dependent, and everyone presumably feels obliged to pay. Furthermore, the principle of the 'social democratic' regime type is not to wait until the family is no longer able to cope, but to socialise the costs of family-hood. The ideal is not to allow dependence on the family to predominate, but to promote individual independence. The outcome is a welfare state that grants benefits directly to children, and assumes direct responsibility for the care of children, the aged and the helpless. As a result, it is committed to a heavy social service burden, not only in responding to the needs of the family but also in allowing women the freedom to choose to work rather than stay at home. Typical examples of this type of regime are found in Denmark, Finland and Sweden (Esping-Andersen, 1990; Taylor-Gooby, 1991).

In order to complete the picture, one should add, as Leibfried (1993) does, the 'rudimentary' type of welfare state regime. In this system, there is no fundamental right to social benefits nor is there a history of full employment. However, for the further purposes of this study, this possible fourth model of welfare regime is, compared with the other three, relatively unimportant. Therefore the study will - like several others (See, for example, Kemeny, 1995; Bräutigam and Schmid, 1996) - continue to use the expression 'Three Worlds of Welfare Capitalism', when Esping-Andersen's classification is concerned.

Roughly similar models to the above illustrated in some detail by Esping-Anderson have been developed by a number of other writers such as Korpi (1982), Cass (1990) and Mishra (1990). On the other hand, several authors (See, for example, O'Connor, 1993; Orloff, 1993) have attacked Esping-Andersen and other mainstream researchers. For example, Orloff (1993) argues that research on the welfare state has omitted an analysis of social policy benefits and services that take particular account of women. O'Connor (1993) observes that comparative research has concentrated too much on the relationship between the state and the labour markets and has not dealt with the relationship between the state and the family. Each of these authors has misgivings about the fact that comparative research on the welfare state is based on a restricted understanding of social rights and citizenship. However, the present study is unable to present evidence on the meaningfulness of distinguishing between three different types of welfare state.

Disregarding the above-mentioned criticism, it is necessary to recognise that there is no single 'pure' type of regime. That the three types of welfare regimes can always be correct for all the different sectors of a welfare state also appears hardly possible in view of the multitude of service provisions (e.g. day care of small children, long-term care for the elderly, unemployment benefits). For instance, Esping-Anderson (1990) argues that although some Scandinavian countries may be predominantly 'social democratic' welfare states, they are not free of crucial liberal elements such as in the insurance schemes for unemployment in Denmark and Sweden that are still essentially voluntary in nature.

As an internationally recognised study by Jamieson (1991) on a cross-country comparison of domiciliary long-term care services (in Belgium, Denmark, England and Wales, France, Germany, Israel, Italy and the Netherlands) has found, at the beginning of the 1990s, the service system features in the countries examined have been to a large extent a manifestation of the general principles of welfare state regimes (Anttonen and Sipilä, 1996). Jamieson further argued that, therefore, policies concerning the disabled elderly in the EU countries are established within the framework of welfare regimes which have existed for a long time, with which people are very familiar and which have led to arrangements being made with regard to the part the state plays, the criteria of welfare provision and its extent (Jamieson, 1991). In the study concerned, this has been illustrated by taking the examples of three countries (each of which represents a different type of welfare state regime, according to Esping-Anderson's (1990) classification). These examples show how the central elements of a long-term care scheme are in harmony with the principles of a country's welfare regime.

Starting with the domiciliary long-term care scheme in Germany (with a 'conservative' or 'corporatist' welfare state), Jamieson (1991) argued that the marked German division of service provision into two distinct domains (health and social services), with their different principles of distribution and access was a major factor in increasing the problems of disabled elderly people. The predominance of the insurance principle in health care in the 1990s, against the background of the vested interests of the labour market, has resulted in older people in need of long-term care being to a large extent excluded. It was also argued that this left older people to depend on fringe domiciliary long-term care benefits, which have always been very explicitly guided by the subsidy principle. Replacing the family with the state or lessening the burden on the family to any significant extent would be flying in the face of well-established principles of welfare. According to the study, the possibility that these principles would cease to be predominant could only arise as a result of labour market demands for women to work. Unlike Germany, Jamieson (1991) suggests that the 'social-democratic' welfare system in Denmark largely takes the form of wide-ranging state intervention and long-term care entitlement which is universal rather than selective. This is to say that the scheme is specially concerned with the needs of elderly people and their families. It is no longer expected of women in the family that they should ever be full-time nurses. The part the state plays is clear and well established, and this is why the welfare services there for elderly people have been more consistent and widespread than in most other EU countries (Jamieson, 1991). Finally, Jamieson (1991) explains how policies are developed and service provided in a 'liberal' welfare system by taking Britain as an example. First, she makes the point that the British system of about 1990 had more in common with the Danish than the German system. Britain and Denmark both have a national health service that is financed from tax income and is accessible to and supported by all classes. The British system, however, has never been as universal and wide reaching as the Danish system. In addition, it was suggested that while, in Germany and Denmark, the underlying principles of the welfare state have from the outset been strongly embedded, a welfare system covering everyone did not fully develop because it lacked the general support it needed, especially that of the middle class. When, in addition, one remembers that the electoral system in Britain has tended to lead to the dominance of one particular political party, it is obvious that social policies have been liable to take different forms, depending on which political party was in power. More often than not it has been the Conservatives. This was the case in the 1980s, for example, with a radical, neo-liberalist regime. As Esping-Andersen puts it, the British welfare state at the beginning of the 1990s was becoming increasingly 'liberal'. Where domiciliary long-term care is concerned, this 'liberal' tendency is particularly illustrated by the provision of benefits limited to people of low income and the assessment of entitlement according to strict regulations (Jamieson, 1991).

4.3.2 Division into 'Bismarck' and 'Beveridge' welfare states

Apart from Anderson's 'Three Worlds of Welfare Capitalism' (1990) discussed above, the division into welfare states of the 'Bismarck' and 'Beveridge' models is probably the most important classification of such states. This second approach reaches some conclusions that are closely compatible with Anderson's (1990) findings (See, for example, Bräutigam and Schmid, 1996). In general, one can say that the 'Bismarck' model of the welfare state is characterised by its orientation towards social insurance. This means that the scheme involves a direct payment to a fund designated for a specific purpose such as long-term care. The main source of funding comes from ear-marked contributions, often paid by employees and/or employers and provisions are frequently limited to employees. Essential parts of benefits and services are, usually under the control of non-state bodies, e.g. associations and corporations (the third party payer), provided in the form of transferred payments and not through social institutions owned by the state. The group of EU countries which is known usually to manage their schemes of social protection mainly based on the 'Bismarck' model are the Benelux countries (Belgium, Luxembourg and the Netherlands), Austria, France and Germany. In contrast to this, coverage in the 'Beveridge' model is usually universal, which means that all residents in a country are included within the provision. However, this does not necessarily mean that the benefits and services offered, which are mainly financed from general taxation, will be of a high standard. In this model, contracting usually plays no role in the relationship between third party payers which are government units and (public) providers, as both financing and delivery have been subsumed within the same organisational structure. Since the state is usually both the main provider and controller of benefits or services, it is frequently characterised as an active welfare state. The group of EU countries which traditionally is known to be predominantly marked by 'Beveridge' elements in their social protection systems comprises the Republic of Ireland, the United Kingdom, the Scandinavian EU countries (Denmark, Finland and Sweden) and the Southern EU countries (Greece, Italy, Portugal and Spain) (Pfaff and Nagel, 1994; De Roo, 1995; Saltman and Figueras, 1997; Saltman, Figueras and Sakellarides, 1998).

4.4 Domiciliary long-term care arrangements in the EU countries

4.4.1 General description

Having discussed basic principles theoretically underlying the provision of social protection services (including those for domiciliary long-term care) and based on this, having illustrated different models of welfare states that historically have emerged out of the ways countries are known to combine these principles, the following section illustrates how EU domiciliary long-term care schemes are organised and funded in practice. However, as noted in earlier parts of this study, there is a huge diversity in the individual arrangements across the Union. For example, the same service provided for the care of disabled elderly people is frequently administered by different bodies in different countries. In other words, the long-term care provision in a particular country is often covered by the benefits and services of a number of different institutions such as the health care scheme, social assistance scheme or pension scheme. In some countries, domiciliary long-term care provision is part of the health care scheme or is separately administered within the framework of the health care scheme (with responsibility for the health-/long-term care funds) whereas in other countries it is administered by the social services and is organised by and is the responsibility of local authorities (See, for example, Anttonen and Sipilä, 1996; Edvartsen, 1996). Another major difficulty already mentioned is that there are some very fundamental and important differences in relevant definitions, not only among the countries, but also across scientific literature (See, for example, Walker and Maltby, 1997). In other words, there is still no international agreement on what is precisely meant by ′domiciliary long-term care services‵ (See, for example, Anttonen and Sipilä, 1996). A further important difficulty is that existing literature in the field of international comparative research on national long-term care services for the elderly can still be described as inadequate. This subject is still one of the most insufficiently researched areas in social welfare and consequently there is hardly any data available from international agencies, which might otherwise provide a basis for comparative analyses (See, for example, Alber, 1993; Antonnen and Sipilä, 1996; Österle, 1999).

It nevertheless appears possible to reduce the existing diversity, at least conceptually, by focusing on selected common categories, while looking at the different arrangements in the individual countries. This may allow a comparison between national long-term care schemes and enable differences and common features to be clarified on a very general basis. Appropriate categories for such an overview, which have been useful, for example, within comparative studies about health care schemes (See, for example, Pfaff and Nagel, 1994; Saltman and Figueras, 1997), are the major source of funding and the major type of service provision. In what follows, the various domiciliary long-term care schemes are compared by predominantly orientating the discussion towards these categories. The data for this is derived from separate national data sources and to some extent from the extremely limited comparative literature available on the subject.

4.4.2 A cross-national overview

Starting with Denmark, the responsibility for domiciliary long-term care services lies with the local authorities. In addition, local authorities, which run their own domiciliary long-term care services, also act as the major provider (Danish Ministry of Social Affairs, 1995). Private and voluntary, non-profit providers are comparatively scarce, but contracts by the municipalities with this type of service provider is significantly increasing. At best they work on instructions from the local authorities and are only able to offer their services within the framework of the legal regulations (Gottschalk, 1995; OECD, 1998). As the provision of services is locally administered and regulated, there are wide differences between areas with regard to the availability, quality and cost of services (OECD, 1996a). The cost of these services is mainly derived from local taxation and from general financial allocations from the national government (European Commission, 2000). In Denmark, permanent domiciliary long-term care services for the disabled elderly are usually free of charge (OECD, 1996a).

A similar situation to that in Denmark exists in the next Scandinavian EU country, Sweden. Here, the responsibility for the care of disabled elderly also lies with the local authorities and, there is considerable public provision. The local authorities provide the main bulk of their help during normal working hours, but help is also available at weekends and at night (OECD, 1996a). In addition, there are also a few local authorities, which contract domiciliary long-term care services out to private, for-profit organisations (OECD, 1998). The financing is mainly provided through local taxation. In addition, the local authorities receive a considerable amount of funding from central government (Hutten and Kerkstra, 1996). Since 1992, this has been in the form of block grants, which are related to a number of area characteristics, including the number of elderly people. In Sweden, each local authority fixes its own fees for domiciliary care, and these take the user's income into account (OECD, 1996a).

In the third Scandinavian EU country, namely Finland, domiciliary long-term care is the responsibility of the 460 Finnish local authorities. In Finland likewise, the public sector is the predominant provider of services for the disabled elderly. However, compared to the other two Scandinavian EU countries, there is a higher number of contractual relationships between municipalities and voluntary non-profit organisations, such as the 'Central Union for the Welfare of the Aged', the 'Finnish Red Cross' and 'National Association of the Disabled' (Hutten, 1996a). In addition, municipalities buy some services from private, profit-making organisations (about 10%). The major financial cost (about 90%) is paid out of local and national taxation.

All individuals have to pay a fee, which is based on their income and the number of persons in the household (European Commission, 2000).

In Greece, which is the first Southern EU country in this overview, there are virtually no domiciliary long-term care services available that are controlled and directly subsidised by state authorities. Both public health insurance schemes and social service schemes have in reality no overall coverage for domiciliary long-term care services (Giaoutzi, 1991). The probably most important services available are provided by voluntary non-profit (e.g. the 'Hellenic Red Cross' and the 'Greek Orthodox Church') and private organisations. But these organisations operate independently of public contracts. In areas where these services are available, patients themselves usually pay, although the payments for some of these services are quite low (in particular, the services of the non-profit voluntary organisations are often considerably subsidised by these organisations' own resources and by voluntary contributions). However, even where this alternative type of service provision is concerned, usually only urban areas are covered, mainly in Athens and Thessaloniki (Boerma, De Jong and Mulder, 1993). As a result, the majority of disabled elderly in Greece still rely on informal solutions (e.g. care by family, friends and neighbours). In addition, many middle class families make their own arrangements for the long-term care of their elderly relatives, in the absence of state provision, by employing immigrant labour (Salvage, 1995).

In the following Southern EU country, Italy, the scheme of domiciliary care for the elderly is highly decentralised and is mainly the responsibility of the 20 regions. For the most important domiciliary long-term care services, there is no national framework and there are large differences among the available services. In some regions, domiciliary care services have been long established, while other local authorities, especially in the South, have not even instituted this kind of service (Pacolet and Wilderom, 1991; European Commission, 2000). Because of these markedly regional variations, it is difficult to determine who is the main provider of services. Public provision by the local authorities still might be the dominant sector. However, there is a strong tendency to replace public provision by services from voluntary, non-profit and private organisations. Such non-public organisations are usually reimbursed according to the number of hours that domiciliary help is supplied and receive no funding from official sources (Hutten, 1996b). The main source of funding for the domiciliary services of the local authorities is tax revenues that come from the central government. The state contribution is distributed among the local authorities by the regions. The amount of subsidies is based on the number of potential users, the actual users, the available personnel and the functions of the social services (Hutten and Kerkstra, 1996). In Italy, contributory payments usually depend on the financial circumstances of their users or their families. The level of such payments differs considerably from one region or community to another. In some authorities there are no contributory payments because services are only provided for elderly people with a low income (Hutten, 1996b).

In the next Southern country, Portugal, the public organisations are part of the social services system, which means that the central government, in particular the 'State Secretary for Social Security', is mainly responsible for domiciliary long-term care at the national level. This 'State Secretary' integrates services organised at three levels. At the national level, the 'General Directorate for Social Action' is a department in central charge of the development, co-ordination, legal framework and provision of technical support for domiciliary long-term care services. The 23 regional social security centres pay benefits and provide services for disabled elderly people. These regional centres work with the local authorities, which are the main providers of services (supervised by the regional centres) (Hutten, 1996c). Services are mainly funded by the national government from tax receipts. The percentage of the total costs, which the elderly in need have to pay themselves, is based on their income level. There are no formal regulations with regard to the kind of and duration of the domiciliary care. But, owing to the limited number of services that are available in the country, the person concerned cannot have them for an unlimited period of time (Hutten, 1996c).

In Spain, the last in the group of Southern EU countries, local authorities are (under the direction of the regional administration) responsible for ensuring the provision of domiciliary long-term care. It is these local authorities that are also the major provider of services. There is, however, a growing involvement in the provision of these services by voluntary, non-profit associations by agreement with local governments. The regions, in all cases, are responsible for planning, organising and regulating services, co-ordinating resources and undertaking research (OECD, 1996a). Contributions from national and regional government constitute the main source of financing for domiciliary long-term care services (OECD, 1996a). Services are usually free for those receiving the minimum monthly pension, while those with a relatively high income meet the whole cost themselves. Those between pay a fee based on a sliding scale related to income (OECD, 1996a).

In the Republic of Ireland, domiciliary long-term care services in kind are part of the general health services and, the responsibility for the services is based at the eight 'Health Boards'. About two thirds of the service are provided by the 'Health Boards' directly. Direct provision usually means that the 'Health Board' employs a domiciliary care organiser. Sometimes this is a special officer and sometimes a public health nurse acts as a domiciliary care organiser.

However, the size of the voluntary sector is nevertheless worthy of note. About one third (mainly depending on the region) of care is provided by about 900 voluntary, non-profit organisations funded by the 'Health Board' (Boerma, De Jong and Mulder, 1993; O'Sullivan, 1998). The main source of finance is taxation, which accounts for about 80% of the total, followed by health contributions amounting to about 9%, hospital charges for accommodation and other income 6.1% and EU-related receipts 2.3% and one or two other minor sources (Lynch, 1998). In general, the eight 'Health Boards' receive a fixed budget from the 'Department of Health'. It is difficult to say what proportion of the budget individuals themselves pay because methods of collecting these co-payments vary a lot. However, very roughly, the contributions of the disabled elderly might not be too far from 10% of the total budget. The negotiating ability of the individual also plays a part (Boerma, De Jong and Mulder, 1993, OECD, 1998). In addition, to the above, another major pillar of long-term care arrangements in the Republic of Ireland is an allowance granted to those who provide care on an informal basis. The exact amount for this benefit, that was introduced in 1990 as a social security programme, varies with the income of the individual carer and her or his partner (European Commission, 2000).

In the UK, the responsibility of assessing need and paying for domiciliary long-term care services in kind was largely transferred from national level to local authorities with the introduction of the 'National Health Service and the Community Care Act' in April 1993. Services are mainly funded from central sources and local taxation (Tinker, McCreadie, Rostgaard and Fridberg, 1998). In general, the scheme shows a noticeable regional diversity regarding entitlement and services (Walker and Maltby, 1997). Meanwhile, the main bulk of domiciliary long-term care is provided by private organisations that have concluded contracts with the local authorities (Knapp and Hardy and Forder, 2001). The local authorities pay for domiciliary long-term care services mainly from central government allocations. In addition, local taxation and charging are the two other essential sources of funding (Tinker, McCreadie, Wright and Salvage, 1994; Royal Commission on Long-term Care, 1999). In addition to the services predominantly available in kind under the responsibility of the local authorities, the 'Department of Social Security' provides different cash benefits for long-term care on a national basis (Rostgaard and Fridberg, 1998). The most important of these benefits are the 'Attendance Allowance' ('AA') which is directly paid to the elderly person in need and the 'Invalid Care Allowance' that is granted to those people who are unable to work because their caring responsibilities. These cash transfers are both mainly funded out of general taxation (European Commission, 2000).

Turning to Austria, the first of the six countries now following, with a health care scheme that is based on social insurance, domiciliary long-term care is mainly the responsibility of the regional (nine) and local authorities. For instance, they have to ensure that there is a certain minimum standard of domiciliary long-term care. For the provision of the infrastructure, general taxation is used. However, elderly people in need of long-term care receive an attendance allowance to cover the care costs. This scheme was implemented in 1993 by the federal government. The main source of finance for this attendance allowance is general taxation (European Commission, 1998). The disabled elderly mainly receive their cash benefits directly through the pension insurance, which is itself reimbursed by the federal government. The amount of payment depends on medical criteria and 'ADL'-measurements, and on the level of need (altogether seven) in which the patient is classified (Austrian Federal Ministry of Labour and Social Affairs, 1995). The basic idea of this policy is to provide people with a choice in the type of care they receive (Evers, Leichsenring and Strümpel, 1995). If the allowance is insufficient, the disabled elderly person frequently has to pay for the extra necessary care him or herself (Wiegele, 1994). In Austria, between 80 and 85% of the new allowance goes to the sector of informal care (e.g. family members, neighbours). When there are no relatives who are legally responsible, the provinces are expected to provide formal long-term care services for the disabled elderly (OECD, 1998).

In Belgium, the organisation and responsibility of domiciliary long-term care services is mainly at the local level. Domiciliary long-term care services under the responsibility of the local authorities, each of which has a 'Public Social Assistance Centre', are mainly provided (about 75%) by the public sector and additionally by private organisations (about 25%). The largest part of the costs is financed from general taxation (Belgium Ministry of Finance and Budget, 1994; OECD, 1998). In Belgium, all clients have to contribute to the total costs of those domiciliary long-term care services which are the responsibility of the local authorities (Belgium Ministry of Finance and Budget, 1994). In addition to this service provision, a certain share of personal help with 'ADL' elements is also provided within the framework of the health care scheme, which is mainly financed from social insurance contributions (Schneider, Dennerlein, Köse and Scholtes, 1992, European Commission, 2000). If 'ADL'-help is provided within the framework of the health insurance scheme (mainly by voluntary, non-profit organisations, in particular by the 'White/Yellow Cross'), there is no contribution by the individual (Hutten, 1996d).

In the Netherlands, compulsory health insurance is based on two laws: the 'Law on Mutual Health Insurance' ('ZFW') and the 'Law on Special Medical Expenses' ('AWBZ'). Domiciliary long-term care is predominately a matter of the second-mentioned law ('AWBZ'), which covers about 90% of the total costs concerned. The first organisation providing long-term care services was founded nearly 125 years ago. By the beginning of the 20th century, voluntary, non-profit organisations, which are still the main providers for the elderly population in need of domiciliary long-term care, were established all over the country (van der Linden and van Dam, 1997; Dutch National Association for Home Care, 1997). The main source of financing stipulated in the 'AWBZ' is contributory. The social contributions have an upper limit and are made by employees (Van der Linden and van Dam, 1997). The contributions are collected into a central fund and then passed to the individual health insurance funds, mainly according to their respective expenditure. The individual health insurance funds are then responsible for the organisation of domiciliary long-term care services (Winters, 1994). Contributory payments are not required for most aspects of long-term care provision. If such extra payments are necessary, these are usually small amounts for home-making assistance and scaled according to the individual's income (Van der Linden and van Dam, 1997).

In Germany, a long-term care insurance scheme was introduced in 1995 as a fifth branch of social insurance alongside insurance for health, old-age, unemployment and accidents at work. This new scheme that provides benefits for both domiciliary and residential care, has been established within the framework of the statutory health insurance scheme. This meant that a new administration apparatus was not necessary. Instead, the health insurance funds also represent the long-term care insurance funds. Administrative expenses are paid for from these long-term care insurance funds (Clasen, 1997). The providers of domiciliary long-term care services mainly comprises five voluntary, non-profit associations (two of the organisations have a religious basis, having been set up for 'Catholics' and 'Protestants'; one is a traditional social welfare organisation set up for workers; one is run by the 'Red Cross'; and the last is a non-affiliated group called 'Parity') and private providers which meanwhile have become the largest group (Para. 77 German Care Insurance Act, 2000; Vincentz Verlag, 2000). As in several other branches of social insurance, the funding is based on compulsory contributions, evenly split between employees and employers. In the year 2000, the rate was 1.7% of the so-called 'insurable income' (frequently the gross income) up to a limit of € 3,298 (DM 6,450) per month (AOK, 2000). Membership is compulsory for all German citizens, but as with Germans health insurance, the long-term care insurance scheme allows employees with earnings above this level to opt out and join a private fund or a special scheme, such persons comprising about 10% of the insured (European Commission, 2000). In Germany, patients do not, in fact, have to pay for domiciliary long-term care services within the framework of the long-term care insurance scheme. However, benefits from this scheme, which are provided independent of income and amount of contributions, are frequently insufficient to cover all the needs of the disabled elderly (Schneider, 1999).

Luxembourg has used the German social welfare legislation (founded under Bismarck) as a model for the establishment of its social protection system (Köstler, 1997a) and implemented a social long-term care insurance based on the German model in 1998 (Luxembourgian Ministry of Social Security, 1998). The new long-term care insurance scheme was established as a part of general health care insurance. There is a tendency that more and more providers try to arrive at a general agreement with the responsible administrative institution, in order to have the authorisation to provide services within the framework of this new social insurance scheme for long-term care. Providers are private, public, and, quite frequently, voluntary, non-profit associations (Luxembourg Ministry of Social Security, 1998). The main source of funding for this new insurance scheme is contributions from all types of income - from employment, capital gains and interest on capital and rental income. In addition, considerable state subsidies are used for the long-term care scheme. If the provision from the insurance is not sufficient to cover all the care costs an elderly person in need usually has to find this extra money (Köstler, 1996a; Luxembourg Ministry of Social Security, 1998).

In France there was a long public discussion on the introduction of social long-term care insurance. The main reason that the scheme was finally not introduced probably was the difficult financial situation of the social insurance scheme ('Sécurité Sociale') as a whole already in existence and in particular the financial difficulties of the health care and pension scheme. As a consequence a new autonomous benefit scheme ('Prestation Spécifique Dépendance' - 'PSD') for the disabled elderly was implemented in 1997, as an alternative for social long-term care insurance (Köstler 1996b; French Law No. 97-60, 2000). Responsibility for administering the service provision under the 'PSD' scheme is in the hands of the regional authorities (departments). The predominant, authorised organisations that provide formal domiciliary long-term care services under the scheme are voluntary, non-profit organisations. In addition, a significant number of carers work on a freelance basis and the majority of elderly people in need directly employ a carer, e.g. a member of the family (with the exception of the spouse or partner), to care for them (Martin, 2000; Faessel, 2001). For the latter group of people with a directly employed carer, the 'PSD' allowance is paid in the form of a monthly cheque or voucher to the disabled elderly person so that the carer can be reimbursed. In the case where the disabled elderly person is cared for by a formal provider, 'PSD' payments usually go directly to this organisation. The main source of funding for the allowance is taxation (Blondeau and Dubois, 1997; European Commission, 2000).

4.4.3 Classification of EU long-term care schemes

The previous section has shown that there exists a huge difference in the way EU countries organise and fund domiciliary long-term care arrangements. Based on the information above, it nevertheless is possible to distinguish the following two groups of domiciliary long-term care schemes in the EU countries (Greece has been excluded since, based on the literature available, it can scarcely be said to have a domiciliary long-care scheme):

1. Domiciliary long-term care schemes where the main source of funding is taxation and services are predominantly provided by the public (private) sector. This group of countries comprises the Scandinavian EU countries (Denmark, Finland and Sweden), the Southern EU countries (Italy, Portugal and Spain), the Republic of Ireland, the UK, Austria, Belgium and France.

2. Domiciliary long-term care schemes where ear-marked contributions are the main source of funding and the services are predominantly provided by voluntary, non-profit (private) organisations, which frequently receive national or regional subsidies in addition to their fees for the services provided. This group of countries comprises Germany, Luxembourg and the Netherlands.

In the first group of countries, benefits and services are usually administered by the social services (except in the Republic of Ireland) and are usually decentrally organised by and the responsibility of local (regional) authorities, whereas in the second group of countries they are part of a social insurance-based health care scheme or long-term scheme within the framework of the health care scheme under the responsibility of the authorities administering the health- or long-term care funds.

Moreover, the previous section has shown that in the majority of the EU countries contributory payments for domiciliary long-term care are required (in those countries where no co-payments are required, the benefits provided are frequently insufficient, which means that the disabled elderly often have to pay for a certain proportion themselves), mostly scaled according to the income of the disabled elderly or their families. However, it is not possible to connect clearly the categories of co-payments and income-related benefits with the two groups of domiciliary long-term care schemes identified. Co-payments and means-related provision are found in most of the countries of the first group, whereas in the second group of countries, only some forms of co-payment may be required and there are no income-related benefits at all.

In addition to the above-indicated possibility of categorising the domiciliary long-term care schemes of the EU countries according to the main source of their finance and the predominance of either public or voluntary, non- profit providers, the information in the previous section should also enable us to categorise EU domiciliary long-term care schemes according to the predominant methods of paying providers. This arrangement appears to be particularly interesting, as it has been a major focus of several internationally recognised studies on health care schemes (See, for example, Hurst, 1994; Ham, 1997) and as far as the author knows, has not until now been available for the sector of domiciliary long-term care. Based on the findings in the present chapter, it is possible to identify three major models of paying providers in domiciliary EU long-term care schemes. These three models are illustrated below.

Figure 4 Model 1 of paying providers (repayment of private expenses from public funds)

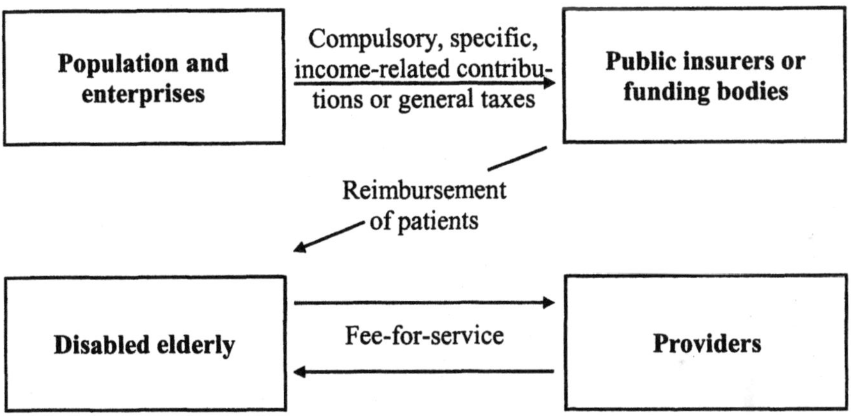

Source: References of Chapter 4

Figure 4 shows a compulsory system, which involves reimbursement by the disabled elderly themselves for care services, in part or in whole. In countries with this model, the premiums for these compulsory schemes are mainly paid from general taxation (income-related contributions). In this model, long-term care providers are usually directly paid by the disabled elderly on a fee-for-service basis. The disabled elderly usually have their expenditure reimbursed up to a certain extent by non-competing sickness (long-term care) funds or funding bodies according to the rate of benefit set out in the scheme. There may well be cost sharing between the disabled elderly and the public funding system. Both the Austrian and French long-term care schemes are predominantly made up of elements of this model.

Figure 5 Model 2 of paying providers (payment for services through public contracts with providers)

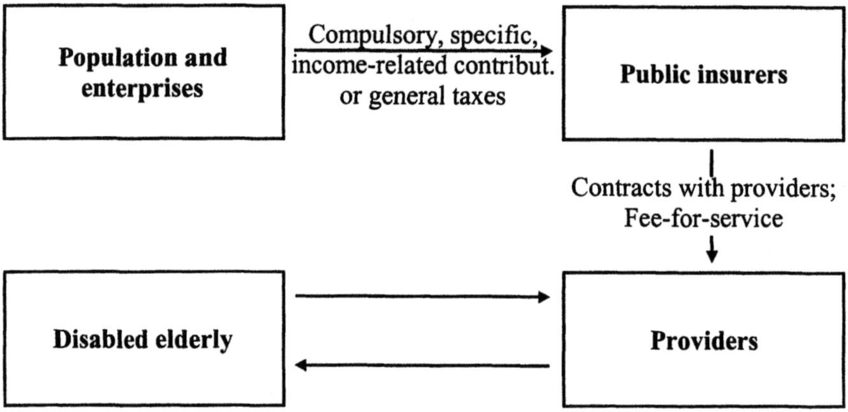

Source: References of Chapter 4

Figure 5 shows a compulsory system with contracts between the public insurers (funding bodies) and the providers. In countries with this model, the premiums for these compulsory schemes are predominantly paid from income-related contributions by employees and/or employers (sometimes general taxation). In this model, independent, long-term care providers are usually reimbursed on a fee-for-service basis by usually non-competing sickness (long-term care) funds. Services are usually supplied in kind to eligible disabled elderly people. The main features of this model are that the responsible organisations are sickness (long-term care) fund authorities, which have contractual relations with the providers. In other words, there is separation of the insurers and the providers. The German, Dutch and Luxembourg long-term care schemes are predominantly made up of elements of this model.

The following Figure 6 (p. 77) shows a compulsory system with integration between public funding bodies and providers. In this model, the local (or national) authority (public insurer) often has a statutory duty to provide domiciliary long-term care through, for example, their social service departments. The local authorities (funding bodies) usually receive a fixed budget (financed from taxation) from the national (or regional) government to pay for the services provided. The available budget from the national (or regional) government usually depends on the number of inhabitants or elderly people in the catchments area or on the number of staff. In addition, finance is also raised through local taxation. The condition that the providers frequently belong to the local authority means in principle that the local government is both the main funding body and the major provider. In general, the choice of providers for disabled elderly is likely to be limited in this model. The long-term care schemes in Denmark, Finland, Italy, Portugal, Spain, Sweden, the Republic of Ireland and the UK are predominantly made up of elements of this model.

Figure 6 Model 3 of paying providers (payment for services provided by public authorities and paid for from public funds)

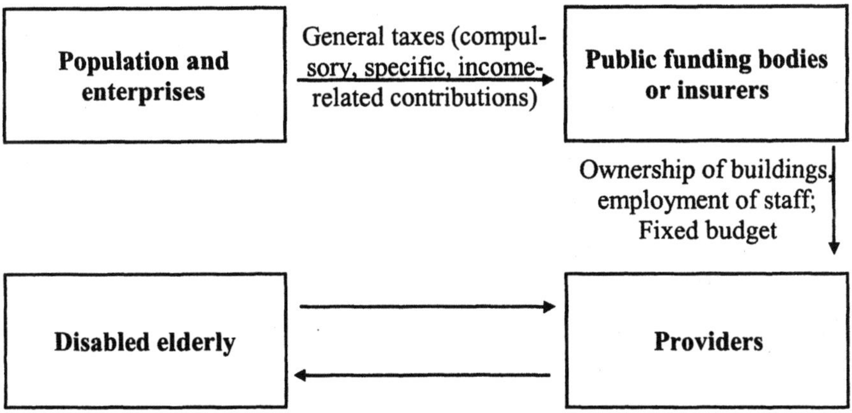

Source: References of Chapter 4

With regard to the major methods of paying providers, combining the models identified with the earlier categories described regarding the main sources of funding and the main methods of providing services, and using these three factors as major pre-defined categories for a classification, the author suggests that there are three different types of domiciliary EU long-term care scheme found among the EU countries. This is shown in the following Table 13 (p. 78).

Of course, this classification scheme only indicates the main characteristics of the various national long-term care schemes. One could equally claim that many of the schemes could be included in more than one category. For example, despite the implementation of the domiciliary long-term care social insurance Act in Germany in 1995, the German scheme is still not a purely social insurance scheme financed from contributions. The services in kind of € 1,432 (DM 2,800) per month for each elderly person with a high level of disability are unlikely to be enough to cover all requirements. Hence, the social assistance scheme (mainly financed from taxation) still (depending on the patient's income and capital) plays a part in the provision of long-term care in Germany (Edvartsen, 1996; Para. 36, Sub-para. 3 German Care Insurance Act, 2000).

Table 13 Classification of EU long-term care schemes

	Category A	Category B	Category C
Main source of funding	Taxes	Taxes	Contributions
Predominant type of providers	Public (Private)	Public / Private	Voluntary non-profit (Private)
Major method of paying providers	Payment for services provided by public authorities and paid for from public funds	Repayment of private expenses from public funds	Payment for services through public contracts with providers
Countries	Belgium Denmark Finland Italy Portugal Rep. of Ireland Spain Sweden United Kingdom	Austria France	Germany Luxembourg Netherlands

Source: References of Chapter 4

4.5 Welfare state changes

As a further step, it would be useful to examine the present relationship between the domiciliary long-term care schemes discussed above and the models of state welfare regimes dealt with (Esping-Anderson's 'Three Worlds of Welfare Capitalism' and the distinction made between welfare states of the 'Bismarck' and 'Beveridge' type). According to the earlier literature at hand, it would seem that the two classifications of welfare states dealt with above covered the various forms that a social protection (long-term care) scheme could take in previous times. For example, as far as Esping-Anderson's (1990) classification of welfare state regimes is concerned, this was clearly demonstrated for the sector of domiciliary long-term care by Jamieson and her colleagues in their internationally recognised study (1991), to which the author has made reference in the second section of the present Chapter, at least for the countries involved in their investigations. Something similar might apply to the division between 'Bismarck' and 'Beveridge' welfare states. This has particularly been illustrated by several studies (See, for example, Pfaff and Nagel, 1994) dealing with the health care sector which includes the provision of long-term care benefits and services in different EU countries.

The question is now if these two models of welfare state regimes which have been useful as a basis for the analysis of social protection systems are transferable to the domiciliary long-term care schemes found in the Union at the turn of the millennium. The welfare state regimes illustrated were constructed based on a certain constellation of economic, political and other contextual factors. An important point in this connection might be that the illustrated models of welfare state regimes were developed on the assumption that the state was able to manage the economy and specifically to maintain the conditions for full employment. As discussed in the previous Chapters of this study, nearly all EU countries are confronted by extreme changes (e.g. ageing of the population, social changes and high rates of unemployed) that have become more and more matters for public discussion since the beginning of the 1990s and which have a great influence on the social protection systems. These changes influence, among other things, in particular the provision of long-term care for the elderly. In addition, as the past has shown, it is possible that not only policy measures can vary, even welfare systems can themselves be subject to change. Therefore, the developments noted in the 1990s may well have contributed to changes in the relation between domiciliary long-term care schemes and traditional models of welfare state regimes.

Searching for scientific studies dealing with the question whether current long-term care schemes are still, to a large extent manifestations of the illustrated models of welfare state regimes is an almost fruitless task. Most of the few existing studies address the relationship of the social protection (or health care) systems to the models of state welfare. An exception is an investigation carried out for the European Commission (1999) which looked at the question of social protection in the case of age-related long-term care in the 15 EU countries and Norway at the close of the 20th century. The study found that it has generally become very difficult to clearly classify the EU long-term care schemes as belonging to the 'Bismarck' type on the one hand or to the 'Beveridge' type on the other. It was further argued that several EU schemes which could earlier be assigned to one of these two models of welfare state have now come closer together. Looking at more widely-ranging publications, a paper put out by the German Chancellor Schröder and the UK Prime Minister Blair (1999) dealing with the future prospects of public policy in the Union appears particularly worthy of notice. It was argued that given the changes in life expectancy, family structure and the role of women, there is a necessity for systems of social protection to adapt themselves to the new situation. The searching for practical solutions for this process of adaptation should be made without insisting on welfare state traditions. It was further argued that new conditions and realities would require a new assessment of old traditions and the development of new concepts. Other sources (e.g. European Commission, 1998; Mossialos, Dixon, Figueras and Kutzin, 2002) likewise point to the considerable change in the economic and social context and the need to modernise and adapt EU social protection systems (e.g. those for health and long-term care) to change, including a re-thinking of existing traditions.

Taking into account the data on domiciliary long-term care arrangements in the Union obtained from the extremely limited amount of available literature and illustrated in the previous section it is clear that this does not allow one to draw any far-reaching conclusions when examining the extent to which current schemes are influenced by the various countries' welfare state traditions. There are, however, at least for some countries, indications that appear to confirm the above-noted findings from the limited available literature, namely, that today's choices of social protection (domiciliary long-term care) arrangements do not necessarily have to be based on historical traditions. For example, the discussion has shown that France, a country well-known for its orientation towards a 'Bismarckian' based social insurance scheme, has chosen a mainly tax-funded arrangement for covering the risk of long-term care. However, much more detailed analysis and empirical evidence is necessary in order to be in a position to arrive at conclusions in this very complex issue. Therefore, a more beneficial approach, after knowledge of empirical experience of selected EU domiciliary long-term care schemes (Compare Chapters 6,7 and 8) has become available is discussed in Chapter 10 of this study.

4.6 Summary

The overall objective of this Chapter has been to give a broader theoretical basis to the discussion on domiciliary long-term care schemes in EU countries, which takes into account the fact that individual schemes are usually embedded in a country's social protection system. In order to achieve this, the first section of the chapter offers a description, in simplified, theoretical form, of basic principles underlying the provision of social protection systems, while giving special emphasis to long-term care provision for the elderly. Attention was drawn to three principles relating to the public sector, the market, and the family. However, all social protection systems in the EU include a mix of these principles, but differences in a country's history, demography, economic and social circumstances, ideological influences, legislative basis, cross-national influences, type of government and the relative influence of stakeholders or even cultural and religious values mean that the mix tends to gravitate towards one dominating principle. This may well split the responsibility between those responsible for financing and those responsible for organising services, such as long-term care for the elderly.

The way a country applies these basic principles, normally in combination, makes it a certain type of welfare state. This aspect has been taken into account in the second part of this chapter. Within the framework of scientific discussions in which welfare states are compared there is often reference to a range of models, of which probably the two most important ones are the classification illustrated by Esping-Anderson (1990) ('The Three Worlds of Welfare Capitalism') that distinguishes between 'liberal', 'conservative' and 'social democratic' welfare states and the division between welfare states of the 'Bismarck' and 'Beveridge' types. Both have become established as a major contribution to the literature on comparative welfare states. The two classifications have firstly been illustrated in general and then, by reference to particular countries as examples, an attempt was made to find out how the respective models of state welfare have had an influence on the development of certain sectors in the individual social protection systems. According to the literature at hand, it would seem that the two classifications of welfare states dealt with above covered the various forms that a long-term care scheme could take previously. For example, as far as Esping-Anderson's (1990) classification is concerned, this was clearly demonstrated by Jamieson and her colleagues in their internationally recognised study (1991), to which the author has made reference, at least for the countries involved in their investigations. For the possible models of welfare states ('liberal', 'conservative' and 'social democratic') - this has been illustrated by presenting a country example for each type. Something similar might apply to the division between 'Bismarck' and 'Beveridge' welfare state models (a typology that appears quite compatible with Anderson's classification).

The aim of the next part of this Chapter was to give a cross-national overview on the organisational structures and the funding arrangements within which EU domiciliary long-term care schemes work in practice. By describing the individual countries' focusing on common aspects, i.e. in particular, the providers responsible for long-term care services and the major source of funding, it was possible to reduce the existing diversity among the individual schemes. In addition, the data at hand made it possible to classify the individual long-term care schemes into two groups. The first group consists of countries in which the long-term care schemes are mainly funded from taxation and services are predominantly provided by public (private) providers. The second group comprises countries in which ear-marked contributions are the main source of funding and the services are predominantly provided by voluntary, non-profit (private) associations. In addition, it was possible to categorise the long-term care schemes found across the EU into one of three different types of paying providers. This includes a model in which private expenses are repaid from public funds, a model in which services are paid through public contracts with providers and, a model in which payments for services provided by public authorities are paid for from public funds.

In the final section of the present Chapter, the goal was to look at the relationship between the domiciliary long-term care schemes and the models of welfare state regime types by Esping Anderson and the division between welfare states of the 'Bismarck' and 'Beveridge' types at the turn of the millennium. Here, in contrast to the situation in previous times, the limited available literature as well as the data on domiciliary long-term care arrangements in the Union illustrated in the present Chapter indicate that it is possible that traditional models of welfare state regimes no longer necessarily cover the various forms a long-term care scheme could take. There is, however, much more detailed analysis and empirical evidence required before conclusions in this very complex issue can be arrived at. Therefore this will be further discussed in Chapter 10 after selected schemes have been studied on an empirical basis.

Part II

5 Methodology

5.1 Introduction

Having set out a definitional as well as a theoretical framework and having discussed the complex issues confronting policy makers in the field of research, it was possible, in Part I of the study, to provide descriptive, standardised information on the financing of domiciliary long-term care for the elderly and on the organisational structures within which care is provided in the European Union countries. This, in turn has facilitated a classification of EU domiciliary long-term care schemes with regard to the main sources of funding, the main methods of providing services, and the major methods of paying providers. In addition to these findings, the relationship of a country's domiciliary long-term care scheme with the two probably most important types of welfare state classifications (Esping-Anderson's 'Three Worlds of Welfare Capitalism` and the division into welfare states of the 'Bismarck` and 'Beveridge` type) has been studied.

However, it is clear that mainly because of the uncertain data situation and the scarcity of relevant literature, recent investigations (on which the first part of this study is based) do not provide sufficient information about the current schemes for financing long-term care for the elderly and about the organisational structures within which care is provided in the EU countries; nor do they tell us enough about experiences with new developments. Moreover, changes are still occurring in the field of long-term care in several EU countries, and this makes it even more likely that the information in existing literature does not accurately reflect the current situation in a particular country. In other words, there might be large gaps in the cross-country knowledge available. Therefore, research into available literature can only be roughly indicative of models and trends. An additional difficulty is that the available data can hardly be adapted to the definitional framework of the present study.

This is, therefore, all the more reason for undertaking empirical investigations in order to ensure that the information in the present study is reliable and can consequently fill some gaps in cross-national knowledge, can add to the fund of knowledge about EU long-term care schemes and can inform future policy initiatives. This applies, in particular, when evaluating the respective capacity of selected schemes to cope with future developments and to offer very general strategies for the long-term care policy makers in the Union. As for the first part of this study, the starting point of these empirically-supported investigations will be that private financial arrangements are not the basis for a solution to the funding of domiciliary long-term care. In addition, informal care by family members and relatives appears to be insufficient to meet the future needs of the disabled elderly. In Part I of this study it was shown that the informal care potential is decreasing in most EU countries, is no longer sufficient and that private arrangements are not in any case suited to the sector of long-term care. This, plus the fact that they do play a significant part in the EU schemes, has strengthened the author's intention to focus, in the following investigations, on public solutions for the provision of such care. Nevertheless, the study will be open to possible options regarding the role, which private financial and informal provision may play.

This Chapter on methodology is intended to establish a framework for the following empirically-supported investigations. It first discusses the aims, objectives and research questions. In a further step, a review of the methodology of the comparative analysis follows, including a general description of this approach, remarks on the special circumstances when countries are the subject of the comparison, an examination on the basis of a comparison within the EU as well as a description of an international comparison with its limitations and possibilities. Moreover, in this chapter on methodology there is a discussion of the basic considerations that are necessary before undertaking the present comparative approach. This discussion consists of a general description of the approach, comments on the types of comparative analysis and remarks on the structures and models of comparative analysis. It also looks at ways of reducing complexity. It includes a description of the levels at which the researcher considers his subject and the procedure for selecting countries that will be involved in the investigations, as well as fixing a time for carrying out these investigations. Finally, the sources from which evidence comes are given.

5.2 Aims, objectives, research questions and evaluation criteria

The aim of this Part II of the present study is to show, in more detail than in Part I, how three selected EU countries (for the selection procedure, see 5.4.6) intend to organise their domiciliary long-term care schemes in order to cope with the increasing pressures on the demand for and supply of long-term care. In this connection, existing differences and similarities are brought to light. Furthermore, the intention is to evaluate the respective merits of the selected schemes in catering for future developments. In addition, Part II of the study also offers very general reflections available for the EU long-term care policy makers and examines the relationship between the individual schemes and models of welfare state regime types at the turn of the millennium.

In order to fulfil the above aims and having in mind the large differences among the EU member countries where the provision of long-term care is concerned, a very structured procedure for the following analysis appears useful. In the following Chapters (6-8) the author will first of all present country reports from three EU long-term care schemes. In order to structure these individual reports, particular attention should be given to the following research questions, which were formulated for each country:

1. What institutions are responsible for implementing a domiciliary long-term care scheme?
2. How is the eligibility of individuals for the receipt of domiciliary long-term care to be regulated?
3. What is the type of service provision for a domiciliary long-term care scheme in terms of benefits and services?
4. How is the domiciliary long-term care scheme to be financed?

Since individual schemes are usually an integral part of a country's social protection system, these will be outlined briefly in addition to the research questions and for each country. Finally, as the field of research is in transition in several countries it would seem useful to review the current policy issues and their validity for the future development of service provision in each case.

The single country reports follow a similar format wherever this seems to be advisable and possible. However, the weight given to particular research questions varies markedly. This seems to be unavoidable, as any attempt to harmonise the individual elements of each country would have to work from the incorrect assumption that not only the financing and organisational structures of the EU long-term care schemes have enough similarities for this to be significant, but also that the level of available information is similar in each country. This is obviously not the case. While studying the individual aspects of the countries, the findings within schemes will be examined critically. After the descriptive part of each country report and based on the sources used for data-collection (See, 5.5), an empirically-founded assessment of the schemes of the countries examined follows, including possible options for dealing with the difficulties that have revealed themselves within the schemes.

Based on the findings of the country reports, Chapter 9 includes the comparative analysis. A characteristic feature of this Chapter is that it combines empirical evidence from the countries studied with already published scientific literature on long-term care arrangements. As in the three national Chapters, the formulated research questions are applied systematically and are of an exploratory nature. With each research question the intention is to synthesize and analyse the advantages and disadvantages of the different schemes and based on this, to arrive at alternative policy strategies which can be drawn on for the future provision of long-term care in EU countries.

In order to assess the advantages and disadvantages of different long-term care arrangements, there needs to be an evaluation framework. There are, of course, several criteria which have been suggested in this context. 'Freedom of choice', 'dignity' and 'independence' are criteria often said to be central considerations, for example, by a 'Royal Commission on Long-term Care' (1999) in the UK. Another criterion frequently put forward in public policy discussion is how the schemes might be steered to improve 'social solidarity' (See, for example, Baldwin, 1990). However, 'equity' and 'efficiency' appear to be the most important criteria (Compare Mossialos and Dixon, 2002), both being widely accepted as evaluation instruments and have been used in some of the limited number of existing studies on long-term care for the elderly. For example, the criteria are applied in an analysis of long-term care funding arrangements by Pauly (1996) within the framework of a cross-national research project for EU countries and they have been used in the assessment of the success of community care in England and France in a study by Davies, Fernández and Saunders (1998). In addition, several internationally recognised studies on general health care have also suggested that 'equity' and/or 'efficiency' are essential criteria for assessing the success of different schemes (See, for example, Bayer, Caplan and Daniels, 1983; McKie, Richardson, Singer and Kuhse, 1998).

The terms 'equity' and 'efficiency' are multi-layered and contentious which means they are given many different definitions. Here it is not intended to discuss their meaning at length as this has already been done in other studies (Compare, for more details, Knapp 1984; Ferlie, Challis and Davies, 1989; Österle, 1999). It also appears impossible to deal with all the different interpretations and individual areas of 'equity' and 'efficiency'. Therefore, the analysis in Chapter 9 rather focuses on what is going to be verifiable according to the empirical data available and this is carried out with reference to widely-accepted interpretations of the two terms. Based on recognised international literature, 'efficiency' in terms of the present study is viewed as 'the maximisation of the quantity and quality of output for a specified level of expenditure or as the minimisation of the cost of achieving a given level of output' (Knapp, 1984; Wittenberg, Sandhu and Knapp, 2002). As far as the 'equity' criterion is concerned, it would appear useful to distinguish between 'horizontal equity' and 'vertical equity' (Compare, for example, Knapp, 1984). Basically, 'horizontal equity' is defined as 'the equal treatment of equals' and 'vertical equity' means 'the unequal treatment of unequals' (See, for example, Österle 1999). However, this comparatively abstract definition inevitably poses the question what is meant by the terms 'equal' or 'unequal' when used as substantives. In arriving at suitable definitions for the purposes of this study, it is useful to distinguish between the allocation of long-term care benefits and services on the one hand and their funding on the other. In terms of allocating such benefits and services, 'need' is an area where individuals usually differ, that is, are 'unequal' and where differentiation among elderly people should be made. This means 'equity' is achieved by 'unequal provision for unequal need' ('vertical equity') and 'equal provision for equal need' ('horizontal equity') (Compare, for example, Knapp, 1984; Österle, 1999). In contrast, where funding arrangements are concerned, there is broad agreement in available literature that it is not 'need' which should determine whether the funding is 'equitable' or not, but rather the income and capital of the individual. This means 'equity' requires that individuals with the same income and capital pay the same amount of money into a long-term care scheme ('horizontal equity'), and 'vertical equity' is concerned with the extent to which the funding of a long-term care scheme is progressive (well-off people pay proportionally more), proportional (well-off and poor people pay equal contributions) or regressive (well-off people pay proportionally less) (See, for example, Wittenberg, Sandhu and Knapp, 2002).

Having discussed available long-term care strategies within a comparative approach, the objective in the next Chapter 10 is to re-integrate the findings in the theoretical framework which takes into account that individual schemes to cover age-related disability are usually an integral part of a country's social protection system. Here, the intention is to analyse the relationship between the empirically-studied domiciliary long-term care schemes and the illustrated models of state welfare regimes in Chapter 4 (which are based on a combination of public, market and family provision as found in a social protection system) at the turn of the millennium. Based on this, it is illustrated how the basic principles of the provision of social protection are currently applied in the empirically-studied long-term care schemes and what future developments may be.

In Chapter 11, based on the findings in the present study, the aim is to offer general policy reflections for the development of EU domiciliary long-term care schemes and Chapter 12 offers advice for future work.

5.3 The comparative approach

5.3.1 General description

The comparative analysis of at least two variables (e.g. two countries) is often described as an important method in scientific research (See, for example, Holt and Tarner, 1970; Warwick and Osherson, 1973; Meinolf, Weiler and Antal, 1987) and the following sections will offer a detailed discussion of this approach, with special regard to the comparison of domiciliary long-term care schemes in EU countries.

5.3.2 Countries as a subject of the comparison

A comparative analysis of countries is usually based on the precondition that the individual states are not unique, that they have important elements in common and are therefore comparable. As Hauser (1991) has stated, in order to receive and evaluate results from a comparative analysis, it is very helpful that the countries involved are similar within the following basic structures:

- In their cultural and religious traditions and the existing social values;
- In their democratic institutions and political processes;
- In the main features of a market economy, which is embedded in the same international economic order;
- In the main features of a welfare state, which is characterised by governmental intervention sometimes in conflict with the aim of economic growth, interior and foreign economic stability, equality of opportunity and social mobility, limitation of dissimilarity and active concern for the welfare of its citizens; and
- In the level of economic development and industrialisation (p. 196).

As Hauser (1991) further argued, a comparative analysis of countries that are alike where the above basic features are concerned, may well concentrate on differences within individual systems, e.g. in these countries' systems of social protection. In the scientific literature, this intention is often described as the 'most-similar-cases' approach. As he further said, one might expect more efficient results from a comparison of countries that are similar within these basic structures, for example with regard to the transferability of new knowledge, leading to the efficiency of a long-term care scheme. In this connection it seems noteworthy that several factors over recent decades, for example, world-wide mass communication, economic and cultural exchanges, tourism and immigration, cross-national agreements and contracts, as well as the formation of international organisations (e.g. the EU) in general have contributed to a strengthening of the similarities between many countries in their basic structures. This increasing cross-national dependency and exchange between countries necessarily leads to an increasing need for comparative analyses that may also become easier and more effective (Hauser, 1991).

5.3.3 The basis of a comparison within the European Union

The intention of this study is to focus specifically on the domiciliary long-term care schemes in the EU. There are also clear areas of similarity to other industrialised countries, such as Japan and the USA, for example, with regard to the reasons for the increasing need for formal long-term care and, therefore, additional information could be drawn from a wider comparison (Hugman, 1994). However, there are some important reasons for focusing on the EU only.

The integration of the countries in the EU was greatly stimulated by the Maastricht Treaty of 1992. The Union, which first operated as a purely economic organisation called the 'European Economic Community' and later the 'European Community', is currently involved in mutual co-operation and in the integration of policies in many different areas, such as culture, education, health care and social services. As a result, information about the current situation in different (long-term care) schemes is needed to encourage dialogue and further understanding between different (long-term care) organisations and among EU policy makers.

From a legislative point of view there is no doubt that social protection has a European dimension. In order to avoid any misconceptions in this matter, it should be pointed out that an adaptation of the individual social protection systems in the member countries neither exists nor is aimed at in the foreseeable future. What the EU basically intended was to ensure that all employees and their relatives covered by the contributory insurance schemes of a member country are treated equally by the respective regulations and receive their benefits independently of their place of work and residence[1]. Those areas of national law, which are inconsistent with EU law usually, lose their applicability. In other words, the intention was to co-ordinate the social protection regulations of the individual EU countries. In guaranteeing this social protection, the decree number 1408/71 of the Council of the EEC is of particular importance. It clarifies the areas of social protection benefits that are concerned with transferability within the Union (Zuleeg, 1998). Article 4

---

[1] Since the Maastricht Treaty of 1992, however, the free choice of one's place of residence within the Union is, for all its citizens, no longer linked with the taking up of gainful employment (Zuleeg, 1998).

determines the practical scope of the decree by defining eight different sectors to which the decree applies. This includes benefits in cases of illness, maternity, handicap, old-age, surviving dependents, occupational accidents and illnesses, death, and family benefits (Fischer, 1999).

Those benefits assigned to one of the eight sectors and provided in cash, according to Articles 19 and 28 of the decree number 1408/71 normally have to be transferred to other EU countries (Schumacher, 1998). With regard to services in kind, the decree, according to Articles 19 and 28, intends to prevent the transfer of this type of provision. However, this does not necessarily mean that an insured person abroad is not entitled to any (long-term care) services in kind. The EU law, on the other hand, specifically provides for the receipt of these benefits by an insured person in other countries (if any provided), these being granted according to the regulations of that country. The authorities paying for the provision in the country abroad are reimbursed by the responsible institutions in the country where the person is insured. This regulation should ensure that all EU citizens are treated equally within the Union (Schumacher, 1998).

Because of disagreements within the judiciary, Article 4 of Decree number 1408/71 has been extended by the addition of further guidelines to cover the sector of non-contributory special (cash) benefits through EC Decree 1247/92. According to that decree, such benefits are those that are paid in addition to, as a substitute for or as a supplement to one of the eight sectors in Article 4 of the Decree number 1408/71 as well as benefits that serve exclusively the welfare of people with disabilities. With regard to these special benefits, due to the changes introduced by Decree 1247/92, Decree number 1408/71 now states that they only have to be paid in EU countries if the applicant's place of residence is in the country where he applies for the benefits. Comparable regulations also apply to possible (long-term care) benefits that are provided within the framework of an EU social assistance scheme (Zuleeg, 1998; Fieber, 1999).

Apart from legislative considerations, the fact that the difficulties in securing the provision of long-term care are similar in most EU countries adds to the case for community-wide consideration. As explained in Chapter 2, the main problem in almost all countries is the ageing of the population. This ageing process can be illustrated by choosing France as an example. In the year 1970, 6,473,612 people had reached the age of 65 in France. In the year 2000, this figure had grown to 9,422,797 and for the year 2045, an increase to 16,607,580 people aged 65 and older is estimated (Eurostat data bank, 2002a; Eurostat data bank, 2002b). Similar developments can be seen in several other EU countries (See Chapter 2). Assuming that an ageing of the population leads to an increasing demand for long-term care, a political factor of considerable significance arises. Beside the ageing of their population, most EU countries have also experienced difficulties in providing long-term care where social changes lead to a decrease in the availability of informal carers and therefore to a rising number of disabled elderly who are dependent on formal services (See, for example, European Commission, 1998; Chapter 2).

In addition to the above, the comparatively high rate of unemployment in several EU countries also exacerbates the problem (See, for example, Eurostat data bank, 2002c). Mainly in the same context as the demographic and social components, it leads to an extremely serious financial problem. In different countries with social insurance systems where public long-term care expenditure is commonly financed by the contributions of employers and employees, the falling levels of employment in recent years have reduced the level for mandatory contributions. Similarly, there is a shortage of cash in those EU schemes where the provisions for long-term care are financed by general taxation (Saltman and Figueras, 1997).

Individual EU countries have now initiated detailed investigations into how to solve the growing problem of modernising their long-term care schemes. Different countries seem to be involved in a process of finding their own policy solutions for problems which are, in principle, the same. Again this highlights the necessity for research in the field of long-term care in the EU.

5.3.4 Limitations of an international comparison

As has been shown in the first Chapters (1-4) of this study, national schemes for securing the provision of domiciliary long-term care have been developed to cope with needs in the schemes themselves and also to take into consideration country-specific contextual factors, such as history, the country's macro-economic position, society's values, type of government, etc. (See, for example, Saltman, Figueras and Sakellaridis, 1998).

Influenced by this diversity, any researcher making an international comparison of long-term care provision, which requires certain knowledge of each national scheme, will encounter a range of difficulties. An initial problem is that on viewing the long-term care services provided and benefits granted in the different EU countries, one sees many differences in the financing and organisational structures within which the care is provided. For instance in Denmark, Luxembourg, and Sweden, social (protection) systems exist, which are mainly financed by taxes. On the other hand, the systems in France and

Germany are predominantly financed by the contributions of employees and their employers.

A further complexity is that the same service is often found in different administrative sectors in different countries. For example, the same services provided for the care of elderly people may be part of national health and pension schemes, private pension schemes or social assistance schemes (See, for example, Edvartsen, 1996). In addition, words frequently mean different things to different people, both with regard to the existing services provided and to long-term care in the individual countries. This results in different definitions for long-term care provision, for example, being used in some other comparative studies. Another difficulty might be the fact that the task faced by long-term care benefits and services overlaps with those of other services in various ways. Furthermore, in some countries services exist that are not described as 'long-term care' although they may have similar functions (Jamieson, 1991).

As a direct result of the complications caused by the problems of definition and the variety of providers of long-term care, the compilation of reliable international statistics is extremely difficult. The collection of such cross-country data is additionally complicated by the fact that disabled elderly often change the type of long-term care that they benefit from over a period of time and sometimes can even change from domiciliary care to residential care or vice versa. This can result in the omission of a case or alternatively in the repeated inclusion of a single case. Another problem in many countries is that several informal care provision schemes have developed which are not administered by public bodies but are nevertheless important (e.g. in the Republic of Ireland) (Walker and Maltby, 1997). Additionally the great variety of services in kind (e.g. free travel, housing allowances) are not recorded in the relatively few statistical data sources available (Nijkamp, Pacolet, Spinnewyn, Vollering, Wilderom and Winters, 1991). Consequently, it is not possible for example to present reliable statistics of long-term care patients aged 65 and over from all the countries of the EU.

What makes a comparison particularly difficult is the fact that even existing scientific literature in the field of international comparative research into national long-term care for the elderly and similar services can still be described as inadequate. An internationally-recognised study carried out for the European Commission (Alber, 1993) notes in this connection that "health and social services for older people is still one of the most neglected areas of social research. In stark contrast to other policy fields where old age is concerned, such as pension schemes or labour market participation, there are hardly any collections of data available from international agencies which would provide a basis for comparative analysis" (p. 100). Therefore, a survey of long-term care for the elderly in the countries of the EU is still one of the pioneer studies in this field and consequently the author cannot fall back on information as detailed as he might wish from recent literature (See, for example, Antonnen and Sipilä, 1996; Österle, 1999).

Given the specificity of mainly nationally collected data one might argue that a cross-country comparison can only be indicative of rough models and trends. However, extreme caution should always be observed if only for the reason that when certain strategies have proved to be effective in dealing with situation in a particular country it does not necessarily follow that the same strategies will be effective in another EU country. This is mostly not possible because of the differences described between the individual long-term care schemes. Within the framework of a European project on health care, Maynard (1975) comments that, in his view, "international comparisons are exercises which must be treated with extreme caution" (p. 265).

5.3.5 Possibilities of an international comparison

The above observations on the limitations of a cross-country comparison of EU domiciliary long-term care schemes do not imply that such an endeavour would not be useful. Instead, there is an urgent need for more reliable and uniformly defined data, but in this study (which is one of the first of its kind) the data, which had to be collected by a single author, with little financial support and not within the framework of a funded research project, should be read with this caution in mind.

However, making cross-national comparisons in general is a long-established method and as old as social science itself. Comparative analysis is, in fact, the social scientist's substitute for controlled experiments (Jamieson, 1991). Despite the outlined limitations, an international comparison offers numerous opportunities for attempting to develop an effective and efficient national long-term care scheme, by analysing the experience of different countries. Referring to this, Hurst (1994) notes that "international comparison provides economists with one of their few opportunities of observing natural experiments within systems and then trying to draw conclusions about causation and performance" (p. 15). An internationally recognised survey by Scharf and Wenger (1995) of cross-national perspectives on domiciliary (community) care for older people has argued that "within the context of their ageing populations, many developed countries around the world are currently promoting health and social care policies for older people which emphasise the importance of non-institutional forms of service provision for elderly within the community.

There is a pressing need to take stock of the international experience of community care policies" (p. XVII).

In the author's opinion, an international comparison of long-term care schemes can provide information for interested countries and particularly for the policy makers. Different solutions to a problem common to many countries can be evaluated. By seeing alternatives developed in different countries and their effects it may be possible to appreciate the structural changes required within the individual long-term care schemes. The existing pool of resources created by the different arrangements in the individual countries allows for a substantial basis from which to extract a lot of information in the search for a long-term care scheme which meets the requirements of both, disabled elderly people and governments. Moreover, from the knowledge and the results of empirically verified investigations of long-term care schemes in different countries, it should be possible to propose targets or possible alternatives for individual countries with regard to modifications of their current schemes. However, one common basis for any cross-country investigation is that the responsible key policy-makers in the individual countries do not assume uncritically, that their own scheme is the best in the EU or that it has exhausted its capacity for reform (For more details compare, e.g. Walker, 1993; Culyer and Wagstaff, 1994; Ritter, 1995).

5.4 Basic reflections on the contents of a comparative approach

5.4.1 General description

Having reviewed the issues surrounding the comparative approach, the focus of this section will be on a discussion of basic contextual reflections that have to be undertaken before carrying out the present comparative research. This is on the one hand inevitable as the possibilities of any comparison are usually very wide-ranging and on the other hand essential in order to inform the reader at the outset about what he/she may expect from this analysis and what aspects will be beyond its scope. This may, for example, include reflections as to whether the comparison is to be based on statistical data or political ideologies. It may also include a debate on what specific criteria are to be applied in selecting a certain number of countries for such an endeavour, as well as considerations regarding the (period of) time from which the comparative data are to be collected. As suggested by Ritter (1997), before undertaking a comparative analysis, such basic reflections, have to be taken into consideration in view of the type of comparative analysis to be made, the classification of the comparative objectives, a reduction in complexity, the level of consideration and, the period of time to which the research is to relate. The author of the present study follows these suggestions and will offer a study-specific discussion of these points in addition to the criteria being used for selecting the countries involved in this comparison.

5.4.2 Type of comparative analysis

As Ritter has noted (1997), there exist four different types of comparative analysis. These are the 'systems comparison', the 'political-economic comparison', the 'phenomenon comparison' and the 'problem-orientated comparison'. In what follows, these four types of comparative analysis will be briefly described.

The 'systems comparison' examines the way in which a system (order), in particular an economic system, works. The development of the 'systems comparison', which is a separate sub-discipline of economics, is originally based on the growth of the economic system in the Soviet Union. With its centrally-planned economy and its extension to other socialist countries, the comparison of systems has become an interesting field of research. The 'political-economic comparison' deals with the responsible bodies, institutions, concepts, aims and tools of economic policy. In addition to the economy, this type of comparative analysis may, for example, also focus on systems of social protection or compare individual institutions such as of banking. The 'phenomenon comparison' deals with the occurrence, range and form of (economic) phenomena among different national economies or at different periods of time. Such phenomena include, for example, the inflation rate, public expenditure and the unemployment rate. The aims of this type of analysis are first of all to develop theories and to verify hypotheses. Aims like learning from experiences or giving guidance for further action are not important in this type of comparison. Finally, based on the assumption that systems of society in different countries are often confronted with similar difficulties which they may intend to manage by using different types of strategies, the 'problem-orientated comparison' intends to examine and compare these different ways of dealing with problems (e.g. the ageing of the population and the unemployment rate). This type of comparative analysis departs from the belief that there has to be a uniform solution for different types of societies and for a longer period of time. It usually takes into consideration the increasing integration of different types of complex factual connections between the systems of society, which may have an influence on a range of problems and may well prevent the establishment of a 'clear cause and effect' relationship (Ritter, 1997; Fieber 1999).

Within the framework of the present study, it appears unsuitable to speak of a 'political-economic' study, as this type of comparative analysis does not claim, for example, to consider political constraints or ideologies in the first place within the framework of its reflections, although some sections may well contain one element or another of this type of comparison. Something similar holds true for the 'phenomenon comparison', as the present study will not in particular deal with elements like the occurrence, range and form of phenomenona found in different national schemes or at different periods of time. Nevertheless, the study may also include some estimates of this type of comparison. For the purposes of the present study, the 'problem-orientated' comparison will be applied. The main problem is that a combination of demographic, social and macro-economic developments has imposed pressure on most existing EU domiciliary long-term care schemes they were usually not designed to deal with. This has led to the challenging question as to how to adapt the individual schemes to the present circumstances, how best to provide sustainable long-term care funding for good quality care of the elderly and how costs should be shared between the working population (paying contributions and/or tax) and the individual in need of care. Based on an examination of the strategies adopted in three selected countries for dealing with these problems and on the sources used for data collection, this study aims at providing access to very general reflections for a long-term care scheme in order to cope with the above-mentioned problems. In addition to this problem-orientation, the present comparative research will also include elements of a 'systems comparison'. The system is the long-term care scheme. This type of a comparative approach can mainly be found in the first part of the present study (Chapters 6-8 containing reports on individual countries), where a descriptive account of the long-term care scheme is offered. However, in the second part of these reports as well as in the cross-national comparison described in Chapter 9 options to resolve these problems will be offered. This means that the present analysis is a mixture of a 'systems comparison' and a 'problem-orientated comparison' (Compare Fieber, 1999).

5.4.3 Structures and models of comparative analysis

In order to be in a position to compare a certain number of countries and to identify specific similarities and differences, it is necessary to develop certain criteria (structures) under which the appropriate systems will be considered. If specific countries show certain similarities when comparing them by using different criteria, it may well be possible to arrive at models. This has been the case in Part I (Chapter 4) of this study where one goal was to look at the domiciliary long-term care arrangements in the 15 EU countries by using three main criteria (main source of funding, predominant type of providers and major method of paying providers). This has indeed led to a typology showing three different types of long-term care schemes. However, as the development of such criteria usually depends on the interests and scientific background of the researcher, the number of corresponding models is extremely great and there exists no agreement on one certain type. The intention behind this procedure is rather to identify such criteria and corresponding models that are generally accepted as distinctive features and appear to be useful. The goal is to offer a well-founded, not necessarily complete, series of criteria and corresponding models that serve as a means of communication (Ritter, 1997).

The intention within the framework of this second part of the study is not to identify further typologies or models of long-term care schemes. The aim is to establish criteria that allow the comparison of three selected countries of interest. With regard to the evaluation procedure of the data to hand it seems useful to apply the already established research questions and the additional fixed areas of interest as a basis for acquiring the structure (criteria) under which the descriptive (first) part of the three country reports (Chapters 6-8) will be studied. These are as follows:

- An outline of the social protection system;
- A review on the responsible institutions for implementing the domiciliary long-term care scheme;
- An investigation into the eligibility criteria for the receipt of domiciliary long-term care;
- A description of the type of service provision for the domiciliary long-term care scheme (benefits and services);
- An examination of the funding arrangements for the domiciliary long-term care scheme; and
- An outline of current policy issues with a bearing on the future developments of service provision in the domiciliary long-term care scheme.

The second part of the country reports then offers an empirically-founded assessment of the respective schemes, including reform options, which are structured according to the formulated research questions and these are applied systematically. The chapter following the country reports, which contains a cross-national discussion that aims to arrive at alternative strategies for coping with the growing need for domiciliary long-term care, is similarly structured. In contrast, Chapter 10 that is intended to link the findings from the comparative analysis on long-term care for the elderly to the broader theoretical framework is formulated on a more general basis without using the structure given by the research questions.

5.4.4 Reduction of the complexity

An important issue that should be dealt with before carrying out a comparative analysis is to reduce the existing complexity. This is unavoidable because of the existing number of different and non-uniform (national) areas that effect such a comparative study of two or more variables (countries). However, in intending to reduce the complexity of a comparative field of interest one may well experience several difficulties. For example, controversy frequently exists concerning the establishment of criteria that on the one hand justify excluding all areas, which have to be left out and, on the other hand to establish criteria that support the inclusion of others. As often noted by the supporters of purely national studies, another difficulty arising as a result of reducing the complexity of a cross-national comparative analysis is that the usefulness of a study disappears following a limited or reduced consideration of national characteristics. The argument is that only painstakingly acquired knowledge of the national scheme and insider information would allow a correct analysis and, the translation into action would only be possible within the framework of national reports. Such national studies are, of course, necessary and useful and a researcher carrying out a comparative analysis has to consider such studies in order to protect him/herself against making mistakes and false generalisations. However, also within a national study, a complete description of, for example, a long-term care scheme appears to be impossible. The author of such a study also selects, but there is a risk that the selection procedure will not be clearly explicable and therefore the reader has to be cautious about the information included (Ritter, 1997; Fieber, 1999).

In the present study, the reduction of complexity has already been carried out within the development of the conceptual framework in Chapter 1 (pp. 5-18). It appeared necessary to do this at such an early stage as the high level of divergence in national definitions in the field of domiciliary long-term care as well as the large variations in dealing with relevant objectives in existing comparative literature made it difficult to carry out transparent information at any other stage of the study without this procedure. Additionally, as the topic of this study is extremely complex a clear conceptual framework has been indispensable from the very start. The practicability of the reduction of complexity achieved in Part I of the study has already been tested successfully in Chapter 4 where standardised information on the 15 EU long-term care schemes has been developed on this basis. Therefore, the same framework will be applied for Part II of this study. It should again be noted that owing to the high level of divergence between the national schemes, the conceptual framework has to be seen as a guideline rather than a binding definition with regard to further proceedings, since any attempt to harmonise the individual elements of each EU long-term care scheme might lead to essential national elements being left out. However, the chosen definition will be adapted wherever it seems possible and useful during subsequent chapters of this study.

To summarise, one can say that the following empirically-supported chapters will focus on 'EU long-term care for people aged 65 and over who are normally permanently unable to perform a particular number of 'Activities of Daily Life' and therefore receive domiciliary long-term care provision (personal care and home-making assistance) which is controlled and subsidised by state authorities'. This means, for example, that the analysis of residential long-term care will remain unconsidered. As the study is limited to long-term care for people aged 65 and over and therefore to a type of disability that is mainly a result of age-related changes, a review of care provision for disabled persons under 65 or for persons who are prevented from working by disability will also not be included. In addition, (domiciliary) nursing care arrangements will not be taken into account. Moreover, those types of informal and private services and benefits that are not controlled and subsidised by state authorities will not be considered within the following three country-related reports. Furthermore, tax relief, which may be granted within the framework of calculations that are usually difficult to understand and requiring an explanation of the national tax systems, will also remain disregarded or will at most be briefly mentioned, for the sake of completeness.

5.4.5 Level of consideration

The next decision to be made before carrying out this comparative analysis is to determine the level of consideration that will be used. Altogether, there exist four different options in this matter. First of all there is the 'macro level' which relates to the whole (national) economy. For more specific questions, e.g. in the case of comparing branches of industry and schemes of social protection, the 'meso-level' is often applied. A next possible level of consideration is the 'micro-level' which for instance relates to comparisons of individual companies or households. Finally, where the 'individual level' of contemplation is applied, single individuals such as blue-collar workers or consumers will, for example, be asked about their job satisfaction or about a judgement of their own financial situation (Ritter, 1997; Fieber 1999).

Within the present comparative analysis, the respective consideration will take place on the 'meso-level'. Nevertheless, there will be some points of contact with one or the other issue at another level. For example, there will be a relation to issues of the national economy and therefore with the 'macro-level' that needs to be considered when looking for financing options. The analysis will also include elements from the 'micro-level' as well as from the 'individual level`. However, the contacts with these levels will only be marginal. A more clear contemplation for the 'individual level` would for instance exist if the author intended to question individual elderly people in need of domiciliary long-term care as to whether they were satisfied with the care received (Compare Fieber, 1999).

5.4.6 Selection of countries

The following section discusses the reasons for selecting particular countries for a comparative study. In this matter, the researcher usually selects a number of countries and a study of these countries provides information on which hypotheses or conclusions can be based or, if already formed, confirmed or rejected (Leichter, 1979). According to the 'most similar cases` approach, as described above (See 5.3.2), it is useful that the countries involved in the comparison are similar within different basic structures (Hauser, 1991).

In this study, the selection is already limited to the 15 EU countries because this has been the intention from the outset. The author assumes that these EU countries have far-reaching fundamental similarities in their cultural and religious traditions (in all countries, the Christian faith is predominant), as well as social values, political institutions and processes, which are all influenced by EU guidelines, in particular when considering them in relation to most non-EU countries. Furthermore, the EU countries are similar in that they all display the main features of a market economy, which is particularly embedded in the economic structure of the Union. With regard to economic development and type of industrialisation, there may well be some minor differences among the member countries of the Union. From a more global point of view it is nevertheless possible to describe all EU countries as highly industrialised countries. All 15 member states also include elements of the main features of a welfare state, although research exists (See, for example, Jamieson, 1991) that classifies individual EU social protection systems within different models of state welfare. However, as the discussion in Chapter 4 has shown with regard to the current situation, one has to be very careful with such classifications as important elements of state welfare schemes (e.g. the sector of long-term care) seem to be changing in several EU countries. Finally, in addition to the comparability in the countries' basic structures, as suggested by Hauser (1991), the resemblance among the EU member states in demographic and social structures also underline their fundamental similarities.

Fischer (1992) has said that if the researcher has the option of choosing from a pool of countries that are widely similar in these basic structures (or independent variables), a condition which we are taking for granted in the

EU countries as outlined above, it is useful to focus on such countries, which show sufficient differences in the field of interest in question (dependent variable). This may give the researcher the option of falling back on a wide-ranging field of information when searching for possible reform options or a basis for conclusions. This leads the author to the first of three main reasons for choosing particular EU countries for this comparative approach. This first reason is the extent to which they represent the different types of domiciliary long-term care schemes identified in Table 13 in Chapter 4, with regard to the main type of funding, the primary type of service provision and the predominant methods of paying providers. This afforded the opportunity of bringing a very broad spectrum of long-term care regulations into this empirical part of the study, although research is limited to a selection of countries. The second selection criterion is the importance of reforms EU countries made in the 1990s or are being contemplated for the future. This afforded the author the opportunity of examining those countries in which there has possibly been an innovative reaction to the difficult circumstances surrounding the sector of long-term care from which other countries may learn. The third consideration in making a selection is to choose from countries with a comparable number of inhabitants and a similar level of affluence. This was decided in view of the convincing evidence of the impact of the already existing different factors on social policy. Therefore, the author felt it necessary to keep some of these variables constant, thus possibly accounting for the similarities and differences among the various schemes. The author of course recognises the differences between a nation with a population of say 80 million people and one of 60 million people. Nevertheless, it seems that this difference in scale or magnitude is of less consequence than, for example, the difference between nations of 3 million and 10 million people. Similarly, although the difference between a gross domestic product (GDP) at current market prices per head of € 24,000 and a GDP of € 22,000 needs to be recognised, it nevertheless lies within a framework where it seems justifiable to speak of approximately comparable basic financial conditions between countries.

In the light of these three main reasons, the countries that have been selected for the case studies are France, Germany and the United Kingdom. In France, where a new autonomous benefit scheme for the disabled elderly (based, with regard to the main method of paying providers, on the public reimbursement model) was introduced in 1997 and tax receipts are the main source of long-term care funding, the services being predominantly provided by private bodies. In contrast, since the introduction of the new and autonomous social insurance scheme for long-term care in 1995, Germany pays for domiciliary long-term care mainly from contributions evenly split between employees and employers. In addition to the large measure of voluntary, non-profit as well as private provision, a significant characteristic of the German scheme is that the main method of paying providers is based on the public contract model. A different approach is currently being found in the UK where general taxation is the predominant method of funding, where private organisations are meanwhile the largest group of providers and where the main method of paying providers is based on the public integrated model. However, what makes the UK particularly interesting is the fact that there is a quite lively public discussion regarding a possible new organisation of the long-term care scheme. The expectation that it is likely that there will be changes in the UK is reinforced by the fact that a 'Royal Commission' has been appointed to look into how best to provide sustainable long-term care funding for good quality care of the elderly and how costs should be shared between taxpayers and the individual. The selected countries are at the same time the three EU member states with the highest number of inhabitants. With populations of about 82 million (Germany) and about 59 million (France and the UK), the total population numbers are still close enough to make comparison valid. Altogether they comprise about 200 million people, that is, about 53 per cent of the total EU population (376 million) (Eurostat data bank, 2002a). Their gross domestic product (GDP) at current market prices per head of population in Euro is likewise not so different (22,250 in France, 23,540 in Germany and 23,560 in the UK) (Eurostat data bank, 2002g) as to put the countries into a completely different financial basic position regarding the resources available for providing such public services as long-term care for the elderly.

In addition to the above-mentioned three main reasons for choosing the countries, other more pragmatic reasons have also contributed to the selection of France, Germany and the UK. As Fischer (1992) has argued, making a comparative analysis can only be useful if the researcher has a good command of the language of a country that he or she studies. This seems to be particularly true in the field of domiciliary long-term care as suitable literature is often only available in national languages. In addition, ability to speak the language of the countries involved in the investigation makes it easier - or is often a necessary precondition - to communicate with experts from the countries involved.

Although the chosen countries fulfil the selection criteria, some readers may wonder why the three selected countries do not include any of the four Southern EU countries. However, the author argues that this fact would appear to make the countries chosen particular suitable where the empirical results of the present study are concerned, particularly, since the long-term care schemes in the four Southern EU countries are not very well-developed, or hardly exist at all - at least in some parts of these countries - perhaps partly owing to the fact that there is a comparatively well-developed informal network which seems to reduce the necessity of introducing such a scheme. However, as the topic of this study is public policy responses to the problem of long-term care of the elderly, case studies of the southern EU countries would not seem to serve a useful purpose. In addition to leaving aside the Southern EU countries, some readers will be surprised at the omission of the Scandinavian countries, perhaps, in particular, at the omission of Denmark which has a highly developed social protection system. However, as, for example, an international study on the reform of community and long-term care by Davies (1995) found, the Danes like their scheme the way it is and have done little to adapt it to deal with the currently more difficult economic problems. In this connection it seems obvious that although further and common EU difficulties, such as the ageing of the society and social changes in Denmark have a lesser influence on long-term care provision than in many other EU countries, nevertheless it appears likely that they will contribute to an over-burdening of the Danish scheme in the future developments. Therefore, the authors doubts if the Danish scheme is a useful model for other countries when searching for ways of adapting their own schemes to the existing, difficult circumstances.

5.4.7 Time fixing

A final basic consideration that has to be made before carrying out a comparative analysis is to fix a time to which the research is to relate. It is then possible to compare the data for a specific year or a specific period of time (Ritter, 1997).

For the descriptive part of the present study, the year 2000 has been chosen as the time to which the information in the following Chapters will relate, whenever this is possible. There will, however, be some divergence in the descriptive part of the country reports dealing with individual schemes and, in particular with regard to the added statistical information. This is unavoidable, as cross-national and even national analysis in the field of research is just at the beginning and, in this connection reliable statistical data often simply does not exist for the one or other relevant aspect or time. The data for the empirical part of the comparative analysis that includes an assessment of the descriptive part as well as very general strategies for the long-term care policy makers in the Union, will be mainly gathered in the third and fourth quarterly period of 2001.

Another decision that has to be made in connection with this selection of a time period for this study is the fixing of the date, which is relevant for the exchange rates that will be used in the following Chapters. As this is a European study, the figures will be offered in the European currency 'Euro'. It is hoped that this uniform presentation of all figures will contribute to a clearer comprehensibility of the information given. The date that will be used for this is the 31st December 2000. However, for those 12 EU countries that have already joined the monetary Union (except, Denmark, Sweden and the UK) and therefore have had fixed exchange rates among each other and in relation to the Euro since 1st January 1999, this fixing is rather of subordinated importance. It should be noted that in the course of this study, one or other figure is rounded off if this appears to contribute to a clearer understanding. The exchange rates used in the study can be seen in the Appendix (A).

5.5 Collecting the evidence

Evidence for this empirical part of the study comes from documents and interviews. The concrete use of these two sources is illustrated below.

As Yin (1984) has argued, except for studies of pre-literate societies, documentary information is likely to be relevant to every comparative study topic. This type of information can take many forms and in the present study, the following variety of documents will be used:

- Agendas, announcements of meetings, and other written reports of events;
- Administrative documents - proposals, progress reports and other internal documents;
- Formal studies or evaluations of the same 'site' under study;
- News clippings and other articles appearing in the mass media; and
- Web sites.

The second type of source to be used for this empirical part of the study (interviews) is generally recognised as one of the most important for such an intention and is often referred to within a range of scientific investigations in the field of comparative and case study research (See, for example Warwick and Osherson, 1973; Stake, 1995). As Lamnek (1989) has said, the interview technique enables questions to be asked when something is not clear. This might, in particular, be useful in such a field as domiciliary long-term care for the elderly, where the existing complexity and differences in interpretation of essential terms often leads to misunderstandings and therefore requires some type of explanation. Lamnek (1989) further argued that it is easier to question individual experts in the field of research than to gain access to and gather information through 'participatory observation'. However, such interviews may take several forms, e.g. the narrative (See, for example, Schütze, 1977) or the focussed interview (See, for example, Merton, Fiske and Kendall, 1956). In this study the interviews are of a semi-structured and open-ended nature (often described as problem-centred interview) (See, for example,

Witzel, 1982), carried out on the telephone, tape-recorded and supported by a guide-line.

This guide-line deals with four subjects (institutions, eligibility criteria, benefits and services and the funding of domiciliary long-term care) and related sub-divisions that will come up in the interviews and is based on the research questions of the study. Each of the four subjects has two main aspects. The first aspect focuses on an assessment of the respective national domiciliary long-term care schemes of the interviewee, and the second aspect focuses on strategies for improving domiciliary long-term care arrangements. As Meuser and Nagel (1997) have argued, such a guide-line is necessary, as the renouncement on all thematic pre-structuring would bring with it the danger that the researcher would seem incompetent in the interview and, therefore not be taken seriously and this could easily lead to the interviewer not being able to get access to the full knowledge of the expert in question. As Meuser and Nagel further argued, it is helpful to use this guide-line flexibly and unbureaucratically in the sense of a topic and not in the sense of a fixed interview pattern. This can ensure that the expert's knowledge and experience are presented as comprehensively as possible in the interview.

As the topic of this study is extremely complex and in addition is hardly characterised by precise facts, it appears necessary to indicate that, from this investigation involving interviews with experts, it cannot be expected that one single solution will be found for each of the individual parts of the domiciliary long-term care schemes. Apart from the uncertainty arising from the data itself, the assessment of the national long-term care schemes and possible reform options, is strongly influenced by the individual (social, political) position of the interviewee. It appears likely that this element of uncertainty will be at least equally relevant, if the interviewee makes cross-national recommendations. It is, of course, impossible to remove this dilemma completely. However, it is possible to combat it by selecting experts with different empirical background for the interviews.

The intention in selecting the interviewees was to ensure that statements of different theoretical views are represented in the investigations. In particular, care was taken to ensure that the 30 key stakeholders (ten each from the three countries selected for this comparative analysis, namely France, Germany and the UK) included five persons at the scientific and five at the practical level of long-term care for the elderly from each country involved in the empirical investigations. Moreover, concerning the interviewees with a scientific background, the goal was to get access to people with specialized knowledge in the sector of long-term care for the elderly. In the first place, specialized knowledge relates to the scheme of the expert's country of origin.

In addition, it would be desirable if the interviewees also had experience in the field of cross-national analysis. The respective knowledge of the experts has been verified in the areas of research and/or teaching. With regard to the key stakeholders from the practical level it had to be ensured that the two areas of administrative (financial) responsibility and service provision are represented virtually equally. Furthermore, the interviewees with a practical background should, if possible, have positions that allow an assessment of the provision of long-term care on the 'meso-level`. These can, for example, be executive personnel of national parent organisations or national syndicates.

The selection of these interview partners has been made in knowledge of the arrangements within the long-term care schemes of the selected countries that has been acquired during the procedure of research for this study. It was also possible to use contacts that have been made in the course of research so far, for example, during conferences. In addition, within the framework of the interview procedure, it was also possible to extend the number of possible experts that may participate in the research through the so-called snowball effect (See, for example, Köhler, 1992). The persons that have been contacted for the interview procedure can be seen in the Appendix (B).

The author first established contact with the experts by a brief letter that mainly offered information on the field and aims of research as well as on the rough content of the planned interview. This gave the expert the possibility of determining the extent of his or her interest to participate in an interview. An inquiry over the telephone (after the letter) has then either led to a direct interview, to a binding agreement for the interview time or to a negative reply by the expert. In all, 30 experts have participated in the interview procedure. The 30 interviewees comprise 15 experts with a practical background and 15 experts with a scientific background. 10 of the participating experts come from France, 10 from Germany and 10 from the UK. The average length of interviews was 40 minutes.

The evaluation of the interviews will orientate towards contextual matching thematic units and not on the sequence of statements. These thematic units are analogous to the guide-line being used for the interviews and, compatible with the research questions as set out for the present study. However, within the framework of the evaluation procedure for the interviews, the first step will be to write down those tape-recorded passages of the individual interviews which are of relevance for the research (i.e. to transcribe the interviews). In doing this, certain sections of the interviews will be reproduced directly and, other sections will be given by using an explanatory description. This decision, if it appears useful to reproduce individual sections from the interviews, whether directly or not, will be made with the research questions in mind. However, in order to avoid the loss of important elements of reality from the interviews, it is also necessary to ensure that those sections of the interviews that are reproduced by an explanatory description include reference to what the interviewee said as a whole. A next step to be taken is to put the reproduced passages in a thematic order, analogous to the guide-line being used for the interviews. In a next step, the simultaneous thematically units arising among the different interviews will be grouped together. As this step includes the unification of a number of data, it is indispensable to verify the assigned material and, if necessary, to make revisions. Only now, a partial removal from the units that have emerged from the interviews will take place. Similarities and differences will be conceptualised and contexts will be combined. Furthermore, remarks on statements made by the interviewees and generalisations based on the empirical material available will be made (Meuser and Nagel, 1997). The presentation of the results will be made systematically according to the division of each thematic unit from the guide-line. In this connection, the results will first be presented within the respective chapters dealing with individual countries (after the descriptive parts) in order to assess the individual schemes and to present reform options. Second, the results will be applied in the comparative Chapter (9) where, based on the experience from the country reports, general strategies concerning long-term care arrangements will be discussed.

5.6 Summary

The present Chapter has set out a methodology for establishing the procedure for this empirical part of the study. First of all, the aims, objectives, research questions and evaluation criteria (i.e. 'efficiency' and 'equity') of the following Chapters have been discussed.

Second, aspects of the comparative approach have been reviewed. This includes a general description of the comparative methodology, followed by remarks on the facts when countries are the subjects of the comparative approach. In addition, the essentials of a EU-wide review of domiciliary long-term care schemes have been given and limitations and possibilities of an international comparison of long-term care schemes have been described. This consideration of the above points has shown why an international comparison of different ways of ensuring the provision of long-term care is necessary and of considerable value.

Third, basic considerations necessary before undertaking this comparative approach have been taken into account. Based on a general description of this concern, thought has been given to the type of comparative approach. It became apparent that the most suitable approach would be a mixture of a 'systems comparison' approach and a 'problem-orientated' one. In a further step, the focus has been on the structures and models of a comparative approach and a corresponding establishment for the following empirically-supported chapters has been made. Moreover, the reduction of the complexity of a comparative approach has been reviewed and, with regard to the current study, it was determined that the definitional considerations already established within Chapter 1 will also be applied for this second part. Furthermore, the level of consideration has been examined and the 'meso-level' has been selected. In a further step, the criteria for selecting individual countries have been discussed. The EU long-term care schemes which were selected for the Chapters that follow were chosen for a combination of three main reasons. The first is the extent to which they represent the different types of domiciliary long-term care schemes identified in Table 13 of Chapter 4, with regard to the main type of funding, the primary type of service provision and the predominant methods of paying providers. The second is the importance of reforms EU countries made in the 1990s or have been contemplating for the future. The third reason was the relatively close similarity between the countries chosen in terms of the number of inhabitants and the level of affluence. France, Germany and the UK were selected for these three main reasons. Finally, this section on basic considerations of the comparative approach has established general time conditions for carrying out the present study, whereby the year 2000 was chosen as a time to which the descriptive data should relate. The empirical data will predominantly be collected in the third and fourth quarterly period of 2001.

Fourth, this Chapter has indicated the sources used for collecting the evidence for this Part II of the study. In addition to several types of documents, it comes from several interviews with key stakeholders, either theorists or practitioners from France, Germany or the UK.

6 Domiciliary long-term care in France

6.1 Introduction

The French long-term care scheme for its elderly inhabitants has a complex range of benefits and services from different types of sources. The most important benefits and services, which often differ between regions, are available within the framework of the social assistance scheme, followed by those provided by different pension schemes. Provisions of both types of schemes are, however, usually means tested and therefore limited to a certain part of the disabled elderly population. In contrast, nursing care, which is only of marginal interest in this study, in France is paid for from national health insurance funds. It covers practically all elderly people and pays about 75 per cent of the costs in this sector (about 83 per cent of the inhabitants in France have a complementary insurance plan that usually covers the rest of the expenditure). However, in the case of domiciliary long-term care (personal care and home-making assistance), the limitation of provision to those with lower income means that the individual frequently depends on the help of the family (Rostgaard and Fridberg, 1998).

As noted above, the main type of domiciliary long-term care provision for elderly people in France may be available under the social assistance scheme where it has, since 1975, been possible to receive a means tested allowance paid for by the regional authorities ('Départments'), the so-called 'Allocation Compensatrice pour Tierce Personne' ('ACTP'). The allowance was originally designed for handicapped people but step by step the number of elderly people in need of long-term care receiving 'ACTP' provision increased and was leading to uncontrolled costs (Rostgaard and Fridberg, 1998). This has led to several debates regarding improvement of long-term care provision. Already at the end of the 1980s and at the beginning of the 1990s, different bills and proposals focused on the development of a specific provision for the disabled elderly out of this 'ACTP' (Kerschen, 1998). During the French presidency election campaign in 1995 the elected President Jacques Chirac had promised the introduction of an autonomous benefit scheme ('Prestation Autonomie') for age-related long-term care provision. However it was argued that owing to financial difficulties the introduction of such a comparatively wide-ranging approach has for the time being to be postponed indefinitely. Instead, a more limited dependency allowance ('Prestation Spécifique Dépendance' - 'PSD') was introduced in 1997 following a mainly experimental scheme in 12 'Départments' ('Prestation Expérimentale Dépandance' - 'PED') (Swiss Federal Office of Social Insurance, 1997). The experimental scheme had been administered by the main fund for old-age, but the new dependency allowance which came into force on 24th January 1997 (French Law No. 97-60, 2000) is part of the social assistance scheme and is mainly the responsibility of the regional authorities ('Départments'). This new scheme provides limited and means tested benefits for disabled elderly from the age of 60 and usually replaces the 'ACTP' provision. Only those people in need that were, according to the previous legislation, entitled to the 'ACTP' allowance before the age of 60 have, should provision after the age of 60 be approved, the option of choosing between 'ACTP' and the 'PSD' payments (Rostgaard and Fridberg, 1998; European Commission, 2000). It appears noteworthy that there has been intensive opposition to the introduction of the 'PSD' scheme from different organisations, while the promised autonomous benefit scheme for disabled elderly, that would have covered substantially more people in need than the 'PSD' scheme, has been demanded. This strong opposition has obviously contributed to the fact that within the framework of the 'PSD' act it is noted that the allowance has been introduced while awaiting a new long-term care scheme to increase the independence of the disabled elderly (Pijl, 1998).

In addition to the above noted service provision, a variety of other benefits and services may be available for elderly people in need of long-term care. For example, in some regions a telephone, alarm system has been established, a range technical aids and care aids are available under different programmes, meals-on-wheels services can be claimed by some elderly people and it is possible to benefit from certain forms of tax relief (Verheij, 1996). In this country-report (particularly with regard to the assessment procedure based on interviews with experts), the main focus will be on the 'PSD' allowance, which represents virtually the only benefit quite specifically provided for the disabled elderly in France during the time period established for collecting the data of Part II of this study. However, in the year 2002, one may expect expanded coverage for the disabled elderly through the so-called 'Allocation Personnalisée d'Autonomie' ('APA') (French Law No. 2001-647, 2001) which seems to be in accordance with the political promises made, in combination with the introduction of the 'PSD' and is to replace the existing scheme (French Ministry of Employment and Solidarity, 2001a). Therefore, it appears at least necessary to deal briefly with these forthcoming changes in the section 'way forward' as well as in the empirically-founded sections.

6.2 Social protection system

In France, different social insurance schemes ('Sécurité Sociale') form the main part of the French social protection system. The main source of funding for these schemes comes from employers and their employees. Social insurance benefits are mainly conditional upon a record of these contributions having been made. In addition to the social insurance schemes, the second important part of the French social protection system is the social assistance scheme which is mainly financed from taxation (Kaufmann, 1997; Rostgaard and Fridberg, 1998).

The social insurance scheme consists of a basic scheme and a supplementary scheme for pensions. The basic scheme can be divided into three different groups. Firstly a general scheme ('Régime Général') that represents the main fundamental scheme and covers the majority of the population (e.g. employees in trade and industry) for sickness, maternity, invalidity, surviving dependents, occupational accidents and diseases, old-age and family. Secondly, there are numerous special schemes ('Régimes Spéciaux'), e.g. for officials and employees in the public sector and thirdly exist independent schemes ('Régimes Autonomes'), e.g. for the self-employed. The main differences between these schemes lie in the provision of pensions. As the general scheme covers more than two thirds of the population and is considered to be a model for the special and independent schemes (European Commission, 1997; Kaufmann 1997), it appears justifiable to limit the main focus (within the discussion of basic social insurance schemes) to this major type.

The general social insurance scheme itself is divided into three different sectors of provision. These three sectors are represented by respective institutions at the national level. First, there exists the national health insurance fund ('Caisse Nationale d'Assurance Maladie des Travailleurs Salariés' - 'CNAMTS') that is responsible for managing the risks of sickness, maternity, invalidity, surviving dependents, occupational accidents and diseases. Second, there is the national fund for old-age ('Caisse Nationale d'Assurance vieillesse des Travailleurs Salariés' - 'CNAV') which is mainly responsible for the management of pension arrangements. Third, there exists the national family fund ('Caisse Nationale d'Allocations Familiales' - 'CNAF') that is predominantly responsible for managing the family benefits. The three national funds are quasi-autonomous, non-governmental institutions, which come under the jurisdiction of the appropriate national ministry. They are mainly responsible for the funding of benefits provided under their respective authority and control as well as instructing the administrators' regional and local funds. At the regional level, 16 health insurance funds exist ('Caisses Régionales d'Assurance Maladie' - 'CRAM'), which are mainly responsible for the payments of pensions. At the local level, there exist 123 health insurance funds ('Caisses Primaires d'Assurance Maladie' - 'CPAM') which are responsible for the admission of the insured and paying out the benefits in the case of sickness, maternity, invalidity, survivors, occupational accidents and diseases. The family funds at local level ('Caisses Locales d'Allocation Familiales' - 'CAF') deliver the different types of family benefits. At local level, a further 105 institutions exist ('Union Locales de Recouvrement des Cotisations de

Sécurité Sociale et d'Allocations Familiales' - 'URSSAF') which are responsible for collecting the social contributions. These 105 institutions are supervised by an institution at the national level ('Agence Centrale des Organismes de Sécurité Sociale' - 'ACOSS') which is responsible for the contributions of the three illustrated funds of social insurance. As mentioned above, the three sectors of social insurance are mainly funded by contributions from employers and their employees with some national tax funding (Kaufmann, 1997; Köstler, 1997b). Within the contribution-related source of funding, two third come from employers and one third from employees. However, there has been a tendency since the 1980s to increase contributions that come from the employees (Rostgaard and Fridberg, 1998). For the sake of completeness, one should point out that the unemployment scheme is not classified as a social insurance scheme ('Sécurité Sociale'), but is equally provided by the unions and management. Governmental institutions have, among other things, responsibility for the agency of employment (Kaufmann, 1997).

As noted above, in addition to the basic scheme, the French social insurance includes, furthermore, a supplementary scheme for pensions which is compulsory. This is unavoidable as the provision for old-age in the basic scheme is insufficient. The supplementary scheme is administered by special funds and there are considerable differences between these funds, e.g. in the services they provide. As in the case of basic insurance, the supplementary scheme is mainly funded by contributions on a 'pay-as-you-go' basis (Kaufmann, 1997).

In addition to the social insurance sector there is a social assistance scheme. The responsibility for providing and funding benefits and services from this scheme is held by the regional public authorities (95 'Départments') (Köstler, 1997b). For example, the scheme provides domiciliary and residential care as well as meals-on-wheel for those who are, according to a means test, entitled to such help (Rostgaard and Fridberg, 1998).

6.3 Analysis of the current domiciliary long-term care scheme

6.3.1 Responsible institutions

In France, at national government level the 'Ministry of Employment and Solidarity' predominantly oversees the responsibility of the social protection system that includes social insurance and social assistance. At this level, the main tasks are to establish the framework for the system by legislation, to support the development of activities at subordinated levels and to contribute to the funding of social protection benefits and services.

Based on the decentralisation process since 1982, the regional level that is mainly represented by 95 'Départments' has been given a decisive role in the provision of benefits and services under the social assistance scheme, in particular by administering the budgets. Each regional government ('Départment') consists of two main authorities: the general council ('Conseil Généraux') whose members are elected and the civil services, e.g. the departmental section of sanitary and social matters ('Direction Départmentale de l'Assurance Sanitaire et Sociale' - 'DDASS') or the regional commission of social and medico-social institutions ('Conseil Regional des Institutions de Soins Médicaux et Sociaux' - 'CRIMS'). These regional authorities have decisive power, for example with regard to the accreditation of service providers (Spinnewyn, 1991; Gabanyi, May and Schneider, 1992). As noted above, with regard to the disabled elderly, social assistance payments have, particularly in past years, been made by the 'Allocation Compensatrice pour Tierce Personne' ('ACTP') and has, since 1997, mainly been replaced by the 'Prestation Spécifique Dépendance' ('PSD') which is also paid within the framework of this minimum income scheme. A disabled elderly person who intends to receive 'PSD' payments has to claim them from the Presidents of the regional government general councils ('Conseils Généraux des Départments'). For this, it is necessary that the elderly person submits a certificate from a medico-social team of experts (that works for the 'Départments') which examines the applicant (usually in his or her home) and provides a plan of care as well as verification of his or her financial situation. In addition, it is the 'Départments' that have to promote structures at regional level in order to ensure the availability of care services (Faessel, 2001).

At the local level, communal centres of social action ('Centre Communaux d'Action Sociale' - 'CCAS') act as one possible drop-in-centre for the disabled elderly. These communal centres also have the responsibility of setting up and running long-term care institutions (Rostgaard and Fridberg, 1998). In addition to the 'CCAS', the offices of individual pension institutions and the different formal service providers likewise are intended to be drop-in-centres for those elderly people who apply for provision from the 'PSD' scheme. However, all of these possible centres pass the application papers to the appropriate 'Départment' (Faessel, 2001).

Besides long-term care benefits and services within the framework of the social assistance scheme, it is also possible to apply for the one or other type of social insurance-based long-term provision. Within the different schemes based on social insurance, the general scheme for old age probably plays the most important role in providing long-term care for the elderly. Nursing care, which is only of marginal interest within the present study, is usually covered by the general health insurance scheme (Rostgaard and Fridberg, 1998). For details regarding the different institutions responsible for the schemes of old age and health care in France see the previous section (6.2).

The individual domiciliary long-term care services in France are provided by different types of organisations. However, the predominant type of recognized organisation that provide domiciliary care is made up of voluntary, non-profit bodies (e.g. 'Association Bas-Rhinoise d'Aide aux Personnes Âgées' - 'ABRAPA' and 'Association du Service à Domicile' - 'ADMR'), followed by private organisations. In addition, a significant number of carers work on a freelance basis and many disabled elderly people employ a member of the family (with the exception of the spouse or partner) to care for them (Faessel, 2001; Martin, 2001). Those domiciliary services that are provided by the public sector are usually placed at the communal centres of social action ('CCAS') which thus in addition to the above-mentioned area of responsibility (e.g. act as drop-in centre for those in need), may also operate as direct service providers of domiciliary long-term care. For this service provision, the centres normally employ different types of nursing staff. The public as well as the voluntary, non-profit and private providers can offer comprehensive services including personal care, home-making assistance and nursing care or their area of provision can be limited to one particular type of service. Both types of providers have to be accepted as well as accredited by the regional government (Köstler, 1997b; Pijl, 1998).

6.3.2 Eligibility criteria

The criteria of eligibility for the 'PSD' are legally defined. In order to be entitled to the provision of the scheme, it is first of all necessary that a person lives permanently in France and is aged 60 or above. In addition, the law demands that an applicant for provision requires help in performing the 'Personal Activities of Daily Life' ('P-ADLs') and 'Instrumental Activities of Daily Life ('I-DALs') or needs to be generally supervised and guided (Para. 2 French Law No. 97-60, 2000). Furthermore, the scheme distinguishes six different degrees of 'disability' ('Groupe-Iso-Ressource' - 'GIR'). A medical-social team of experts, of which one member has to be a physician and the other two or more, for example, social workers or deputies of the national fund for old-age ('CNAV'), identifies these degrees by using a national assessment scale, the so-called 'AGGIR' ('Autonomie, Gérontologie, Groupe Iso-Ressources') (Davies, Fernandéz and Saunders, 1998; Para. 2 French Decree No. 97-426, 2000). This 'AGGIR' scale consists of 17 items in all which can be seen in the following Table (See p. 115).

Table 14 'AGGIR' scale

Item	**Assessment criteria of the applicant**
Coherence	Is able to have a coherent conversation
Orientation	Is aware of time, period of the day, place
Washing	Is able to wash him- or herself
Dressing	Is able to dress and undress him- or herself
Eating	Is able to eat prepared meals
Toileting	Is able to manage bodily functions
Transfer	Is able to get in and out of bed
Mobility (inside)	Is able to walk indoor with or without stick, wheelchair, etc.
Mobilitv	Is able to walk outdoor without using means of transport
Communication	Is able to use the telephone alarm system
Administration	Is able to manage own finances, possessions, etc.
Kitchen	Is able to prepare and serve meals
Housework	Is able to do housework tasks
Transport	Is able to use means of transport
Shopping	Is able to shop directly or through correspondence
Medication	Is able to follow instructions given by a physician
Hobbies	Is able to undertake leisure activities (e.g. of a sporting, cultural or social nature)

Source: Appendix I French Decree No. 97-426, 2000

Basically, the seventeen items shown in Table 14 are all rated at one of three different levels (A, B and C). Level A applies if the person is regularly able to perform the task without help and normally correctly, level B is the case if the person can at most partially perform the task concerned or not correctly and, level C holds true if the person cannot perform the index at all (Appendix A, French Decree No. 97-427, 2000). However, the precise procedure of classifying the applicants into one of the six degrees of disability by using this 'AGGIR' scale is a complex procedure and is carried out by using a points system. This procedure may include the passing through of up to eight assessment categories for an applicant. Starting with the first category, the performance of the individual in the first 17 items of the 'AGGIR' is tested. This means that each of the 17 items is assessed by the above-noted three-level scheme (A, B and C). Corresponding to the appropriate level an applicant gets a fixed number of points for each item. The resulting total for the 17 individual items either leads to a specific rating of 1, 2 or 3 (in the case of the first category in the classifying procedure) or - depending on the points total - to moving the applicant to the next (second) assessment category. In the next category, the applicant is similarly handled with the exception that the points given for each of the 17 items differ (the points differ between each of the total eight categories). The applicant who meets the requirements for this second category gets the rating 4. Those applicants that do not get the necessary score for this category will again be passed to the next category (three). This procedure may continue up to the last of the eight assessment categories. Finally, the ratings given (11 in total) entitle the applicant to be classified in one of the six degrees of disability in the 'PSD' scheme, e.g. rating 1 gives entitlement for degree I and ratings 2,3,4,5,6 and 7 for degree II (Appendix II, French Decree No. 97-426, 2000).

Within the six different degrees of disability that may have emerged from the above-illustrated procedure of classification, it is roughly possible to identify specific syndromes. This is shown in Table 15 (p. 117).

If the applicant is classified in the degrees I to III and also fulfils the other eligibility criteria for the benefits from the scheme, the 'PSD' is granted (Para. 3 French Decree No. 97-426, 2000). In addition to the classification of the individual in need into one of the six degrees of disability, it is also the responsibility of the medico-social team of experts to recommend an individual plan of care (including a fixing of costs for this plan) (Kerschen, 1998).

Finally an applicant for the 'PSD' also has to pass an income test. The maximum level of the 'PSD' payment according to the individual's need may be granted to people with a net monthly income (including the 'PSD') of less than € 1,597 (FR 10,477) for a single person and € 2,207 (FR 14,477) for couples (€ 2,890 / FR 18,954 if both members are recipients of the 'PSD'). Those with an income at and above these limits get a maximum allowance that is reduced by the amount, by which the net income, including the 'PSD` payment, exceeds the income limit. Those applicants who have a net income which, without the possible 'PSD` benefit, is already above the income limit consequently get no provision (Caullychurn, 1997; Köstler, 1997b).

Table 15 Six degrees of disability ('GIR`)

Degree of disability	Includes in particular people aged 60 and over:
I	• Those who are confined to bed or chair and whose mental functions are considerable disturbed, so that the person needs to be looked after permanently. This group mainly includes people who are in the final stage of life;
II	• Those who are confined to bed or to the chair and whose mental functions are not fully disturbed but who need extensive help with the 'ADLs`; • Those whose mental functions are disturbed but who are still able to move without help (this group of people mainly includes people with 'dementia`);
III	• Those whose mental functions are complete, whose locomotive ability is only partly limited but need help with washing, dressing, etc. In addition, most persons in this group suffer from incontinence;
IV	• Those who need help to change their posture but are able to move indoors without assistance. They occasionally need help with washing and dressing. The majority of people in this group are able to eat without help; • Those who are able to move without help but need assistance with washing, dressing, eating and similar activities;
V	• Those who are able to move indoors, to eat and to dress themselves without assistance but need specific help with washing, preparing meals and with household tasks;
VI	• Those who are able to cope with the 'ADLs` without help;

Source: Appendix A French Decree No. 97-427, 2000

With regard to the numbers of recipients of domiciliary care provision from the 'PSD' scheme, at the end of the first quarterly period in 2001 about 71,000 people living at home received 'PSD' payments (the total number of recipients at the same time, including those in residential care facilities, was 134,000). The majority of disabled elderly persons in this period fall into the categories of care degrees II (about 44 per cent) and III (about 49 per cent). The proportion of those that are entitled to care degree I amounts to only about 7 per cent (French Ministry of Employment and Solidarity, 2001b).

If an applicant does not meet the criteria of eligibility for the 'PSD' scheme, which means that the person is classified in the degrees IV to VI, it is further possible to apply for a long-term care provision under a public pension insurance plan (European Commission, 2000). It is not possible to give detailed information on this matter, as the assessment procedure to determine the eligibility of a person for long-term care provision dealt with by the individual schemes for old age is freely determined by each scheme, leading to a broad dissimilarity. However, in general one can say that the income limits up to which provision is granted are, in some of the different old-age schemes, above those under the 'PSD' scheme (Rostgaard and Fridberg, 1998). From the year 2002, a new autonomous, long-term care scheme ('Allocation Personallisée d'Autonomie' - 'APA') will be introduced which provides benefits for the degrees I to IV according to the 'AGGIR' scale and will replace the 'PSD' scheme (See, 6.5). For the long-term care provision under a pension plan, this means that only the persons that are classified in the degrees V and VI remain entitled to apply for this type of benefit (Faessel, 2001).

6.3.3 Type and amount of provision - benefits and services

6.3.3.1 General Description

As illustrated above, the main provision for elderly people in need of long-term care may be available under the social assistance scheme through the 'PSD'. This scheme should, up to the introduction of an autonomous scheme for long-term care with extended service provision, meet the needs of disabled elderly people as well as possible. It also largely replaces the long-term care provision for people aged 60 and over under a scheme called 'Allocation Compensatrice pour Tierce Personne' ('ACTP'). This 'ACTP' allowance, which is also available under the social assistance scheme, was originally meant for (younger) people with handicaps, but in the past the number of disabled elderly people that applied and were found eligible increased rapidly. As an alternative to 'PSD' provision within the framework of the social assistance scheme, some disabled elderly may be entitled to receive social insurance benefits through a pension plan (European Commission, 2000).

6.3.3.2 Domiciliary care provision under the social assistance scheme

For a person in need of long-term care hoping to get 'PSD' provision under the social assistance scheme the law requires application to be made to the president of the regional government general council, with a certificate from a local level medico-social team of experts, as well as verification of his or her finances, usually based on a tax assessment. According to the president's decision, the 'PSD' may be granted for a restricted time, after which a renewal of the assessment procedure by the medico-social team of experts is necessary (Rostgaard and Fridberg, 1998).

At least 90 per cent of the 'PSD' provision granted to a disabled elderly person has either to be paid as the salary (or part of the salary) of a person that is directly employed by those in need or to an approved care-providing organisation. If the carer is directly employed by the disabled elderly person (this may also be a family member, but not the husband, wife or partner, as these persons are excluded from this regulation), the 'PSD' is directly paid by cheque or voucher to the person in need so that the carer can be reimbursed. It is not possible to receive 'PSD' payments and use them for the salary of a directly employed carer who personally receives a benefit within the framework of old age provision. In the second case when the long-term care services are delivered by an organisation in the formal sector, 'PSD' payments normally go directly to the provider. A small part of the 'PSD' allowance (up to 10 per cent) may also be used to cover other expenses (e.g. technical aids, care aids and meals on wheels services), if this is indicated in the individual plan of care (Blondeau and Dubois, 1997; European Commission, 2000).

The exact amount of the 'PSD' allowance a disabled person receives depends first of all on the income of the applicant (See 6.3.2). Secondly, the need of care that has been established by a medico-social team of experts, which assesses the degree of disability, influences the 'PSD' payment. Thirdly, the respective tariff (per hour) to be paid for the individual types of provision and fourthly the number of hours granted, likewise determine the amount of provision. Finally, the social circumstances of the applicant also influence the provision (European Commission, 2000; Para. 5 French Law No. 97-60, 2000; Faessel, 2001). The maximum 'PSD' amount is, nationwide, limited to € 717 (FR 4,706) per month (French Ministry of Employment and Solidarity, 2001b). However, there neither exist nationwide recommendations regarding the amount of payments for the individual degrees of disability nor are there guidelines for tariffs (per hour) to be paid for the provision of care as well as no national regulations for the maximum number of hours to be granted (Grignon, 2001). These allowed differences among the regions also lead to a variation in the maximum 'PSD' amounts provided by the individual 'Départments'. Thus, some regions, such as a wealthier Paris suburb ('the Hauts de Seine'), have set the allowance at the maximum level allowed by law. On the other hand, there are some hard-pressed rural regions that have fixed a maximum allowance that amounts to only about 30 per cent of what is allowed by law (Davies, Fernández and Saunders, 1998). The average monthly domiciliary 'PSD' amount provided to those in need was € 518 (FR 3,400) in the first quarter of 2001 (French Ministry of Employment and Solidarity, 2001b).

6.3.3.3 Domiciliary care provision under the social insurance scheme

In the framework of the social assistance scheme, some disabled elderly may receive long-term care benefits under their individual pension plan (European Commission, 1999). However, there are large variations in the regulations of service provision, including the exact amount of benefit, among the pension schemes that offer such allowances. This is a result of the fact that each scheme quite freely determines the amounts of provision. However, in general the maximum amount of domiciliary care granted is 30 hours monthly (Rostgaard and Fridberg, 1998).

6.3.4 Funding

The long-term care provision under the social assistance scheme ('PSD') is the responsibility of the presidents of the regional government general councils ('Conseils Généraux des Départments'). The regions fund the allowance through taxation which is the main source and charges (European Commission, 2000). The charges that are used for the 'PSD' allowance come from resources of the national solidarity fund for old-age ('Fonds de Solidarité Vieillesse'). This fund itself is predominantly financed through a general social charge which is raised on all types of income (Köstler, 1997b). The total costs of the 'PSD' scheme in the year 2000 amounted to about 0.52 billion Euro (3.4 billion French Francs) (Martin, 2001).

An additional (indirect) type of funding the 'PSD' exists because of the regulation that the allowances paid will later be reclaimed from any inheritance of the recipient. In contrast to benefits for residential care, this is made in the sector of domiciliary care only with that type of heir whose legacy exceeds € 45,735 (FR 300,000). Moreover, only the allowances above € 762 (FR 5,000) can be recalled (Para. 15 French Decree No. 97-426, 2000). As Köstler (1996c) has said, with this regulation the legislator intends to promote informal care.

The provision under the individual pension plans is usually financed by contributions from employers and employees. The amount of contributions paid varies between the individual plans for old-age, making it difficult to provide detailed data. The contribution rate for the old-age fund within the framework of the general social insurance scheme is fixed at 16.35 per cent of the employee's gross salary (9.80 per cent of this amount is paid by the employers and 6.55 per cent by the employees) (Kaufmann, 1997).

6.4 Ways forward

In the year 2002, a new autonomous long-term care scheme to extend the independence of the disabled elderly, the so-called 'Allocation Personnallisée d'Autonomie' ('APA'), will be introduced and will replace the provision under the 'PSD' scheme. By raising the income limits as well as by entitling those elderly persons with an average degree of disability (Degree IV) within the framework of the new 'APA', it is expected that the total number of disabled elderly persons who are entitled to long-term care provision will rise from about 135,000 people (aged 60 and over) in need ('PSD' scheme) up to about 800,000 people ('APA' scheme). The figures given include the recipients of domiciliary as well as residential long-term care services (French Ministry of Employment and Solidarity, 2001b; French Ministry of Employment and Solidarity, 2001c).

Like the 'PSD' the scheme which will follow is not a social insurance-based coverage, but mainly administered under the responsibility of the regional authorities ('Départments'). As in the 'PSD' scheme, a national scale ('Autonomie, Gérontologie, Groupe Iso-Ressources' - 'AGGIR') (which has been partially modified for the new 'APA' scheme) will be used for assessing the degree of disability and for laying down a plan of care (French Ministry of Employment and Solidarity, 2001c). The benefits available under the new 'APA' scheme, which will be provided in kind, as well as the number of expected beneficiaries, is illustrated in the table below (Table 16, p. 122).

The table shows that the maximum amount of allowance between the 4 degrees of disability that gives entitlement to provision varies between € 1,067 (FR 7,000) and € 457 FR (3,000). It is expected that the majority of elderly people in need will be allocated to care degrees II, III and IV, whereas a comparatively low number will be entitled to the allowance available for degree I. In contrast to the 'PSD' payments, the allowances as well as the tariffs (per hour) to be paid for the provision of care by associations under the 'APA' are harmonized nation-wide (Faessel, 2001; French Ministry of Employment and Solidarity, 2001d).

Table 16 'APA' allowances and beneficiaries

	Care degree I	Care degree II	Care degree III	Care degree IV
Maximum amount of allowance per month	€ 1,067 (Fr 7,000)	€ 915 (Fr 6,000)	€ 686 (Fr 4,500)	€ 457 (Fr 3,000)
Expected number of beneficiaries	69,000	262,000	201,000	264,000

Source: French Ministry of Employment and Solidarity, 2001d

As noted above, there is still an income test within the framework of assessment. This, however, in contrast to the 'PSD' scheme, does not mean that an elderly person in need will completely be excluded from 'APA' provision, but the co-payments that a recipient of the benefit has to make vary between 0 to 80% according to his or her income situation. To put it another way, this means that the 'APA' payment varies between 20 and 100% of the established costs within a plan of care. Actually, this means that those elderly people with income up to € 915 (FR 6,000) per month are entitled to the full amount of allowance for their degree of disability. Those with a higher income get the allowance with certain reductions and disabled people with a monthly income of € 3,049 (FR 20,000) and above are only entitled to a fixed minimum amount according to the degree of disability. For example, an elderly person who is classified in care degree I and has a monthly income of € 915 (FR 6,000), the monthly 'APA' payment will be € 1,067 (FR 7,000). If the same person has an income above € 3,049 (FR 20,000), the allowance will only be € 213 (FR 1,400) (20%) per month (French Ministry of Employment and Solidarity, 2001d).

The total costs for the new scheme are expected to be between about 2.29 and 2.59 billion Euro (15 and 17 billion French Francs) for each of the two first years (2002 and 2003). As in the case of the preceding scheme ('PSD'), the new 'APA' allowance will be funded mainly by the regional level ('Départments') (mainly through taxation). This source of funding is expected to cover about 1.7 billion Euro (11 billion French Francs) which is more than two-thirds of the total expenditure. A certain proportion (about 381 million Euro or 2.5 billion French Francs) of that first source of financing may not be directly raised in the area in which it will be used, but will come from a fund (mainly from national taxation) from which the poorer regions in particular will receive payments. The second source of funding that contributes about 762 million Euro (5 billion French Francs) to the new scheme will come from the general social charge ('Contribution Sociale Généralisée' - 'CSG') which is raised on all types of income and for its contribution to the 'APA' will be raised by 0.1 points. Thirdly, a comparatively low source of funding for the new scheme, amounting to about 76 million Euro (500 million French Francs), will come as a contribution from social insurance funds. In addition, as in the case of the 'PSD' scheme, the law initially intended that any inheritance of the beneficiary above the exemption limit of € 45,735 (FR 300,000) will later be used to reclaim the domiciliary 'APA' allowances provided (French Ministry of Employment and Solidarity, 2001c; French Ministry of Employment and Solidarity, 2001d). This provision for repayment out of a beneficiary's inheritance has, however, been cancelled following strong public protest, e.g. by different bodies representing elderly people's interests (Faessel, 2001).

6.5 Assessment and options for reform of the current domiciliary long-term care scheme

6.5.1 General Description

The subsequent sections will offer an assessment of the domiciliary long-term care scheme as existing in France as well as possibilities for reform. The data given will be empirically-verified and come from semi-structured interviews with French experts in the field of research (See Appendix B). These are experts with a scientific background and experts with a practical background (the latter included persons representing service providers and persons representing potential funders of the provision). The main focus within this procedure will be on the 'Prestation Spécifique Dépendance' ('PSD') scheme representing the major benefit for domiciliary long-term care during the time to which the research relates. However, because of the forthcoming changes in the French provision of care by the introduction of the 'Allocation Personnallisée d'Autonomie' ('APA') scheme in 2002, the sections that follow also aim to offer first judgments on these new arrangements as far as this is possible for a scheme of which no practical experience exists thus far. In the same way as in the above descriptive part of this country report, the research questions set out in Chapter 5 ('Methodology') lead to the structure of the following discussion.

6.5.2 Assessment and options for reform of the responsible institutions

Starting with a consideration of the institutional responsibilities for domiciliary long-term care in France (See 6.3.2), the departments have been given a decisive role in the provision of payments under the 'PSD` scheme and will keep this position under the new 'APA` scheme that will be introduced in 2002. This fact was welcomed by an interviewee with a practical background. As has been argued, this administrative structure ensures that those in need usually live near the institution responsible for administering the scheme. The idea of decentralisation is a welcome step and, represents progress compared to the provision under the individual pension plans as the institutions responsible for this social insurance-based provision (e.g. the fund responsible for the general scheme for old-age) are normally located at a further distance from the elderly people than the 'Départments`.

However, quite a number of interviewees criticised the fact that the administrative responsibility for the 'PSD` scheme as well as for the 'APA` scheme is located at the departmental level. For instance, as an expert from a scientific background said,

> *the fact that the responsibility for a long-term care scheme is based at the level of the 'Départments` and not within the framework of the national health insurance scheme is totally illogical having in mind the system of social protection in France including its tradition of social insurance. Of course, the main reason for this questionable location of the provision of long-term care for elderly people is based on the financial difficulties surrounding the health funds, leading to limitations of the possibilities for providing long-term care from this sector. Nevertheless, the existing organisational structure is not acceptable.*

Another interviewee representing a service provider stated,

> *if long-term care were to be organised within the framework of social insurance, it would mainly be funded from contributions. This would inevitably lead to people supposing that there was universal public coverage for cases of need. Also, an insurance based solution does not usually include any type of income test, which, unfortunately, is a significant element of both the 'PSD` and the 'APA` scheme. However, a social insurance approach would also lead to much higher and in my opinion a much more appropriate total amount of expenditure for those in need. But this appears currently undesirable to those responsible.*

As argued by another expert in this context, the co-ordination between the 'Départments' which are responsible for providing services for personal care and home-making assistance on the one hand and the health care funds that are e.g. responsible for nursing care on the other hand, is not regulated by law and their relationship is very bad in many regions. Many elderly people are in need of a provision from both types of institutions. They are usually assessed by different bureaucratic bodies and receive individual services, which are often poorly coordinated. However, with regard to the co-operation of services at the departmental level, it was also emphasised that there exist strong geographical variations. As described by a scientific expert

> *in the best situation, there exists a model where the head of all co-ordination is the administrative body of the general council that is mainly responsible for managing the 'PSD' or 'APA' scheme. This institution co-ordinates the assessment of elderly people in need of help as well as the services accordingly granted. In this situation, it is of secondary importance which institution is responsible for paying the individual services as, overall, the provision is arranged and co-ordinated as a service package by one authority. As the departments meanwhile employ social workers as well as physicians and therefore should be able to consider different aspects of need while developing service packages for elderly people, this authority currently appears to be most suitable to co-ordinate the different services available for elderly people.*

He further argued that only in a few departments would the co-ordination work in the way illustrated or similarly. This may at the same time mean that the general role of the department in providing elderly people with help is very weak and in such a situation it is often the general practitioner who is more important for co-ordinating the services that an elderly person receives. As pointed out by another interviewee working for a service provider,

> *in many, many cases, it seems that differences in the funding mechanisms, assessment procedures and accountability of individual services are leading to serious difficulties with regard to co-operation and arrangements between the institutions involved in the provision of different type of services for the elderly.*

A number of experts would like to see the provision of domiciliary long-term care administered within the framework of the social insurance scheme ('Sécurité Sociale'). Of those experts preferring a social insurance solution, there have been voices that would place such a social insurance-based long-term care provision in the hands of the funds which are predominantly responsible for managing pension insurance plans. An interviewee with a scientific background commented that such a view would usually be based on the quite common opinion in France that growing old inevitably means getting ill or that illnesses such as Alzheimer's disease are a normal phenomenon of age. This view, for instance, is also found in the French law that regulates the provision of care, where it is stated that elderly people will be provided with someone to look after them if they develop age-related infirmity. A further example that may underline this common misconception that the need for long-term care is automatically linked with old age is the circumstance that long-term care benefits are made available under individual pension schemes. The assumption that the disability of elderly people must be age-related appears to be illogical as,

> *long-term care is mainly required owing to the results of an illness such as a stroke or some type of dementia and not only because of the ageing process itself. Therefore, it appears logical to place the administrative responsibility for care needs very close to the local health insurance funds ('Caisses Primaires d`Assuarance Maladie`) or, preferably to new long-term care funds. The work of such care funds should be carried out by the existing health funds which then at the same time would act as health insurance funds and as long-term care funds . . . This approach seems very efficient since, on the one hand, no new bureaucracy has to be installed and, on the other hand, it would make it possible to administer long-term care independently and therefore to establish the exact amount of long-term care costs.*

Different interviewees approve, in principle, this model of organising long-time provision care and therefore are in favour of a long-term care coverage that should be implemented by the local health insurance funds.

As a further aspect, consideration was given in the interviews to providers of services whereby services under the 'PSD` scheme are normally carried out either by carers who work on a freelance basis, by different types of recognized care services or by a person (very often a relative, except the spouse or partner) who is employed by the disabled elderly person. In view of the availability of service providers, a number of experts mentioned the large geographical inequality across the country and therefore inequity towards those in need. As pointed out by an expert with a practical background,

> *there exists on the one hand some, often built-up, regions where those in need may choose between the whole variety of providers. On the other hand, there are, frequently rural, regions where there may only be one, or in the worst case, no formal provider available.*

As the new 'APA' scheme that replaces the 'PSD' scheme in 2002 will entitle about six times more disabled elderly people to receive some type of publicly-funded long-term care services, several experts are expecting the insufficient supply of service providers to increase. As stated by an expert with a scientific background, the establishment of an appropriate infrastructure of service provision in the individual regions has simply not been considered adequately while the new 'APA' scheme has been worked out. As further argued, in order to meet this increasing need for service provision, the regulations governing contracts for providers of publicly-financed services should be made easier so that more potential carers are encouraged to enter the market. In this connection, there should be no preference within the department for contracting any particular type of service provider. It would rather be helpful if the voluntary, non-profit bodies, private organisations and carers that work on a freelance basis as well as public providers had the same starting point. This might help the elderly person in need to choose from a broader supply of service providers in different regions.

Basically, a range of interviewees welcomed the fact that a multi-disciplinary (medico-social) team usually carries out the applicant assessment procedure. However, some regretted that the way these teams act in practice varies widely across the country and is highly influenced by the basic financial capability for providing long-term care within the individual departments. As stated by an interviewee with a scientific background, it would be very welcome if the duties of these teams went further than just classifying an applicant into a particular degree of disability. For example, it would be useful if the assessment could include giving advice with regard to rehabilitation and trying to encourage the elderly person to fight against his or her disability. As the expert further said, such an extended and desirable course of action by the multi-disciplinary teams is only identifiable in very few of the departments.

6.5.3 Assessment and options for reform of the eligibility criteria

With regard to the eligibility criteria of the 'PSD' as well as for the 'APA' scheme, the national assessment scale ('AGGIR') which is applied within both schemes for classifying an applicant in one of six degrees of disability (See 6.3.2 and 6.4), was an important consideration for several interviewees. Some experts pointed to the fact that the scale was originally developed by the French society of geriatrics for assessing the help needed by people in a hospital or an old people's home. The scale was not intended initially for the sector of domiciliary long-term care provision. However, different interviewees acknowledged this national assessment scale as an excellent instrument for determining a claimant's state of health and explaining the reasons for the individual's needs. Unfortunately, the decision to provide appropriate long-term care services that are needed to cope with the applicant's infirmity is at best only partly based on this assessment. As an interviewee representing a service provider explained,

> *to be able to provide elderly people with appropriate long-term care, not only is detailed information about the elderly person' state of health required but rather the kind and/or extent of help they need resulting from their infirmity. The 'AGGIR' scale is not a very suitable instrument for establishing the need for care, owing to its strong emphasis on medical issues and its neglect of social issues.*

As stated by another expert with a scientific background, the main weak point of the 'AGGIR' scale is how to relate the established syndrome of an elderly person to one or other degree of disability, each related to a different amount of long-term care payment (as intended in the new 'APA' scheme). He said that it may well be that because of the difficulties in allocating the disabled elderly to different degrees of disability according to their needs an applicant will be classified in degree II although he or she has a greater need of care than someone who is classified in degree I (actually intended for people in extreme need of care). An interviewee with a practical background also sees too strong a weighting of the 'AGGIR' scale towards physical restrictions and a neglect of forms of mental disturbance. He further said that this leads to significant disadvantages for those elderly people who suffer from any of the different types of dementia (e.g. Alzheimer's disease) and need to be generally supervised and guided, but this need is not considered adequately.

Some experts mentioned the lack of comprehensibility of the eligibility criteria (which are based on a complicated point-awarding procedure) both for people working in the field and in particular for those in need or their relatives. Therefore, they would like to see a simplification of the very complicated and hardly understandable assessment procedure.

Another interviewee with a scientific background referred to the subjective application of the 'AGGIR' scale by those carrying out the assessment procedure. It was said that

> *there exists evidence that this tool is not used in the same way in the North and South of France. According to research concerning this, it is much easier to be classified in a higher degree of disability in South of France than in the North. This difference is often seen even when individual cases are comparable - people of the same age and same type of disability, for example. This is the result of using an*

instrument that offers too much room for subjective assessment by those carrying out the procedure and those behind them (department).

In addition, a scientific interviewee criticised,

the degree of dependency that is assessed through the 'AGGIR' is not only based on the physiological or functional situation of those in need, but also depends on the degree of help the individual can get from informal care. For example, a disabled elderly person who is married will usually have a very low rate of dependency according to the scale but on the other hand a person who lives alone with the same degree of disability will normally get higher benefits. This means that the scale is not only a matter of the individual's degree of disability but also reflects the help that the environment may be able to provide. This means that there is an implicit trade-off between what the spouse is going to do and what the state is going to do.

Another expert commented on this aspect,

in French the idea is still widespread that providing care for the elderly inhabitants is a family matter. In this concern, it is quite common for provision within the family to be regarded as a maintenance obligation ('Obligation alimentaire') in a legal sense. Having in mind the social changes occurring in France (e.g. the decreasing potential of informal carers as a result of the increase in the numbers of women in paid employment), there is an urgent need that the state rethinks the role of the family in the social welfare mix. There is an urgent necessity to redistribute the burden between what the state provides and what the family can provide. It therefore is wrong that the family situation should influence the assessment of the need for care that an elderly person has.

A range of experts emphasized the missed opportunity to reform the 'AGGIR' scale significantly before the introduction of the 'APA' scheme in 2002. It was noted that the 'AGGIR' scale, with the exception of some minor changes that in particular offer some improvements for those suffering from dementia, will largely remain the same for the 'APA' scheme. It was also mentioned, greatly influenced by criticisms from a very large number of professionals in the field of long-term care, that enshrined in the 'APA' law is the provision that there will have to be a scientific commission to analyse the 'AGGIR' and develop proposals for its modification. A number of experts welcomed the move towards rethinking the 'AGGIR' scale on a scientific basis but at the same time regretted that results from this venture are not to be expected before the year 2003. Some experts were also of the opinion that it would be more effective to look for a new instrument for assessing the care need of elderly persons instead of trying to modify the 'AGGIR' scale. For instance, the 'Activities of Daily Life' scheme, put forward initially by the Australian doctor Katz, was mentioned as a suitable basis for developing a more preferable instrument for identifying needs.

One expert with a scientific background was in favour of an assessment procedure that works free of nationally fixed criteria and is also not intended to classify applicants in different degrees of disability. He suggested that examinations should be free from national guidelines and simply carried out on the basis of an elderly person's need in terms of what the applicant is able to do without help and for which items care is necessary and to which extent. The necessary care should be provided based on an individually-based assessment procedure. In contrast to such an approach, several experts were clearly in favour of national eligibility criteria for accessing the need for care. As argued by an expert working for an institution funding care services,

> *the absence of fixed eligibility criteria would certainly have the advantage that it would then be possible to consider each individual applicant independently of any guidelines. Using national criteria of course include the risk that an elderly person's needs may more likely not be satisfied as well as is possible with an individually-based assessment. However, among other reasons, such considerations would appear to be unsuitable simply because of the problem of funding such a scheme without reference to established degrees of disability and, therefore, fixed maximum amounts of payments.*

Other interviewees argued that local criteria would reinforce the risk that even in the case of the same type of disability the care granted to elderly people may well vary significantly with the place of residence. As further pointed out, having geographical variations in assessing need is simply inequitable. Instead of contributing to clarity about what an elderly person may expect from long-term care provision, not knowing what to expect from the scheme would more probably lead to insecurity for many people in need. In this connection it was also noted that having a locally based set of criteria would mean that it is not clear how much money nation-wide has to be raised for long-term care. As an additional consideration, an expert with a scientific background who was, in principle, also in favour of a uniform set of criteria underlined the necessity that in the case of a national assessment procedure it is very important that they are far-reaching fair and equitable to those in need, independently of the type of disability (e.g. do not put those who suffer from dementia at a disadvantage in comparison to those with a more physical illness). Therefore, it is extremely important how these criteria are defined.

As shown in the descriptive sections, the amount of long-term care an elderly person is entitled to under the 'PSD' and 'APA' schemes is not solely decided on the basis of help needed. It is the income of those in need that is the main barrier for many elderly people when applying for benefits and services. The experts commented very critically on this situation. In the 'PSD' scheme, the income test has lead to an exclusion of the majority of elderly people in need of long-term care. A scientific expert said that about 135,000 people in need have been shown to be entitled to some kind of 'PSD' provision. Considering the need of care according only to the 'AGGIR' scale, the number of elderly people who would be put in care degrees 1 to 3, i.e. would be entitled to receive a 'PSD' on the basis of help needed, without looking at the income situation, would be about 532,000. This means that without the existing income test, the number of elderly people entitled to the provision would be nearly four times as great.

An interviewee with a scientific background suggested that one option for improving the unsatisfactory situation of so many people in need excluded from support from public funds would be to adjust the income limits for the 'PSD' scheme in such a way that provision is available in many more cases. Other interviewees flatly refused to agree with any form of income or savings test in a long-term care scheme. For example, an interviewee working for a service provider argued,

> *it is not understandable why, for example, on the one hand, a disabled elderly person who suffers from Alzheimer's disease is not entitled to publicly provided care while those elderly person with a heart condition or cancer usually get the main bulk of care free.*

A number of other experts argued similarly by just saying that the current situation is very inequitable. In contrast to elderly people who need medical care and mainly get this type of help free of charge, many of those who require long-term care do not get adequate public support for their needs. The experts did not see a justification for the differences in the provision of public money to deal with the individual problems of an elderly person. A better balance in the provision of public support for individual syndromes an elderly person may be confronted with was desirable. Therefore, the existing income test for long-term care should be dispensed with. Those interviewees that commented on the fact that the allowances paid from the 'PSD' scheme will later be reclaimed from heirs whose legacy exceeds € 45,735 (FR 300,000) disapproved of this regulation, largely on the same grounds as those cited for rejecting the income test.

A number of experts stressed that in the 'PSD' scheme many people are excluded from provision not only on income grounds but also on the basis of their disability status according to the 'AGGIR' scale. A scientific interviewee explained that services are exclusively provided for elderly people in extreme need of care (Degrees I to III). This means that a large number of disabled elderly (about 264,000) with a considerable need for care (Degree IV) are already excluded on the basis of their degree of disability.

With the introduction of the 'APA' scheme that replaces the provision under the 'PSD' scheme in 2002, eligibility will be substantially broadened. By entitling those elderly people with a considerable degree of disability (Degree IV), raising the income limits and abolishing the regulation that the allowances paid may later be reclaimed from an inheritance, nearly all interviewees saw an improvement in the 'APA' scheme (that is expected to provide long-term care for about 800,000 elderly people) compared to the 'PSD' scheme. An expert with a scientific background stated,

> *the main advantage of the 'APA' is that no disabled elderly person is excluded from the scheme on the basis of a means test and, in addition, those elderly people with a considerable degree of disability are no longer left out. This means that the new scheme will be universal and may in principle offer care for any elderly person, if a need exists.*

The condition that basically no one is excluded completely from provision was also highlighted by other interviewees as a very important necessity in a long-term care scheme and this condition will be fulfilled in France with the introduction of the 'APA' in 2002. As argued by one of these experts, covering all elderly people in a uniform scheme appears to be effective and the national uniform assessment procedure should give people a clear idea of the availability of long-term care services paid for from public resources in cases of need. The expert further said that excluding no-one will help the scheme to be accepted by the population and should ensure that the need of all disabled elderly is equitably assessed and an appropriate plan of care drawn up for them.

However, although the 'APA' does not exclude anyone completely on the basis of an elderly person's means, the scheme includes a co-payment that a beneficiary has to make. This varies between 0 and 80% and will be fixed according to the elderly person's income. An advocate of this regulation with a scientific background said the regulation makes it easier to ensure the provision of care for elderly people of higher incomes and helps to improve the situation for those who are unable to pay for long-term care services out of their own pocket. It was further argued that the provision of support without considering the individual's financial resources would lead to an unfair distribution of public funds and the wealthier would profit from this. In opposition to this view, a range of other experts regretted that the income of an elderly person is considered when assessing the 'APA' provision, even though this will be done in a less stringent manner than in the 'PSD' scheme. These experts are nevertheless in favour of treating age-related disability as a social risk within the framework of social insurance, which would mean that there is no income test. Where fixing the exact amount of the co-payments in the 'APA', one of these experts stated that charges of up to 80% will lead to extreme inequality as some elderly people will only get a fraction of the public provision compared to others. Apart from the large differences in the provision of free services among elderly people, the criticism was expressed that the income limits for the 'APA' scheme are still fixed comparatively low. As illustrated in the descriptive sections, only those elderly people with a monthly income up to € 915 (FR 6,000) are entitled to the full amount of payments according to their degree of disability and all others have to make co-payments that vary between 20 and 80% (the maximum co-payment of 80% has to be made from a monthly income of € 3,049 or FR 20,000).

Among the criticism of several experts regarding the income test in general, one expert with a scientific background further said that it is still not clear which type of income we are talking about for the 'APA' scheme. He said that

> *it is not clear if it is net income as assessed for tax purposes or gross income, with or without income from assets or other sources. Therefore, there is an urgent need to arrive at a very clear definition about what is meant by income where the 'APA' scheme is concerned.*

In addition, as suspected by another interviewee with a practical background, having a means test exclusively based on the income of those in need and not taking account of their property (e.g. houses) as planned for the 'APA' scheme is, on the one hand, a positive approach as it usually does not force those in need to sell their house or flat before becoming entitled to public long-term care provision. On the other hand, it offers incentives for elderly people to transform some part of their regular income into property. He further said, it appears very doubtful if hidden incentives for such transfer can be deliberately taken account of in a scheme of public provision.

6.5.4 Assessment and options for reform of the type and amount of provision - benefits and services

With regard to the type of provision available for disabled elderly people in France (See, 6.3.3), many interviewees first of all pointed towards the low amount of benefits and services available under the 'PSD'. As was said, in most cases the provision only covers a small part of the individual's total long-term care costs. In most instances, this holds true even if the national fixed maximum amount of payment is granted. In addition, the amount of provision is not only inadequate, but also distributed inequitable fashion among those in need. As explained by an expert with a practical background, this inequity mainly arises from the fact that each department has a broad term of reference for establishing the exact amount of long-term care provision that an applicant who falls within their responsibility may be entitled to. This latitude first of all exists in the fact that while there is a nation-wide regulation that determines the maximum 'PSD' amount to be paid by a department per month, there is no directive concerning a minimum payment. The expert further said that this means, in practice, that some wealthier regions or regions where care for elderly people is very high on the political agenda, provide 'PSD' payments up to this maximum amount. In contrast to this, many departments grant only a comparatively small part of the nationally fixed maximum amount. Various interviewees criticised this disparity in departmental provision and pointed to the consequence for elderly people, i.e. that the extent of care a person receives under the 'PSD' scheme is highly influenced by where he or she lives. For example, as one of the interviewees with a scientific background commented,

> *the inequity in the 'PSD' scheme is a logical consequence of the lack of national guidelines. There neither exist national recommendations concerning the tariff per hour to be paid for the individual types of provision nor are there guidelines for the number of hours to be granted for the individual degrees of disability. Nevertheless, at the departmental level, the services are often, but not necessarily, granted according to the applicant's degree of disability. This, however, is done on a very individual basis by each department and is leading to a wide variation in the amount of provision. The result of this is that although the degree of disability often influences the total amount of provision in the individual departments, it may well be, for example, that an elderly person who is put in degree I (the highest degree) in one department gets lower payments than an elderly person who is put in degree III in another.*

In addition to the difficulties arising from the comparatively low amount of provision and the geographical variations in the application of the law, a number of interviewees found it extremely problematic that 'PSD' provision is only available for elderly people in extreme need of care (Degrees I to III). Those with a considerable need (Degree IV) are not covered by the scheme. In this connection, an expert from a scientific background noted,

> *doing nothing at an early stage for people in need and also doing nothing for family members caring for them may well lead to admittance into a nursing home since, without support, it simply is extremely difficult to cope with the problems that caring for the elderly infirm brings. In addition, doing nothing for elderly people at an early stage also includes the risk that such people will in the future be in greater need than would be the case if help is provided at an early stage.*

An expert working for a funder of care services took up a further point. He noted that the geographical variations in provision make it almost impossible to inform those concerned about the services of the 'PSD' scheme and to calculate its total cost, now and for the future, on a national basis. Another interviewee representing a provider of care stated that owing to the different and often unclear provision in the individual departments, many people are neither very clear about what (financial) support they may expect from the 'PSD' scheme nor do they have sufficient information about the different options regarding those who may provide support.

In 2002, the 'APA' scheme will start making provision available and in this new scheme the interviewees generally recognised clear improvements in service provision compared with the 'PSD' scheme. As mentioned, the improvements will be found, in particular, in the fixing of nationally uniform maximum amounts of monthly benefits and services depending on the degree of disability and income. In addition, it was acknowledged that the provision the individual may get from the new scheme will normally be higher than in the former 'PSD' scheme and also that those elderly persons with a considerable need of long-term care (Degree IV) will now be entitled to the benefits and services. An expert with a scientific background commented on this,

> *the new 'APA' scheme means that people can now be clear about what to expect in the case of need; no disabled elderly person is completely excluded from the scheme and the amount of provision will no longer depend on where a person lives.*

However, although the ´APA` in general is seen as an improvement, several experts commented critically on different elements of the service provision under the new scheme. As pointed out by some, the limited amount of payment under the ´APA` scheme in most cases is still insufficient to meet the need of care a disabled elderly person has, even if the maximum provision is paid. The amount of public support will remain unsatisfactory, particularly for those who receive reduced payments following the income test. Therefore, different interviewees would welcome a uniform provision for all elderly people in need without a reductions related to income. An expert with a practical background suggested, long-term care provision should not be provided up to fixed monthly maximum amounts, but free on the basis of the individual's need. He said that society was rich enough to take on this responsibility for its elderly fellow citizens. Different experts opposed such an approach and emphasized the necessity of having upper limits. For example, as asserted by a scientific interviewee,

> *even if the provision of long-term care is made part of a social insurance-based scheme, there has to be an upper limit of benefits. While providing long-term care free on the basis of need would be an appropriate step for those in need, it would mean having to disregard the realities of restricted public means. Having in mind the forecasts of demographic as well as social changes, one must assume that the need for and the cost of care will rise in future years and provision only according to need would lead to non-fundable, incalculable costs.*

Another interviewee said that cost-free care would lead to an increase of people's expectations in terms of the extent and quality of publicly-funded long-term care. The necessity of having clearly fixed benefits and services instead of a free provision according to need was also stressed in view of the need to keep control of the expenditure on long-term care schemes.

A major point of criticism was expressed by a range of experts regarding the barely available support for informal carers, both in the ´PSD` and in the new ´APA` scheme. It was said that the ´PSD` scheme includes the option of using the benefit for formal help to make payments to one or more relatives who do not necessarily have to be trained carers. However, this is not possible in the case of the spouse or partner and, with the introduction of the ´APA` scheme it is also no longer possible to use the public benefit to pay for the services of any other unskilled relative. As explained by a scientific expert, the complete exclusion of the spouse or partner from ´PSD` provision is based on the notion of the family's moral maintenance obligation, which is still present in France, namely, that the spouse or partner is considered obliged to provide maintenance without any payment. This notion, it was said, needs urgent discussion. An interviewee with a practical background declared that

> *the current situation not only puts the provision of care on an informal basis at a disadvantage, people do not even have any real choice about the way care is provided. It would be desirable if the elderly person in need were given support to retain a certain degree of autonomy in making his or her individual care arrangements. This failure to cater for the reimbursement of informal care appears all the more surprising, as there are still some areas in France where the supply of formal care providers is insufficient to meet the demand. This may for example lead to the strange situation that only care by the spouse is possible as no formal provider is available, but there will be no public support for this single option.*

As stated by an expert with a scientific background, the discussion in France about long-term care has mainly concentrated on benefits for the elderly person in need and has largely excluded reference to the huge number of family carers who are almost exclusively women. He further said that even under the 'PSD' scheme where it is possible that a comparatively low sum can be paid out to relatives who are employed by the person in need, the benefit is at best only a kind of 'social acknowledgement' of those who have no other paid employment. For those informal carers who left their job to care for the infirm relative, the normally low payment means a substantial cut in income. It was recommended that the status of the informal carer should be clearly defined, with reasonable compensation being paid for their work, including social protection (e.g. pension and health care). Other interviewees likewise stressed the urgent need that any long-term care scheme (whether the 'PSD' or the 'APA' scheme) should officially support informal care. It was said that elderly people should have the chance to choose between services in kind, benefits in cash or a combination of both. The availability of an adequate benefit in cash which can be used to pay for the work of the informal carer gives them a fair choice when they are not able to work because of the responsibilities of caring for a relative. An interesting consideration with regard to the reserved handling to give support to informal carers or to provide cash in benefits was highlighted by a scientific interviewee who was also in favour of a better balance between supporting formal and informal care. She said that

> *according to EU law, cash benefits from a long-term care scheme often have to be transferred to entitled people who are living abroad. In contrast, benefits in kind normally only have to be paid if the elderly person lives in the country where the provision is paid for. As there exists a general resistance in France against transferring*

> *any benefit abroad, it currently seems a difficult undertaking to persuade the public policy makers to see the necessity of providing long-term care benefits in cash in addition to services in kind.*

However, although there have been a lot of comments in support of informal care, there where also experts who stressed that there are limits to the value of such informal care. In this matter, an expert representing a service provider argued that for people in extreme need of care, formal and qualified help (at least in addition to informal care) appears to be necessary. Another interviewee stressed that

> *there may well be problems in accepting informal care in performing tasks that concern intimate areas of an elderly person's body. It may be easier for many disabled elderly to accept formal care in such spheres. There are also fields where the same elderly person may prefer help on an informal basis, for example, with more general care. As this is all individually based, it is important that a long-term care scheme offers the possibility to arrange the care largely according to the wishes a person has.*

6.5.5 Assessment and options for reform of the funding

The funding mechanism of the 'PSD` scheme which is mainly based on regional government taxation (See 6.3.4) has been excoriated by several of the participating interviewees. As stated by an interviewee with a scientific background,

> *with the main source of funding being the individual departments, probably the worst solution was chosen. In general, it appears difficult to have an equitable funding scheme if it is administered by different regional governments. The fact that there exists a comparatively large number of such regional authorities (about 100) makes the situation even more difficult and means that there is a lot of room for inequity, because there are very rich departments and very poor ones. In addition, there are departments with a very high proportion of elderly people, which means that the demand for care services and the strain on financial resources required in such areas is likely to be higher than in departments with a comparatively young population. Another aspect is that some departments have less than 100,000 inhabitants, which means that from an organizational point of view it appears rather unwise to put the funding on such a narrow basis. For the funding of long-term care provision at the departmental*

level to be equitable it would be necessary to construct a very complicated scheme of re-allocating resources to the different departments. This however, still seems to be a very questionable solution.

Further experts indicated that some departments simply couldn't cope with the financial burden of providing adequate long-term care arrangements for their elderly inhabitants. It was suggested that instead of leaving the main financial responsibility to the departments with the differences between them, funding on a national basis would lead to more equity across the country.

When considering the basis of funding for the new 'APA' scheme, a range of experts saw improvement compared with the 'PSD' scheme. It was pointed out that spreading the funding of the 'APA' among the departments, a fund (mainly from national taxation) to support the poorer regions, the general social charge ('Contribution Sociale Généralisée' - 'CSG') as well as on social insurance, means that there will be some progress in terms of equity compared to the former 'PSD' scheme. However, as further argued, the fact that the funds again come from the regional authorities means that there remains some inequity since the amount of the individual's contribution to the funding of long-term care still depends on where he or she lives. As pointed out by an interviewee with a scientific background

already now before the new scheme starts, considerable doubt has been expressed in public discussion as to whether the departments will be able to bear the burden of their share in the funding of the 'APA'. It appears likely that some of the poorer departments will, in spite of the newly established fund to support them, not be able to cope with this financial burden. The difficulty of funding the 'APA' scheme appears even greater when considering that the probable total amount to be spent by the departments will in most cases be much higher than it was in the 'PSD' scheme. In addition, it is estimated that the costs of the new scheme will rise rapidly from the year 2004 onwards which means that the new 'APA' is based on very weak funding arrangements.

As indicated above, many interviewees are in favour of funding the provision on a national basis. It was also recommended that long-term care should be financed on a (national) 'pay-as-you-go' basis under which the current costs of the scheme would be funded through present social contributions. As explained by one scientific interviewee, a contribution-based long-term care scheme is therefore a preferable solution than a scheme which is paid for from national taxation, as it fits well within the framework of the already existing social insurance-based schemes, e.g. the schemes for health and old-age. Another interviewee representing a service provider said

> *in contrast to a scheme which is funded by general taxation, a social insurance-based scheme enables people to be aware of the relationship between what they are paying for insuring themselves against the risk of being infirm and needing long-term care on the one hand and what they may expect in return for their contribution in the case of need on the other. People will pay their contributions more willingly if they know what their money will be spent on.*

Different experts suggested implementing long-term care insurance as a new source of finance among the already existing schemes. As stated by a scientific interviewee, a scheme involving individual contributions specifically for long-term care allows a better control of expenditure than if the benefit is provided within the framework of funding that includes other types of social spending, e.g. within the framework of the health insurance scheme. Considering the close relationship between illness and age-related disability, another expert said, however, that he could well imagine the financing of long-term care being within the health insurance scheme. But the interviewee also pointed out that owing to the current difficult financial situation in health insurance, this would be very difficult to implement. Another interviewee was of the same opinion and said

> *currently it seems reasonable to introduce long-term care insurance as an independent sector of the social insurance scheme for a time. Later, after experience of separate financing of the provision has provided detailed knowledge of the costs and the funds available from such insurance, and when it is hoped that there has been an improvement in terms of the control of health expenditure, consolidation of the two sectors can be considered.*

A difficulty in the provision of long-term care within the existing social insurance scheme or rather a questionable feature of the existing scheme was stressed by an interviewee with a practical background. It was said that within the general social insurance scheme ('Régime Général') which covers the majority of the population (e.g. employees and their families), there exists a range of special schemes ('Régimes Spéciaux) (e.g. for civil servants) and also independent schemes ('Régimes Autonomous') (e.g. for self-employed persons). There may well be differences between the individual schemes, in the contributions to be paid for and also inequality in the provision of benefits and services. The interviewee went on *a universal scheme would be much fairer and would not entitle certain groups of the population to certain privileges. However, it is an extremely complicated issue and a desirable change in the current situation seems far from being achieved. Therefore, the question now is how to integrate a new long-term care scheme into the existing complexity of different types of insurance. One way of dealing with the present situation might be to implement a long-term care scheme with equal contributions and equal benefits determined by law and independently of the question which scheme a person is covered by. However, the administration should be left with the different schemes and the individual should be covered by that scheme which is providing cover against other risks, such as health insurance. Such a uniform model would seem fair as it would put people in equal starting positions.*

Although some experts were in favour of a social insurance-based long-term care scheme, some of them raised doubts as to whether it would be possible to fund such a scheme from contributions by employers and employees as traditionally intended. Here, it was argued that the demographic changes already occurring, which are expected to gather pace in the future, raise doubts that a social insurance scheme mainly funded by the working population will remain affordable in the future. As stated by another interviewee,

one does not need not to be a prophet to realize that calculations based on the reasonable assumption that fewer and fewer working members of the current population will be required to pay for a continually increasing number of pensioners, who are the main beneficiaries of social insurance, will not be reliable.

In light of the difficulties arising from the 'traditional` way of funding any social insurance-based scheme, e.g. for long-term care, scientific experts pointed to the method of funding benefits and services by an ear-marked taxation ('Contribution Sociale Généralisée - 'CSG`), already applied in some branches of social insurance in addition to the social insurance contributions through employers and employees. As explained by one of these experts

the 'CSG` is a special tax or charge for social purposes and is raised proportionally with a fixed rate on all types of income, for example rental income. This means that the procedure is similar to that of imposing social insurance contributions, which are also raised proportionally and not progressively as normal taxes are. In contrast to normal taxes, which may be used for different public expenditure, the 'CSG` is an ear-marked tax and, for example, used to cover *benefits not linked to contributions (i.e. entitlements arising from time spent bringing up children) under the pension scheme.*

It was further said that the 'CSG' is a welcome step towards putting the funding of social insurance on a broader basis. Leaving the burden of paying for social insurance on the decreasing working population alone would not only lead to a questionable balance between the working population who pays on the one hand and the increasing proportion of elderly people on the other hand, it would also inevitably lead to a collapse of the whole funding mechanism. As concluded by experts regarding the provision of long-term care within the framework of social insurance, a new sector for the disabled elderly should not be paid for exclusively by employers and employees, but the costs should likewise be distributed. Ear-marked taxation in the sense of the 'CSG' (which by the way is also intended to pay for a certain proportion of the new 'APA' scheme) offers the appropriate tool for dealing with this.

As a final point, different experts commented on the option of funding long-term care through private insurance contracts. However, those who made a statement on this issue in general expressed some doubts concerning the efficiency and equity of a market solution for insuring against the risk of long-term care becoming necessary. An expert representing a service provider suspected that private companies would select the risk of age-related disability, which may mean that either only healthy people will get insurance contracts or that those exposed to some special kind of risk have to pay very high premiums. He further noted that women, who on average have a higher life expectancy than men, on average also spend a longer period of life needing long-term care and have to pay higher premiums for a private insurance contract. An expert representing a funder of care pointed out that in private insurance the premiums are not raised progressively or proportionally with income and those with lower usually have to pay exactly the same premiums as the more wealthy. This clearly puts those with lower means at a disadvantage, as they have to pay the same contribution from smaller financial resources. As stated by a scientific interviewee, private insurance does not offer an adequate approach to insuring against the risk of needing long-term care. They may, however, be helpful to those who intend to have coverage for what is needed in addition to a public scheme which normally provides a fixed amount of care.

6.6 Summary

The present Chapter has given an overview of the French domiciliary long-term care scheme. This has included a descriptive outline of the social protection system where it has been shown that different social insurance schemes

('Securité Sociale') form the main part of social protection in France. This, for example, comprises the sectors of pensions and health. In addition to social insurance, another fundamental part of social protection is the social assistance scheme. The main provision for domiciliary long-term care between 1997 and 2001 ('Prestation Spécifique Dépandance' - 'PSD') is not integrated together with the different sectors of social insurance, but is part of the social assistance scheme. Following this general overview on social protection, a review of the responsible institutions for implementing long-term care, a discussion of the eligibility criteria for the receipt of benefit and services, a description of the type of service provision and an examination of the funding arrangements have been given. As a final descriptive aspect, an outline of future developments was given. This brought to light that the French long-term care scheme will undergo essential changes from the year 2002 onwards when a new autonomous scheme for covering the risk of long-term care (Allocation Personalisée d'Autonomie - 'APA') will replace the 'PSD' scheme. In addition to the descriptive part of this country report, an empirically founded assessment of the long-term care scheme, including options for reform, has been put forward. This firstly contained an examination of responsible institutions, secondly the eligibility criteria, thirdly the type of service provision and fourthly the type of funding from the 'PSD' scheme as well as from the new 'APA' scheme. The results of the empirical analysis including an overview of the descriptive findings relating to these findings are given below.

Regarding the institutions responsible for implementing domiciliary long-term care in France, administrative responsibility for the 'PSD' as well as for the 'APA' scheme is in the hands of the departments ('Départment'). The recognized organisations that predominantly provide domiciliary care is made up of voluntary, non-profit bodies, followed by private organisations. In addition, a significant number of carers work on a freelance basis and in order to be granted entitlement to provision from the 'PSD' scheme another option that many elderly people in need have chosen is to employ a family member (except the spouse or partner). The empirical discussion has shown that putting administrative responsibility in the hands of the departments seems to be a very questionable approach, as it does not fit in with the existing administration of insurance against other risks, e.g. that of health care, where a social insurance fund is responsible for managing these schemes. As was reported in the empirical part of the study, elderly people who are in need of long-term care, frequently need additional help (e.g. nursing care) that is not provided by the department, but by other institutions (quite often by health insurance). The discussion has shown that the 'PSD' services and other kinds of help are poorly co-ordinated in many regions. An option for reforming this unsatisfactory state of affairs would be to institute a system in the individual regions where one institution or care manager (e.g. from the department) is responsible for arranging all the services an elderly person is entitled to as a service package and which institution is paying for the individual services should be a subordinated matter. Another possibility is to implement a completely new scheme, where the provision of domiciliary long-term care is administrated within the framework of social insurance. Due to the close relationship of long-term care with health care, it appears appropriate to place the responsibility in the hands of the health insurance funds or possibly even better to implement new long-term care funds under the aegis of the health insurance funds. This would seem efficient, as no new bureaucratic measures would need to be adopted. Concerning the predominant type of service providers in the 'PSD' scheme, in the empirical analysis it was observed that large geographical inequalities exist with regard to the availability of the different type of providers. In some regions elderly people may choose from the whole variety of providers whereas in other regions the supply is far from adequate. This situation is expected to become aggravated with the introduction of the 'APA', as this new scheme will offer only extended formal care. Therefore, an urgent need exists in several regions to cope with the expected increasing demand by establishing an adequate infrastructure of service providers. A positive element is that the assessment of an applicant for long-term care benefits is carried out by a multi-disciplinary (medico-social) team. Nevertheless it seems desirable that all teams would, in addition to classifying elderly people into different degrees of disability, also give advice with regard to rehabilitation and try to motivate the person in need to fight against his or her disability.

For assessing an elderly person's need, the national 'AGGIR' ('Autonomie, Gérontologie, Groupe Iso-Ressources') scale is applied in the 'PSD' and will also be used in the subsequent 'APA' scheme. As the discussion has shown, the scale is a controversial instrument for assessing the care needs of an elderly person resulting from disability. Moreover, it includes too great an emphasis on physical criteria and neglects mental disturbance. In addition, it is a very complicated and scarcely understandable instrument that is applied unevenly in different regions. Therefore an urgent need exists to reform this scale or otherwise to look for a completely new national tool to replace the 'AGGIR'. In this matter, research is currently going on to find ways of modifying the 'AGGIR' scale. It is to be hoped that this will lead to quick and suitable proposals. In addition to the care needed, income is the second essential criterion in decisions concerning the provision of long-term care paid for from public sources for an elderly person. In the 'PSD' scheme, the excessively strict income test has led to an exclusion of most disabled elderly. In the 'APA' scheme, no one will be completely excluded on income grounds, which shows important progress compared to the 'PSD' scheme. However, the 'APA' scheme includes a co-payment that a recipient of services has to make.

This varies between 0 and 80% according to income. Therefore, those who find it inequitable that elderly people, when, for example, suffering from cancer, get the main bulk of care free from the health insurance (without an income test) whereas someone suffering from dementia possibly has to make a co-payment of up to 80%, may only accept the new law as a temporary solution while waiting for a social insurance-based scheme with no income test. In addition to this, there seems to be a need for action in defining clearly what is meant by the term 'income' in the sense of the new law.

As the discussion has shown, the amount of benefits and services for domiciliary long-term care from the 'PSD' varies widely across the country and is highly influenced by regional circumstances. Given this geographical inequality, it is hardly possible to get information on a national basis about what an elderly person may expect from the scheme. In general, the provision is very low, often only covering a small part of the total cost and people officially have no choice as the 'PSD' is available only in kind (it is, however, possible to employ one or more relatives, with the exception of the spouse or partner, and use the benefit for this). In addition, it is very problematic that provision is only available for those in severe or extreme need of care (Degrees I to III) and those with a considerable need (Degree IV) are not covered by the 'PSD'. The 'APA' scheme will offer an expanded provision. Another positive element of the new scheme is that people with a considerable need of long-term care (Degree IV) will now also be covered. The 'APA' also redresses the geographical variations by fixing of national uniform monthly amounts of provision according to an elderly person's degree of disability and income. However, even though provision under the 'APA' in general brings clear progress compared to the former 'PSD', the empirical discussion has shown that the new scheme includes certain regulations that should be re-assessed. Given the reality of restricted public resources, it is clear that provision of a long-term care scheme has to be limited. Nevertheless, the fixed amount of payment as intended within the 'APA' appears relatively low, as it will in too many cases remain insufficient to meet an elderly person's long-term care needs even if the maximum sum is granted. For those who are only entitled to a reduced services because of their income situation, the support will remain unsatisfactory. A major weak point of the new 'APA' scheme (as was already the case in the former 'PSD' scheme) is the barely available support for informal care. The 'APA' is exclusively available in kind and does not include support for informal carers. This missing assistance means that elderly people have no real choice about the way care is provided. Therefore an urgent need exists to reform this regulation by re-defining the provision of services in kind to include informal care. This may include the option that elderly people can choose between services in kind and benefits in cash or a combination of both, and also that informal carers are reimbursed in the form of social protection benefits.

The departments (Départments) bear the bulk of the expenditure on the 'PSD' scheme, predominantly through regional government taxation. As the empirical investigations have shown, this is a very questionable way of funding a long-term care scheme as it offers room for a range of inequities (e.g. as there are departments with a very high proportion of elderly people in need of long-term care) and many departments simply can not cope with the burden of paying for adequate services for their inhabitants. In the 'APA' scheme, the main source of funding will still come from the departments but support will also be derived from a fund (predominantly from national tax) mainly set up to support the poorer departments, from the general social charge ('Contribution Sociale Généralisée' - 'CSG') as well as from social insurance. Although the funding of the 'APA' is shared out on a broader basis than the 'PSD', one may doubt if this concept with the main source of funding still coming from the regions is a very fair one or even financially viable, especially when considering predictions of an increasing need of long-term care in the future. As the empirical section has shown, spreading the risk of long-term care equally across the whole country by having a national source of funding would lead to a fairer balance of the individual's contribution to the scheme and would help to ensure that the scheme can be paid for now and in the future. Given the traditional French contribution-based scheme of social insurance, it appears advisable to implement a long-term care insurance as a new sector among the already existing schemes but, due to their overlapping areas, incorporated in health insurance. Having in mind the continuing demographic changes, with a growing number of people in retirement and a lower number of people of working age, it seems questionable whether the traditional way of funding a social-based insurance solely from contributions by employers and employees will remain affordable and equitable. Therefore, the ear-marked 'Contribution Sociale Généralisée' ('CSG') which is already raised by a fixed rate on all types of income and used for certain elements of social insurance, should also be used to provide a second source of funding for such a long-term scheme in addition to contributions. This would give the funding of long-term care insurance a broader basis. As the empirical discussion has also shown, funding the long-term care risk in France through purely market solutions seems to be rather unsuitable, as this for example includes the difficulty that private companies would select the risk of age-related disability.

7 Domiciliary long-term care in Germany

7.1 Introduction

In May 1994, Germany's Parliament introduced a new social insurance scheme to cover the risks of long-term care. With this long-term care insurance an autonomous coverage in the field has been offered for the first time. The legislative basis for this scheme is the 'Care Insurance Act' ('Pflege-Versicherungsgesetz'), which was implemented as the eleventh book ('SGB XI') of the 'Social Welfare Legislation' ('SGB') and came into effect in three stages. From 1st January 1995, contributions were required from employers and employees, provision of domiciliary long-term care began on 1st April 1995 and the provision of residential long-term care started on 1st July 1996. It is worth mentioning at this stage that benefits and services are not exclusively granted to the disabled elderly, who are the subject of this study, but also to younger people aged under 65. However, the large majority of eligible people for provision of the scheme belong to the age group of 65 and over. In figures, 77.4% of the beneficiaries from the social long-term care insurance were 65 and older in 2000, while 67.7% were women and just 32.3% men (German Ministry of Health, 2002a).

As Vollmer (2000) has said "the new care insurance has closed the last gap in Europe's oldest social security system" (p. 1). Initiated by Bismarck in the 1880s, the system further includes health insurance (introduced in 1883), industrial accident insurance (1884), provision for old age, surviving dependants and inability to work (1889) and unemployment insurance (1927) (Vollmer, 2000). This new long-term care insurance is divided into social long-term care insurance, which covers around 90% of Germany's total population, and compulsory private long-term care insurance that covers around 9% of the total population. The remainder are covered by special systems or other social protection schemes (European Commission, 2000). Every person that has been covered by the social health insurance becomes a member of the social long-term care insurance. Those who have been covered against illness by a private health insurance organisation have to take out a private long-term care contract (Para. 1 German Care Insurance Act, 2000) and cannot choose to be covered by social insurance (See, for example, Schmidt, 1995). According to law, benefits and services provided under a private insurance plan have to be equivalent to those provided by the social part of the long-term insurance (Para. 110 German Care Insurance Act, 2000). It is therefore possible to speak of similar provision arrangements in private and social long-term care insurance. As a consequence, the following parts of this Chapter are restricted to the social part of the new scheme and, due to the definitional framework of this study, also restricted to the domiciliary part of the social sector. This preference of domiciliary long-term care before residential long-term care is also a basic principle of the new long-term care insurance and is embodied in the law. This commitment is intended not only to promote the sector of domiciliary care in general, it also aims to contribute to an increasing willingness to provide informal care (Para. 3 German Care Insurance Act, 2000). Nevertheless if an elderly person in need is provided with care in a residential facility, services under the new long-term care insurance will be offered according to the degree of disability.

It is important to note that long-term care insurance is not usually a comprehensive scheme covering all the needs of the disabled elderly. The plan of care necessary for the individual in need, that by law has to be recommended by the medical services of the health insurance funds (Para. 18 German Care Insurance Act, 2000), normally schedules a type and extent of service the cost of which if, for instance, provided by formal organisations, is higher than the value of provisions under the scheme. The fact that the scheme in many cases offers rather, a partial coverage, with limited, though generous, benefits and services, has been admitted from the start by the legislator (See, for example, Schneider, 1999). This means that the elderly in need or third parties that are under a legal obligation to support them (e.g. relatives) frequently have to make contributory payments. Only if these people are not able to do so because of their financial situation is it possible for support to be obtained from the social assistance scheme. Another possibility is extra private cover (See, for example, Schneider, 1999). Social assistance is legally established by the 'Federal Social Assistance Law' ('Bundessozialhilfegesetz' - 'BSHG') and represents a minimum-security system that provides income assistance or help in special situations in life, e.g. if elderly people are in need of long-term care (Paras. 1,2 German Federal Social Assistance Law, 2000). However, with regard to the sector of domiciliary long-term care, at the end of 1997 only around 5.5% people in need of long-term care actually received such benefits from the social assistance scheme (German Ministry of Labour and Social Affairs, 2000). This comparatively low rate means that detailed information on this scheme in the following sections can be dispensed with and therefore, the focus can be quite specifically on the benefits and services of social long-term care insurance.

7.2 Social protection system

Provision by the German social protection system is divided into different areas. There are five social insurance sectors. As can be seen in the next figure, these are pensions, health, unemployment, industrial accident and, long-term care insurance (Para. 4 German Social Welfare Legislation - General Part, 2000).

The social insurance sectors are (with the exception of the industrial accident insurance which is solely paid by the employers) mainly financed (within a 'pay-as-you-go` system) by equal contributions from employers and their employees up to an annual fixed ceiling. It is important to note that every dependent employee, up to an annual fixed ceiling of income is legally required to have insurance in the different social insurance sectors (See, for example, AOK - Die Gesundheitskasse, 2000).

Besides the five sectors of social insurance, there are areas of public expenditure for promoting education and employment, providing social compensation for damage to one's health, different programmes for supporting the family, subsidies for appropriate housing, various schemes for helping children and young people, a supplementary minimum security system in the form of the social assistance as well as for integrating handicapped persons. The responsibility for provision is mainly held by various public corporations, institutions or authorities. The financing of those social protection schemes that do not belong to one of the five sectors of social insurance is usually done through the general budget of the administrative body responsible (German Social Welfare Legislation - General Part, 2000). The following figure (p. 150) gives an overview.

Figure 7 The five sectors of social insurance in Germany

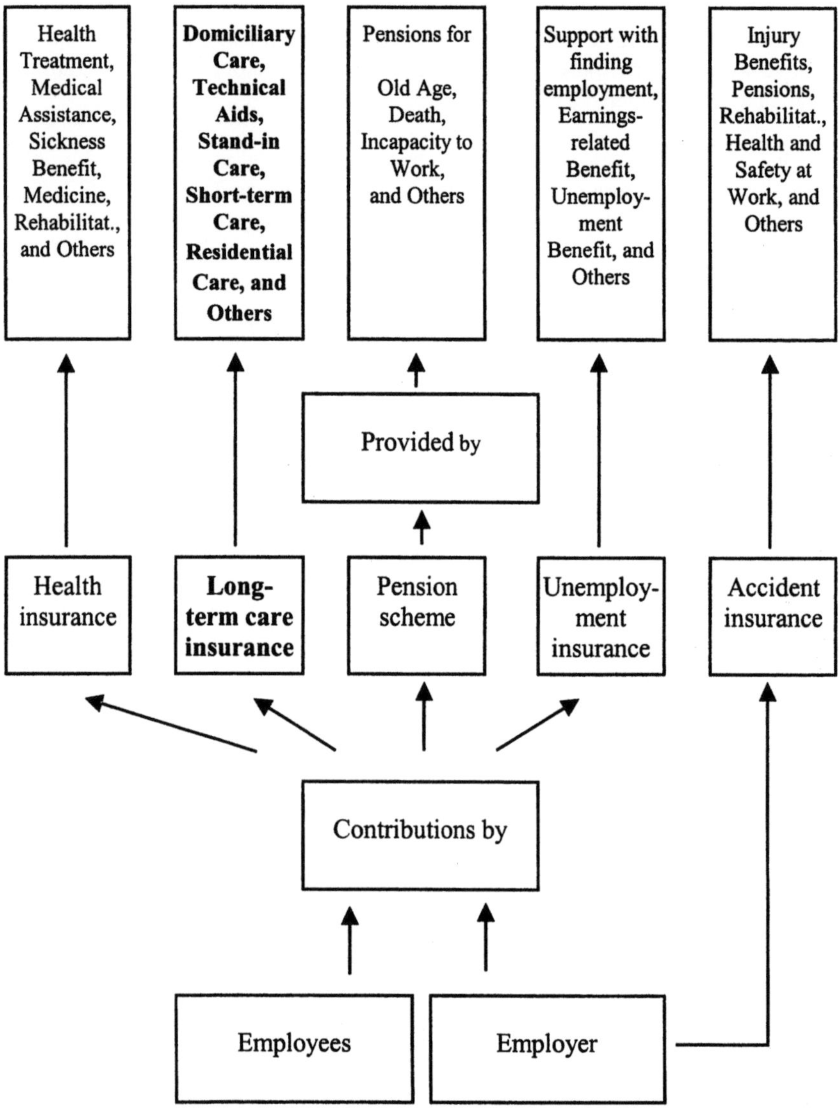

Source: German Social Welfare Legislation - General Part, 2000

7.3 Analysis of the current domiciliary long-term care scheme

7.3.1 Responsible institutions

The 'Care Insurance Act' ('Pflege-Versicherungsgesetz' - 'SGB XI') initially ordered the establishment of a new sector in the social insurance system for people in need of permanent care, that is the long-term care insurance (Para. 1, Sub-para. 1 German Care Insurance Act, 2000). In order to avoid the establishment of a completely new insurance organisation, the bodies responsible for the new insurance are the newly established long-term care funds, but their work is performed through the existing health insurance funds with the help of their comprehensive network of (local) offices. This means that since the introduction of the long-term care insurance, the existing health insurance funds act on the one hand as long-term care funds and on the other hand as health insurance funds (Para. 1, Sub-para. 3 German Care Insurance Act, 2000).

At the moment, there are about 600 long-term care funds, e.g. general local funds ('Ortspflegekassen' - 'AOK') that operate within comparatively small geographical areas (with one fund to a region or a major city), company-based funds ('Betriebspflegekassen' - 'BKK') that initially were frequently organised by employers for their employees but in the meantime are often accessible for a much wider section of the population, funds that are organised on trade or craft lines, e.g. farmers and agricultural workers funds ('Landwirtschaftliche Pflegekassen') or miners ('Bundesknappschaft') and, usually nationwide, substitute funds ('Ersatzpflegekassen'). The different funds are autonomous, non-profit legal entities and have the status of public corporations. The administration of the funds is made by boards of trustees and, these authorities establish the policies and the method as well as the shape of operations by the individual funds. The work of these boards is not independent, but determined by the legislative framework (Vollmer, 2000).

Since the provision of the long-term care scheme is not only granted in cash, but also in kind, long-term care funds have to purchase the services from organisations that provide the care concerned. For this purpose, care contracts are concluded between the long-term care funds or their regional associations and the providers of long-term care services or an association of the same kind of providers. The providers thus approved, between which the disabled elderly may choose without restriction, firstly consist of five voluntary, non-profit associations (or subdivided groups of these associations) that reflect the historical segmentation of German society into denominational and other social groupings ('Arbeiterwohlfahrt', 'Deutscher Caritasverband', 'Deutsches Rotes Kreuz', 'Diakonisches Werk' and 'Deutscher Paritätischer Wohlfahrtsverband').

The importance of private providers, however, is becoming increasingly crucial. By law, these two main groups of provider (voluntary, non-profit associations and private organisations) have to be given priority when concluding care contracts (Para. 72 German Care Insurance Act, 2000). In exceptional cases it is also possible to conclude care contracts with public providers or others, e.g. individual professional carers (Para. 77 German Care Insurance Act, 2000). At the end of 1999 there have been 13,275 organisations that provide domiciliary long-term care services, whereby the private organisations are meanwhile the largest group of providers with a share of 51.8%, followed by the voluntary, non-profit associations with a share of 39%, local public providers with a share of 5.2% and others with a share of 4% (Anonymous, 2000).

The appropriate remuneration, which the organisations receive for the services in kind provided is regulated by a reimbursement agreement. This is usually concluded between the provider concerned, the long-term care funds (or associations of them) and the administrative body responsible for the social assistance. The conditions of that contractual relationship must be such that all disabled elderly persons cared for by the provider concerned are treated equally. The providers are usually directly reimbursed on a fee-for-service basis by the relevant long-term care funds of the disabled elderly (Para 89 German Care Insurance Act, 2000). In contrast to services in kind, provision in cash from the long-term care insurance is mainly paid directly to the disabled elderly (Para. 37, Sub-para. 3 German Care Insurance Act, 2000).

7.3.2 Eligibility criteria

The criteria as to whether a person is defined as disabled and therefore eligible for the benefits and services from the long-term care insurance are defined by the 'Care Insurance Act`. In law, an elderly person in need of long-term care is defined as "a human being that requires for a minimum period of approximately 6 months, permanent, frequent or extensive help in performing a special number of 'Personal Activities of Daily Life` ('P-ADLs`) and 'Instrumental Activities of Daily Life` ('I-ADLs`) due to physical, mental or psychological illness or disability" (Para. 14, Sub-para. 1 German Care Insurance Act, 2000). Consideration of the financial situation of the disabled elderly person or his/her family has no effect on his/her entitlement. The individual activities are illustrated in the following table (Table 17, p. 153).

Table 17 'Personal Activities of Daily Life' ('P-ADLs') and 'Instrumental Activities of Daily Life' ('I-ADLs')

'Personal Activities of Daily Life' ('P-ADLs')	
Bodily cleansing activities:	washing, showering, bathing, shaving, using the toilet, combing, toothbrushing
Nourishment related activities:	preparing food for easy consumption, eating
Mobility related activities:	getting in and out of bed, outdoor walking, dressing, walking, standing, using stairs
'Instrumental Activities of Daily Life' ('I-ADLs')	
Home economics provision related activities:	shopping, cooking, cleaning, laundry, washing up the dishes, heating the accommodation

Source: Para. 14, Sub-para. 4 German Care Insurance Act, 2000

In addition to the definition of 'disability', the scheme distinguishes three different degrees of 'disability'. For identifying these degrees, first of all the number and frequency of activities in which the elderly person needs help is considered. In addition, the three different degrees of disability thus defined are specified by additional time requirements, if care were provided by informal carers. Resulting from this, it is possible to fix three degrees of 'disability'. This is shown in the next table (Table 18, p. 154).

Based on this table, care degree 1 is applied to disabled elderly persons in considerable need of long-term care. They require help at least once a day for at least two activities in the three areas of bodily cleansing, nourishment or mobility. Furthermore they need help several times a week with home economics provision. In addition, care degree 1 requires that the disabled elderly person needs help for at least 90 minutes including 45 minutes of personal care. Care degree 2 is applied to disabled elderly persons in severe need of long-term care. They need help on at least three separate occasions a day with bodily cleansing, nourishment or mobility. Moreover, they need help several times a week with home economics provision. In addition, care degree

2 demands that the disabled elderly person needs at least 180 minutes help a day, of which 120 minutes must be for personal care. Care degree 3 is designated for persons in extreme need of care. They need assistance with the areas of personal care (bodily cleansing, nourishment or mobility) 24 hours a day, as well as help with housework several times a week. Finally, care degree 3 requires that the disabled elderly person needs at least 300 minutes of help a day, including a minimum of 240 minutes personal care (Para. 15, Sub-paras. 1 and 3 German Care Insurance Act, 2000).

Table 18 Degrees of disability

Degrees of disability	**Low**	**Average**	**High**
Frequency and number of cases where help is needed for the 'P-ADL' indices	At least once a day concerning two or more activities in one or more of the three different areas	At least three different times a day in one or more of the three different areas	24 hours a day in one or more of the three different areas
Frequency and number of cases where help is needed for the 'I-ADL' indices	Several times a week	Several times a week	Several times a week
Average daily time requirements for the 'P-ADLs' (personal care) and 'I-ADLs' (home-making), if made by informal carers	At least 90 minutes a day, including a minimum of 45 minutes personal care	At least 3 hours a day, including a minimum of 2 hours personal care	At least 5 hours a day, including a minimum of 4 hours personal care

Source: Para. 15, Sub-para. 1 and 3 German Care Insurance Act, 2000

Assessment of the respective levels of care is the responsibility of the medical services of the health insurance funds (mainly provided by physicians and qualified nurses) which act on behalf of the long-term care funds. In performing this task, the experts are also expected to suggest rehabilitation treatments and establish what technical aids are necessary. Furthermore, it is also the responsibility of the medical services to recommend the type and extent of service provision for the individual in need as well as an individual plan of care (Para. 18 German Care Insurance Act, 2000).

In addition to the criteria of eligibility illustrated above, it necessary that a disabled elderly person has been insured for a certain period before benefits and services can be received from the scheme. From 1st January 2000, the regulation is that provision may be granted if the disabled elderly person has been insured for at least five years within the last ten years at the time he/she applies for benefits and services. In this connection it is worth noting that provision is not granted automatically. Application must be made to the long-term care fund responsible (Para. 33 German Care Insurance Act, 2000).

In the table below, figures are given for recipients of domiciliary care benefits according to the degree of care in total numbers and as a percentage of total numbers for the years 1998 to 2000. However, the figures do not distinguish between disabled people aged 65 and over - as focussed on by this study - and younger people with disabilities. It is, however, based on the assumption that the large majority of the beneficiaries are aged 65 and over (German Ministry of Health, 2002a).

Table 19 Recipients of domiciliary long-term care provision in total numbers and in %, 1998 - 2000

Year	Care degree 1		Care degree 2		Care degree 3	
	Total numbers	In %	Total numbers	In %	Total numbers	In %
1998	616,506	50.2	471,906	38.5	138.303	11.3
1999	668,314	52.2	472,189	36.9	139.876	10.9
2000	681,568	54.0	448,406	35.6	130.696	10.4

Source: German Ministry of Health, 2002b

As can be seen in the previous table, the majority of disabled elderly over the period examined fall into the categories of care degrees 1 and 2 and the total number has increased slightly from 1998 to 2000 (from 1,226,715 to 1,260,760).

7.3.3 Type and amount of provision - benefits and services

7.3.3.1 General Description

If a disabled elderly person fulfils the eligibility criteria of the long-term care insurance, that person may have a range of domiciliary benefits and services at his/her disposal. Besides domiciliary benefits in cash or services in kind, stand-in care, short-term care, day- or night care, technical (care) aids as well as contributions to social protection schemes for informal carers are possible benefit options.

In general it should be mentioned that the available provision frequently does not represent a full service. The benefits and services in each case are provided in the shape of a fixed allowance that depends on the degree of disability. If additional care is needed, this has either to be paid privately or by the social assistance scheme in the case of those entitled.

7.3.3.2 Domiciliary care services in kind

The main types of domiciliary care provision from long-term care insurance may be divided into those that are provided in cash or in kind. If the disabled elderly person chooses formal care, the scheme provides for domiciliary visits (personal care and home-making assistance), e.g. by professional nursing staff. In this event, the benefit is directly paid to the organisation providing the service. Depending on the degree of disability, monthly maximum amounts are set for the disabled elderly. This is illustrated in the following table.

Table 20 Domiciliary long-term care services in kind

Degree of disability	Benefits in kind provided up to a monthly maximum of approx.
Care degree 1 (Low)	€ 383 (DM 750)
Care degree 2 (Average)	€ 920 (DM 1,800)
Care degree 3 (High)	€ 1,432 (DM 2,800)

Source: Para. 36, Sub-para. 3 German Care Insurance Act, 2000

For care degree 3, the maximum sum of € 1,432 (DM 2,800) may be exceeded by the payment from the individual long-term care funds if an unusually high level of care is required. In such specific cases, the monthly benefit may be extended up to € 1,917 (DM 3,750). Such provision may, however, not be extended to more than 3% of the total number of disabled elderly classed as care degree 3 within the individual funds (Para. 36, Sub-para. 4 German Care Insurance Act, 2000).

7.3.3.3 Domiciliary care benefits in cash

As an alternative to benefits in kind, the disabled elderly may receive benefits in cash, if the person is able to secure adequate personal care and home-making assistance for himself/herself from informal carers. Benefits in cash are lower than services in kind and also depend on the level of disability, as shown in the following table.

Table 21 Domiciliary long-term care benefits in cash

Degree of disability	Benefits in cash provided up to a monthly maximum of approx.
Care degree 1 (Low)	€ 205 (DM 400)
Care degree 2 (Average)	€ 409 (DM 800)
Care degree 3 (High)	€ 665 (DM 1,300)

Source: Para 37, Sub-para. 1 German Care Insurance Act, 2000

Elderly people in need of cash benefits are obliged by law to call for a visit by a formal provider at least half-yearly in care degree 1 and 2, and quarterly in care degree 3. These visits are intended to ensure the quality of the care being provided and give advice about domiciliary care. The reimbursement is made by the responsible long-term care fund and is € 15 (DM 30) in care degrees 1 and 2, and € 26 (DM 50) in care degree 3 per visit (Para 37, Sub-para. 3 German Care Insurance Act, 2000).

7.3.3.4 Additional options of service provision

In addition to the provision available either in cash or in kind, the elderly person in need can also opt for a combination of both types of support. This may enable the individual to arrange a service provision according to personal (social) circumstances (Para 38, German Care Insurance Act, 2000). In the event that the informal carer is unable to provide domiciliary care due to holidays, illness or other reasons, the care insurance will pay for a maximum of 4 weeks formal domiciliary care service up to a cost of € 1,432 (DM 2,800) regardless of the care level ('stand-in care'). There is, however, the restriction that the informal carer must have already cared one whole year before the period of absence. In the case that 'stand-in care' is not provided on a formal but on an informal basis, only the normal benefit in cash according to the degree of disability is granted (Para. 39 German Care Insurance Act, 2000). If it is not possible to obtain adequate domiciliary substitute care, the disabled elderly person is entitled to residential care for up to four weeks a year ('short-term care'). The amount of benefit is up to a value of approximately € 1,432 (DM 2,800) regardless of the care degree (Para. 42, German Care Insurance Act, 2000). In addition, if it is not possible to provide sufficient domiciliary care, the person in need may apply for day- or night care up to the cost of the services in kind according to the degrees of disability. Only in the case that the full amount of this provision is not exhausted, is it possible to receive a proportional benefit for domiciliary care representing the remaining amount (Para. 41, German Care Insurance Act, 2000). Furthermore, the disabled elderly are entitled to technical aids and care aids (Para. 42, German Care Insurance Act, 2000).

Finally, the long-term care insurance also offers social protection benefits for those informal carers that provide domiciliary care for at least 14 hours week and are either not employed or do not work more than 30 hours a week in regular employment (Para. 3 German Pension Insurance Act, 2000; Para. 19 German Care Insurance Act, 2000). Such carers are entitled to various social insurance benefits. Firstly, the care insurance funds pay the pension insurance contributions for this group of informal carers, according to the degree of disability of the cared person and the amount of time that care is provided. Furthermore, these informal carers are covered by accident insurance during the time they provide care and home-making assistance. Moreover, they are entitled to paid training if they want to return to gainful employment after they have finished providing care (Para. 44 German Care Insurance Act, 2000). In addition, long-term care funds offer free care courses for those providing informal care (Para. 45 German Care Insurance Act, 2000).

7.3.4 Funding

Funding for the long-term care insurance scheme comes mainly from equal contributions by employers and employees. Children and non-employed spouses are normally covered and do not contribute. The contributions for the scheme are raised within the framework of a 'pay-as-you-go' system ('Umlageverfahren'). In contrast to the rate for the health insurance that varies and is fixed by the individual funds, the contribution for the long-term care insurance is determined by law and equal among the individual organisations. The rate for the long-term care insurance has, since the 1st July 1996, been established at 1.7% of the so-called 'insurable income' (frequently the gross income). However, the insurable earnings are not considered unlimited, but up to a certain ceiling that usually increases every year. The long-term care insurance ceiling is the same as for the social health insurance and corresponds to 75% of the ceiling for the statutory pension insurance (Paras. 54 - 57 German Care Insurance Act, 2000; Vollmer, 2000). On 1st January 2000 it was fixed at € 3,298 (DM 6,450) monthly in the eleven old Federal States and at € 2,723 (DM 5,325) monthly in the five new Federal States. Insured persons earning more must still pay contributions but assessment applies only to a maximum of € 3,298 (DM 6,450) or € 2,723 (DM 5,325) respectively (AOK, 2000).

Those contributions that are raised from employees are normally deducted from their wages or salaries by their employers. The employers transfer the contributions to the health insurance funds and from there to the corresponding long-term care funds. As established by law, the employers have to pay the same share as their employees. For their contribution to funding the scheme, the employers have been compensated through the option in the individual sixteen Federal States of cancelling an annual public holiday (Para. 58 German Care Insurance Act, 2000; Vollmer, 2000). As a result, in fifteen Federal States (the exception is Saxony), the 'Day of Repentance and Atonement' has been cancelled. In Saxony, where this recommendation has not been adopted, employees pay the full contribution rate of 1.7% without sharing it with their employers (Igl and Stadelmann, 1998). Finally, as stated by law, the expenditure within the framework of the scheme has to be borne commonly by all long-term care funds in proportion to contributions paid by the insured. Therefore, a financial balancing process takes place between the individual long-term care funds through a balancing fund that was founded through the 'Federal Insurance Department' ('Bundsversicherungsamt') (Para. 66 German Care Insurance Act, 2000; Vollmer, 2000).

In the table below (p. 160), the financial figures for social long-term care insurance are set out for the period 1995 to 2000. However, besides the amounts for domiciliary long-term care, it also includes the other sectors that are part of the insurance scheme.

Table 22 Financial development of social long-term care insurance in millions of Euro (German Marks)

Term	1995	1996	1997	1998	1999	2000
Total income	8,406 (16,440)	12,041 (23,550)	15,942 (31,180)	16,003 (31,300)	16,320 (31,920)	16,550 (32,369)
Total expenditure	4,970 (9,720)	10,860 (21,240)	15,139 (29,610)	15,876 (31,050)	16,351 (31,980)	16,670 (32,604)
Surplus / deficit[1]	+ 3,436 (+ 6,720)	1,176 (+ 2,300)	+ 803 (+ 1,570)	+ 128 (+ 250)	- 31 (- 60)	- 120 (- 235)

Source: German Ministry of Health, 2002c

As can be seen, in 1995 there was still a considerable surplus of € 3,298 million (DM 6,720 million) in the long-term care insurance funds. This, of course, was clearly influenced by the situation that contributions for the scheme had been collected from the 1st of January 1995 but first benefits and services were not paid out until the 1st of April 1995. In addition, the services in the sector of residential care did not even start until the 1st of July 1996. Nevertheless it is significant that the surplus in the period that followed has decreased progressively up to 1999 when the first deficit was recorded. It is true that the long-term care insurance still has liquidity reserves arising from the surpluses between 1995 and 1998, but the rising deficits in 1999 and 2000 augur badly in view of the protected increases in provision for the future.

While the income for social long-term care is predominantly obtained from contributions, the situation regarding expenditure is more complex due to the different types of provision granted. This distribution is illustrated below in Table 23 (p. 161).

[1] Differences in results arising from rounding off.

Table 23 Distribution of expenditure of the social long-term care insurance in millions of Euro (German Marks)

Term	1995	1996	1997	1998	1999	2000
Domiciliary benefits in cash	3,037 (5,940)	4,438 (8,680)	4,320 (8,450)	4,285 (8,380)	4,239 (8,290)	4,180 (8,175)
Domiciliary services in kind	690 (1,350)	1,544 (3,020)	1,774 (3,470)	1,989 (3,890)	2,132 (4,170)	2,230 (4,362)
Stand-in care	133 (260)	133 (260)	51 (100)	56 (110)	72 (140)	100 (196)
Short-term care	46 (90)	87 (170)	97 (190)	107 (210)	123 (240)	140 (274)
Technical (care) aids	194 (380)	394 (770)	332 (650)	373 (730)	424 (830)	400 (782)
Social protection for informal care	307 (600)	925 (1,810)	1,186 (2,320)	1,156 (2,260)	1,130 (2,210)	1,070 (2,093)
Day- or night care	10 (20)	26 (50)	36 (70)	46 (90)	51 (100)	60 (117)
Residential care	0 (0)	2,700 (5,280)	6,545 (12,800)	7,056 (13,800)	7,378 (14,430)	7,690 (15,040)
Expenses of the medical service	225 (440)	240 (470)	230 (450)	240 (470)	235 (460)	240 (469)
Administrative expenses	317 (620)	363 (710)	552 (1,080)	557 (1,090)	552 (1,080)	570 (1,115)
Other expenses	5 (10)	5 (10)	10 (20)	15 (30)	10 (20)	20 (39)
Total expenditure[2]	4,970 (9,720)	10,860 (21,240)	15,139 (29,610)	15,876 (31,050)	16,351 (31,980)	16,670 (32,604)

Source: German Ministry of Health, 2002c

[2] Differences in results arising from rounding off.

For the sector of domiciliary long-term care, which is the main focus of this study, Table 23 shows that a much greater proportion of the expenditure is accounted for by cash benefits than those in kind, although the proportion of expenditure for services in kind is increasing. However, the ratio of this dissimilarity becomes even clearer if one considers that the possible services in kind for the individual disabled elderly are significantly higher than those benefits provided in cash. For example, in care degree 1 the ratio is € 205 (DM 400) (cash) to € 383 (DM 750) (kind). According to a recent survey carried out in the year 2000, in other words five years after the beginning of domiciliary care benefits on 1st April 1995, around 67% of the disabled elderly living at home still preferred the lower benefits in cash to the higher services in kind. In 1995, the ratio was 88 to 12%. This means that it is the informal carer (mainly family) that is still the main provider of care, although the share of disabled elderly turning to formal care is increasing (Vollmer, 2000).

With reference to long-term care insurance, a dual system is frequently talked about. This is justified by the fact that besides the income from contributions, the sixteen States are also involved in the financing mechanism of the scheme, though to a much lesser degree. In the case of domiciliary long-term care, this means that those organisations which are permitted to provide care services within the framework of the scheme through a care contract may receive public assistance from the States with their investment costs. In other words, the States are encouraged to contribute to the improvement of the infrastructure in the sector of care through their general budget (tax revenues). If a State does assist the providers of care or only provides partial assistance, they may charge the investment costs to their clients (disabled elderly) (Paras. 9 and 82 German Care Insurance Act, 2000).

The financing of benefits through contributory payments by the disabled elderly is not envisaged by the law at this stage. It is, however, important to note that the benefits and services from the scheme, which is not legally required to pay the full cost of the care, are frequently insufficient. In other words, the cost of the care required by the individual in need is in most cases higher than the provision received from the long-term care insurance. This means that the elderly person in need has to pay for additional care from private means if he is not entitled to benefits from the social assistance scheme and has no additional private insurance cover (Schneider, 1999).

7.4 Ways forward

Now, more than five years after the introduction of long-term care insurance, there are several areas where an improvement of the scheme is under consideration. For instance, as the Minister of Health[3], Mrs. Andrea Fischer argued on the occasion of the fifth anniversary of the long-term care insurance in Berlin, "the long-term care insurance has made an important contribution to safeguarding against social risks and has already been useful to many people. However, there are still gaps and a need for reform, such as in the case of care for people suffering from dementia and in the security and improvement of quality standards in domiciliary and residential care. Furthermore, there is a need to improve the coordination between the benefits from the long-term care insurance, health insurance and social assistance scheme" (German Ministry of Health, 2000, p. 1).

The gaps mentioned in the above quotation with regard to the care of elderly people suffering from dementia seem indeed to be a main issue in the discussions surrounding the improvement of the long-term care insurance. Due to the fact that within the framework of the insurance, only needs in the areas of bodily cleaning activities, nourishment-related activities, mobility-related activities and home-making activities are covered, psychosocial and communicative aspects such as general supervision and guidance, which might be particularly important for elderly people with dementia, remain disregarded thus far. Thus benefits and services not provided within the framework of the long-term care insurance, which are of course very important for elderly people with dementia, are mainly provided by informal carers - a job that makes high demands on those involved (Jordan, 2000). In order to improve the situation of the persons concerned, the German Ministry of Health has already put forward a second proposal (which replaces the first one[4] in this matter) that should address these difficulties. The major intention of this proposal is that those disabled elderly who need to be generally supervised and looked after (mainly elderly people with dementia), in addition to the help required with 'P-ADLs' and 'I-ADLs' should be eligible to receive € 460 (DM 900) a year. This amount would be earmarked and used for day or night care services, short-term care, services by formal providers if it concerns the specific supply of general supervision and looking after the person in need and not services of personal care and home economics provision. It would also be possible to use the provision to pay for services by organised groups that look after people suffering from dementia, helper groups that relieve the strain for caring relatives on an hourly basis and care provided by geronto-psychiatric centres. In addition

---

[3] The responsibility for the long-term care insurance scheme has meanwhile moved from the Ministry of Labour to the Ministry of Health.

[4] The first proposal in 2000 which is now replaced by the new proposal intended that those disabled elderly who have a considerable need for general supervision (mainly elderly people with dementia) in addition to the help needed with 'P-ADLs' and 'I-ADLs' should be eligible to receive day- or night care once a week in addition to the general domiciliary care benefits (German Ministry of Health, 2000).

to the above, the group of persons concerned receiving benefits in cash would be entitled to receive twice as much consultations from a formal service provider as the current regulation has provided for till now (one visit half-yearly in care degrees 1 and 2, and quarterly in care degree 3). Finally, it is intended to support the development of new care concepts for people suffering from dementia (German Ministry of Health, 2001). Additionally, the second major plan dealing with the improvement of the long-term care insurance scheme by the Federal Ministry of Health focuses on the quality of care (Jordan, 2000). However, as this aspect of the long-term care scheme is beyond the scope of the present study, these ideas will not be pursued any further.

7.5 Assessment and options for reform of the current domiciliary long-term care scheme

7.5.1 General Description

In the following, an empirically-verified assessment of the German domiciliary long-term care scheme is outlined and options for reform are suggested. The established research questions discussed in the chapter on methodology guide the structure of what follows. The compatibility of this empirically-supported part with the above country report facilitates a certain transparency. The information for the following sections was obtained from semi-structured interviews with experts in the field (See Appendix B). These experts included scientists and practical workers (the latter included persons from long-term care funds and service providers).

7.5.2 Assessment and options for reform of the responsible institutions

With regard to the institutional establishment of the new scheme (See, 7.3.1), several interviewees appreciated that the risk of long-term care is now (partly) covered within an autonomous scheme. The fact that the provision of domiciliary long-term care began only three months after the new scheme came into effect was praised. In this connection, some experts also pointed out that those elderly people who had already been in need of long-term care when the scheme started and fulfilled the criteria of eligibility under the new scheme were entitled to provision from the very first day. As the long-term care insurance has been established as a new sector within the framework of the social insurance system, there was a far-reaching consensus between the interviewees that it was useful to give the administrative responsibility for the scheme to the newly-established long-term care funds. The work of these long-term care funds is actually performed by the existing health insurance funds through their existing network of offices. As different experts stated, this made it possible to take advantages of the expertise in health care and, moreover, prevented the establishment of a new bureaucracy. However, some experts with both scientific and service provision background mentioned difficulties arising from this close connection or the somewhat 'artificial separation' between long-term care and health care funds. For example, it was argued that some funds have tried to transfer different domiciliary services of nursing care at home (e.g. giving medicines, taking blood pressure, etc.), which were originally classified as part of health care provision, to the area funded from the long-term care insurance. Another expert mentioned the area of rehabilitation as a further example that has to be observed very carefully because of the close connection between the two funds. According to law, all medical and complementary services connected with rehabilitation should be used to help the disabled elderly to improve their health or to prevent a change for the worse and should be mainly financed as part of the service provision of the health care funds. According to this same interviewee, the provision of such services under the health care scheme is extremely limited.

There were those who would expect better results from long-term care provision within the framework of health insurance, while other interviewees from different backgrounds did not agree with these reflections, arguing, in particular, that such an association would in the first place be helpful for improving the extremely difficult financial situation of the health care funds but would probably lead to less satisfactory care provision for disabled elderly persons. Another expert stated on this issue that within the long-term care scheme, some important elements have been introduced (e.g. a contribution rate fixed by law or the possibility of choosing between or combining benefits in cash and services in kind) that cannot be found so far within the health insurance scheme. This same interviewee further argued,

> *the inclusion of these elements within the framework of the health insurance scheme hardly appears conceivable.*

In addition to these reflections on the current regulations, thought was given by some experts to placing the administrative responsibility elsewhere. However, no expert was of the opinion that it would be advisable to opt for other solutions in this matter, e.g. putting administrative responsibility in the hands of local authorities, as long as the provision is regulated within a social insurance scheme.

In order to guarantee the provision of service for those in need, the long-term care funds or their regional associations conclude care contracts with providers of long-term care services or an association of the same kind of providers. As pointed out by an expert working for a provider,

> *the appropriate remuneration, which the providers receive for the services is regulated by a reimbursement agreement which is usually concluded on a regional level for a certain period of time. These agreements exactly determine the individual services provided and their costs. Thus, each individual provider, as well as the two big groups of providers, i.e. private and voluntary, non-profit organisations, is bound by contract to these prices.*

In particular, experts working for service providers, but also scientific experts, are of the opinion that the current prices are at a very low level. At the moment, the reason for this seems to be that supply is much higher than demand. It was further mentioned that the share of the private providers, in particular, has been increasing since the introduction of the long-term care insurance. As stated by another expert with a practical background,

> *many private providers entered the market in the first year of the long-term care insurance scheme (1995/96) but some of these providers left the market as fast as they came in. Nevertheless, it is a fact that the private providers' share of the market is continuing to grow and the proportion of voluntary, non-profit providers is declining.*

As declared by another expert in this context,

> *in the hope that a supply arises that is higher than the need, the legislator has deliberately abstained from a regulation of the demand.*

It was also pointed out by several experts that private providers are often better placed because of their flexibility in the application of certain modalities. For example, private organisations, in contrast to most voluntary, non-profit organisations, are not bound by tariff contracts and this gives them the freedom, for example, to be more flexible when paying nursing staff. The fact was also mentioned that voluntary, non-profit organisations frequently have long-established organisational structures that are more extensive and therefore more expensive, compared to private organisations. As noted by an expert working for a voluntary, non-profit service provider,

> *in the meantime, quite a few service providers, private as well as voluntary, non-profit organisations, have had to close because of*

financial difficulties. From a supplier's point of view it is, of course, difficult because of the over-supply, for example to conclude reimbursement agreements with long-term care funds that are cost-covering.

However, as several interviewees have argued, from the point of the disabled elderly, one clearly has to welcome the existing mix in service provision as this, on the one hand, guarantees an elderly person's right to choose between different suppliers and, on the other hand, prevents a standard care procedure being implemented without the possibility of selection. As stated by an expert from a scientific background,

the introduction of long-term care insurance has led to competition and a certain 'push` towards higher quality in care. This 'push` has had a useful impact on the whole market where support for elderly people is concerned. In particular, through the newly-established private providers and the situation of a quasi free market the traditional, voluntary, non-profit organisations are now being forced to make improvements, for example, in terms of economic efficiency. On the one hand, this can generally be described as positive, in particular with regard to those in need of long-term care who are usually free to choose between different providers (altogether there are about 13,000 services nation-wide with about 135,000 employees). On the other hand, this development has unfortunately led to there being more and more dubious service providers on the market, particularly private organisations. This, for example, tends to lead to under-supply and can foster greed.

In order to counteract any such abuse, but also to improve the quality of the services provided, different interviewees call for more frequent and more accurate quality controls by the medical services of the health care fund administrations. These are obliged by law to do this but their resources appear to be insufficient. As experts from a scientific background suggest, it appears very likely that an expansion of these controls would lead to a reduction of the service providers as some may not fulfil the necessary requirements, for example, in their accounting procedures. As recommended by one of these latter,

these controls should be seen less in the sense of a supervision of the providers but more as a benchmark and a means of identifying the better providers. The worst providers would then be able to learn from those identified as better.

Referring to the co-operation between the different institutions involved in long-term care provision, a number of experts pointed towards existing causes of friction between long-term care funds and service providers, for example when concluding reimbursement agreements - mainly at regional level. Nevertheless, the experts that commented on this issue said the co-operation at the regional level where, for example the rates of payment for service providers are discussed, as well as co-operation at the national level where, for example the basic orientation and development of the additional insurance benefits are discussed, is not so problematic. The main difficulties in co-operation are at the local level, where the actual provision takes place. Here, difficulties frequently occur in the coordination between long-term care funds, service providers' and physicians, as well as other participants. It was emphasized that these difficulties are not only limited to participants with different backgrounds such as long-term care funds and providers, but also arise between different service providers. For example, if the provision for a disabled elderly person guaranteed by a combination of domiciliary services as well as day care services, these two different types of provision may well be supplied by two separate organisations. Because of these difficulties in coordination, some experts urged an improvement in the integration at the local level as this is inadequate in many areas. In this connection, it would be useful to organise periodical meetings (under the auspices of the community) consisting of the participants involved in long-term care provision such as long-term care funds, private and voluntary, non-profit providers and local authorities. As further suggested, at these meetings it would be helpful to have discussions about of the coordination of the demand or debates focusing on conceptual reflections with regard to future developments.

As a final point regarding the institutions responsible for the long-term care scheme, some interviewees with a scientific background doubted the effectiveness of home visits by formal providers to those receiving benefits in cash in order to ensure the quality of the care being provided and give advice about domiciliary care (as obliged by law at least half-yearly in care degree 1 and 2 and quarterly in care degree 3). The interviewees commented critically both with regard to the low frequency of these visits and in view of the fact that these visits are made by formal providers, as this includes a conflict of interests. As formal providers are in a competitive situation, it appears possible that these tend to offer their own services instead of giving advice about care to the relatives or friends of elderly in need. As a consequence, transferring these visits from the service providers to the local authorities was recommended by scientific experts.

7.5.3 Assessment and options for reform of the eligibility criteria

Of the participating experts, several identified the current eligibility criteria of the scheme (See 7.3.2) focusing on the help required in the areas of bodily cleansing activities, nourishment-related activities, mobility-related activities and home-making activities as insufficient and therefore as a clear weak spot of the long-term care insurance scheme. It was argued that general supervision, looking after and guiding the person do belong to the help considered within the scheme as far as these aspects are connected with the above-mentioned activities. However, that part of general supervision and looking after which has nothing to do with these activities and might be particularly important for the disabled with dementia remain disregarded thus far. As different experts have said, the current exclusive orientation towards physically related needs in the eligibility criteria either leads to the condition that several people with dementia are not entitled to any benefits and services at all as they do not even fulfil the criteria for care degree 1, or to the condition that those people with dementia that are entitled to provision have nevertheless a considerable disadvantage with regard to the extent of the benefits and services. This condition was said to be the major weak point of the long-term care insurance. However, apart from the urgent need for reform regarding the entitlements of people with dementia, experts with a practical background also argued that on no account should one expand the eligibility criteria so far that almost all individual needs would be covered.

As described in the first part of this Chapter (7.4), the Ministry of Health is planning to improve the situation of people with dementia, mainly by providing about € 460 (DM 900) a year for those disabled people who have a considerable need of general supervision and need to be looked after in addition to the need in the areas of 'Personal Activities of Daily Life` ('P-ADLs`) and 'Instrumental Activities of Daily Life` ('I-ADLs`) (mainly elderly people with dementia). According to this proposal, disabled elderly may use the additional and earmarked benefit for the provision of day or night care, short-term care and services by formal providers if it concerns the specific supply of general supervision and attention. Those experts that did comment on this new proposal agree that these plans of the Ministry of Health would only marginally improve the situation of some people with dementia because the additional provision is very small. Other experts also pointed to problems arising from the fact that the intended plans do not consider those people with dementia whose requirement of help in performing 'P-ADLs` and 'I-ADLs` is insufficient to qualify them for care degree 1. In addition, an expert with practical background doubted that the framework of the proposal included the option of using the additional provision for services of day or night care. It was argued that *for people with dementia it is important to look after them in their own home surroundings. If one moved them, for example, once a week to a day care centre, it could lead to additional confusion for these people and therefore more likely to a change for the worse in their health instead of an improvement.*

The recommendations offered by the experts for dealing with the above problem are different in nature. An expert with a scientific background advocated the establishment of new eligibility criteria for the long-term care scheme as a whole and that the development of such criteria should be scientifically supported. It was further argued that an extension of the existing criteria would result in an inadequate 'patchwork'. Another expert recommended forming a judgement as a whole, irrespective of already existing eligibility criteria, whether a need to be generally supervised and looked after exists and if so, to provide separate benefits and services.

However, in contrast to the above experts, the majority of interviewees suggested adding such elements to the existing eligibility criteria that consider the particular help required by people with dementia. This additional element should be applied within the assessment procedure by the medical services. An expert from a scientific background suggested specifically how the existing criteria might be extended. He said,

it would be useful to give the need for general supervision and attention a certain extra daily time value within the framework of the help required with personal care. This extra time value, that might for example amount to 45 minutes a day, should then be considered within the framework of assessing disability and classifying elderly people within the different degrees of care. This would mean, that in the case of a disabled elderly person with dementia to whom, within the current procedure, daily requirements of 30 minutes of home-making assistance and 40 minutes of personal care have been granted (and therefore does not even fulfils the conditions of care degree 1), the suggested extension changes would lead to an additional time of 45 minutes in the sector of personal care resulting in 115 minutes of personal care. Thus, this disabled elderly person would meet the requirements for care degree 1 of needing at least 90 minutes help a day, of which 45 minutes must be for personal care. Analogous to this condition one could imagine a situation in which, for example, a disabled elderly person with dementia would be moved up from care degree 2 to care degree 3 . . . Such an extra time value could likewise amount to 35 or 40 minutes instead of 45 minutes.

The higher these values the more additional expenses would be required to put them into practice.

An expert working for a service provider made, in principle similar proposals, however the above-mentioned ideas do not go far enough according to his view. He said that the above idea includes the risk that a disabled elderly person with dementia who is already classified in care degree 2 and needs say 3 hours and 45 minutes help a day including 2 hours and 45 minutes of personal care, an extra time value of 45 minutes would be meaningless as this would only lead to a total need of 4 hours and 30 minutes including 3 hours and 30 minutes personal care. The next degree of care (3) requires that a disabled elderly person needs at least 5 hours of help a day including a minimum of 4 hours personal care. Such a case, the expert described as inequitable and therefore he suggested the provision of additional benefits and services for those people with dementia where the additional extra time value for general supervision and attention would not lead to re-classification into a higher degree of care.

Despite the problems in the case of people with dementia, some interviewees considered the eligibility criteria from a general standpoint as equitable. As an interviewee with a scientific background said

long-term care insurance can only offer partial coverage. In the public mind the impression arose that the insurance would provide a complete coverage where long-term care is concerned. This never was and never can be the intention. It is therefore necessary to limit the access to benefits and services. The 'P-ADLs` as well as the 'I-ADLs` are suitable areas to which benefits could apply, though these should be complemented with an element that specifically considers the help required by people with dementia.

Another expert stated

from the standpoint of the one or other individual in need, it may well be that he/she feels he/she is being treated unfairly, but because of the very great cost of the benefits and services and the large number of those in need, standardised eligibility criteria are simply necessary. From this point of view the criteria applied appear to be equitable.

Nevertheless, there have been interviewees who critically mentioned that it is often difficult to understand the time requirements for each 'ADL` that are determined by the medical services. The main problem arising from this would be that these time requirements have upper and lower limits. Within the framework of these limits, the exact assessment of help required for the individual activities is incumbent on the medical services. Some experts mentioned surveys according to which, particularly at the very beginning of the long-term care insurance, considerable divergence in the classification of the people in need between different regions (in particular, variations in the proportions of elderly people in need between the 3 degrees of disability) have attracted attention. It was not possible to explain these differences by the age distribution in the population, they have simply been the result of variability in the use of the eligibility criteria by the experts working for the medical services. Other experts also called attention to studies, which show that this imbalance is more significant if physicians carry out the eligibility procedure on behalf of the medical services. In cases where qualified nurses fulfil these tasks, the variability is not so significant. However, a clear majority of experts also indicated that the high rates of variability at the beginning have levelled out over time but there are still several ways of appealing by those concerned.

As illustrated in the descriptive sections, elderly persons who apply for service provision from long-term care insurance are assessed without taking their income (and capital) into account. As suggested by a range of experts, a major justification for this regulation is that a financial adjustment already takes place through the income relation of the contributions to be paid for the scheme. An expert from a scientific background argued,

> *an additional income-related criterion within the framework of the current social insurance scheme would lead to a double-redistribution which would not be comprehensible.*

Moreover, different experts pointed out that those disabled elderly persons who are unable to pay for such services as may be necessary in addition to those provided under the long-term care scheme, still have the possibility of applying for benefits under the social assistance scheme (currently, about 5% of elderly people receiving domiciliary long-term care get benefits from the social assistance scheme). He further said this meant that persons with low incomes did not drop through the safety net of social benefits. In this matter, other experts mentioned that with the introduction of the long-term care scheme the intention was that disabled elderly persons could leave the social assistance scheme but this is hardly possible in all cases as otherwise the provision of too many benefits and services would become the responsibility of long-term care insurance.

7.5.4 Assessment and options for reform of the type and amount of provision - benefits and services

According to a range of interviewees involved in the study, the benefits and services of long-term care insurance (See, 7.3.3) are in general well known by those concerned. In addition, the clearly fixed amounts of benefits and services essentially contribute to transparency and thus to acceptance by the general public. However, it was further stated by different experts that a lack of clarity exists, merely with regard to social protection benefits provided by the long-term care funds for informal carers, particularly in the case of pension insurance contributions. As a scientific expert argued,

> *this arises more from lack of clarity in the pension scheme than is the long-term care scheme.*

An expert with practical a background stated,

> *an essential advantage of the long-term care insurance compared to other sectors of social insurance (e.g. pension scheme) is that the amount of benefit to be expected, according to degree of care and type of provision, is clear.*

In contrast to this, an interviewee declared that there is a need for a more individual provision of benefits and services than is possible within the framework of just three different degrees of care.

However, several experts that commented on the possibility of choosing between benefits in cash and services in kind or a combination of both, judged this element of the insurance as a particularly positive element. This freedom of choice enables those concerned to tailor the help required to individual circumstances. A scientific expert, however, referred to the necessity to give detailed advice to those concerned in the run-up to the process of care with regard to a suitable provision of care for the individual in need. He further said,

> *the informal care provided by relatives or friends for someone in care degree 1 may well be of the necessary quality and not be too great an imposition of the carers. It is however hardly conceivable that for a person in extreme need of care (degree 3), a provision on a purely informal basis is adequate. An elderly person with a class 3 disability under normal circumstances needs at least a combination of formal and informal care . . . A decision whether informal care is possible or if formal services are necessary depends every time on the individual case and within this assessment not only should the*

degree of disability be considered, but also the social relationship between the elderly people in need and the relatives who care for them.

Some experts pointed the condition that at the beginning of the long-term care insurance (1995), there was a significantly higher demand for the lower benefits in cash (informal care benefits) than for the higher services in kind (formal care services). However, it was further noted that there has been an increase in the proportion of services in kind over the course of time which is expected to continue in the future, mainly because of a decrease in the informal care potential.

An expert from a scientific background argued that informal care would be devalued because of the difference between the amounts of benefits in cash and services in kind and therefore suggested the adaptation of these two types. In contrast, several interviewees that commented on this were of the opinion that differences would be justifiable. As some experts argued, this difference would be necessary as otherwise there would be the risk that many of those concerned would prefer the benefits in cash even though this would overstretch them. Other experts also mentioned an increasing danger of 'moral hazard' (insurance-induced overconsumption) in the case of an adaptation of benefits in cash and services in kind. Some experts with a practical background argued that an adaptation of these two types of provision would hardly be conceivable as this would lead to additional loads on the long-term care insurance, which would not be fundable. With regard to the differences in the amounts of provision between the three degrees of care, none of the experts saw any inequity in these classifications.

Considering the amounts of provision generally, a range of interviewees basically agreed that it is justifiable that long-term care insurance in most cases offers only a partial coverage and not full benefits and services, in particular when considering society as a whole. Nevertheless, some of the experts were of the opinion that the current amount of provision, which has remained unchanged since the introduction of the scheme and has not even been adapted to the rate of inflation, appears to be a problem. As established by a scientific interview partner,

this failure to adjust benefits has led to a de facto continuous reduction of the amount of benefits.

An interviewee with a practical background argued that

> *if one multiplies the reimbursement rate for formal care (e.g. hourly wage) by the number of hours of care that a plan of care recommends, this usually results in payments that are higher than the provision from the scheme. This discrepancy has increased over the years, as the reimbursement rate for formal care has increased since 1995.*

He further argued that the increasing discrepancy between the costs of care and the limited provision from the scheme contains the risk that the demand for benefits from the social assistance scheme will increase. In view of the specific situation of people with dementia (Compare 7.5.3), a range of experts who expressed themselves on this point recommended that the limited monthly amount of benefits and services from the scheme, which are granted according to the degree of disability, should not be extended for this group of people. It appeared more favourable to the interviewees that if persons with dementia were classified as needing a higher degree of care, because of additionally established eligibility criteria that consider the specific need of these people, the scheme would give them the choice of using the monthly benefit also for general supervision and attention in addition to help with 'P-ADLs` and 'I-ADLs`. This choice should of course also be conceded if people with dementia were to remain in the same degree of disability in spite of additional disability criteria. In this case, an interviewee from a scientific background noted,

> *an extension of the limited benefits and services for certain groups of people, e.g. elderly people in particular extreme need of care or people with dementia, would be too costly.*

In addition to statements on the scheme's major benefits in cash and services in kind, some interviewees also commented on the provision from the long-term care funds for the half-yearly (care degree 1 and 2) or quarterly visits (care degree 3) of formal providers to elderly people in need receiving benefits in cash. The amounts of provision, e.g. € 15 (DM 30 in care degree 1 and 2) have been viewed very critically. The main argument was that this low amount would hardly offer a good basis for ensuring the quality of care being provided and giving advice about domiciliary care as required by law.

Other scientific interviewees mentioned a structural problem in the long-term care insurance. As they said, the scheme virtually inhibits a possible improvement in the health of the elderly in need by providing lower benefits and services, e.g. in cases when, as a result of good care, it is possible to downgrade a person in need from care degree 2 to care degree 1. One of these experts pointed towards the fact that

> *this unacceptable structural problem did not only emerge in the long-term care scheme, but is unfortunately a general weak spot of most health care scheme in industrial countries.*

In order to improve the situation within the long-term care scheme, it was recommended that comparative studies should be made to examine the changes in the health of the clients from the individual providers. Those formal organisations, which compare favourably with others, should be entitled to additional benefits.

7.5.5 Assessment and options for reform of the funding

With regard to the funding arrangements (See 7.3.4), a range of interviewees doubted that the current scheme would be fundable without reforms in the future developments. In connection with projections for the development of the scheme's finances, some experts noted that it is extremely difficult to make a clear forecast because of the large number of factors that influence a matter of such great concern. Nevertheless, difficulties are expected. As was noted by different experts, these difficulties would first of all be the consequence of an expected growth in the number of benefits and services provided under the insurance scheme because of the predicted significant increase in the number of elderly people. In connection with this increase, both in total numbers and as a proportion of the population, the share of those who mainly pay for the scheme (people of working age) is expected to decrease. This will lead to a reduction in the total amount of contributions that flow into the scheme. Furthermore, the experts agree that the informal care potential will decrease in the future. This will necessarily lead to an increasing demand for services in kind which are higher than benefits in cash. An expert with a practical background referred to different forecasts that the financing of the insurance is guaranteed to the year 2004 inclusive. Other interviewees mentioned a significant surplus in the long-term care funds on its introduction in 1995. It is a fact that the surplus in the years that followed decreased constantly till 1999 when the first deficit was recorded.

Some interviewees pointed to the fact that because of the poor financial situation of long-term care insurance, it is not possible to respond adequately to additional demands placed on the scheme, as for example the care necessary in the case of elderly people with dementia. As a scientific expert has said,

> *the proposal of the Ministry of Health which aims to improve the situation of people with dementia would at most lead to marginal improvements for those concerned and are hampered by limited finance.*

A judgement by the Federal High Court of April 3rd 2001 was mentioned, which additionally complicates the financial situation. The judge said that the German population would inevitably and massively grow very much older in the next 50 years. Since the long-term care insurance that mainly covers the risk of age-related disability is mainly financed by the earning population, up-and-coming generations and their upbringing are of decisive importance for the scheme. As remarked by the judge, parents are at a disadvantage compared with childless people. The judge explained that parents not only pay insurance contributions but also bring up children. For many parents, this (financial) burden leads to reduced spending and wealth creation. Therefore, the judge said that by the end of 2004, the contribution scheme for long-term care insurance will have to be reformed to ease the burden on parents compared to childless people. As an interviewee said about this judgement,

> *a relief of the strain for parents calls for far-reaching changes in the funding of long-term care insurance.*

A range of interviewees agreed on an urgent need to reform the funding arrangements in long-term care, but the solutions suggested differed. In the current situation, different experts recommended reforms within the framework of the existing social insurance scheme which is financed through a 'pay-as-you-go' basis by contributions. However, a numbers of experts from the level of scientific- and service provision said that before the introduction of long-term care insurance, they could well imagine other ways of providing long-term care for those in need. This particularly included the possibility of a national tax-financed transfer scheme with an administrative responsibility exercised by public authorities. As stated by one of these experts,

> *in the current social insurance based 'pay-as-you-go' scheme there is a considerable danger of putting too great a strain on the rising generation because of the ageing German population. The main financial responsibility will, in the future, be shared by fewer young people. This would be less the case within the framework of a tax-financed scheme.*

An expert working for a long-term care fund maintained,

> *a disadvantage of such an idea would be that the current coordination within the framework of the social insurance system that ensures a particular degree of certainty would be dropped and additionally would for a while lead to more expensive and unstable administrative procedures.*

Another interviewee recommended an immediate restructuring of the current 'pay-as-you-go' scheme towards a 'capital resourced' insurance scheme. As this expert argued, this type of funding would be more independent of an ageing population than the current 'pay-as-you-go' scheme. However, another interviewee stated,

> *changing over from the existing scheme to another appears to be inconceivable as it would be extremely difficult to manage such a procedure.*

This expert also said that the introduction of a 'capital resourced' insurance scheme would include the difficulty that in addition to contributions paid for the scheme, additional payments would be necessary in order to cater for those people who are currently in need of long-term care.

However, with regard to the current 'pay-as-you-go' insurance financed from contributions, the retention of which was favoured by a range of interviewees, a significant problem of this scheme appears to be that different groups of people (mainly self-employed persons, employees with income above the ceiling and civil servants) can opt out of the unified community of social long-term care insurance, combined with taking out a private insurance contract. This was criticised by different interviewees. According to law, benefits and services provided under a private insurance plan for long-term care have to be equivalent to those provided by the social part of the insurance, but the contribution that has to be paid by those insured differ. In contrast to the income-related contributions of social insurance, contributions under a private insurance arrangement usually differ with age. Another expert pointed out that the contributions for a person covered by the social part of the long-term care insurance with a monthly income of € 3,272 (DM 6,400) amount to € 56 (DM 109) (1.7% of the income). The mainly age-related contributions under a private plan, e.g. for a person at the age of 35 with a monthly income of € 3,336 (DM 6,525) (the ceiling for social long-term care insurance in 2001) who now changed to a private insurance, would amount to approximately € 27 (DM 53). This means that the contributions of this person who took the opportunity of changing to private coverage would drop to below half the contributions for social insurance by a person with a little lower income. As the expert further said, if the person were, for example 50 instead of 35, the corresponding contributions for private coverage would be about € 44 (DM 87) and therefore still significantly under those paid for social insurance. The expert further said that with regard to the above example, one must remember that the contributions for the private insurance do not take account of possible contributions for non-working spouses and children of the insured who, in contrast to social insurance, are not included without additional contributions. Therefore, the expert said that he was aware that detailed statements on this topic required complicated calculations taking account of different family models. Nevertheless he, as well as other interviewees, said that although the rate of contribution has to be considered for each individual case, the tendency towards inequity as between social- and private long-term care insurance is obvious. Particularly as an employee whose income reaches the ceiling that allows him to change to private insurance, may freely decide, depending on his personal situation, whether he takes this step or remains covered by social insurance.

In addition to the above, some experts also called attention to the fact that the private long-term care funds do not participate in the compensation procedure between the different social long-term care funds, but had a compensation arrangement with other private funds. As further said, the financial situation of private insurance is significantly better than that of the social long-term care funds. According to an expert with a scientific background this is because of the fact that the share of younger people and people earning a good salary is much higher in the private- than in the social insurance sector. As he further said, in private long-term care insurance, only about 0.9% of those insured are recipients of domiciliary benefits and in the social insurance which covers many elderly and also many socially weak people this share amounts to about 1.8%. Another expert argued

> *the division of social insurance implies the risk that the wealthier part of the population is able to obtain private coverage while those with smaller financial resources are left in the social part of the insurance. This is destroying the effect of solidarity in the long-term care scheme, which should include the whole population, and is significantly threatening the scheme.*

With this in mind, a range of interviewees recommended extending the number of people covered by social long-term care insurance. Regarding the existing financial assistance scheme for civil servants (civil servants are usually covered by a semi-private long-term care contract from which, in the case of disability, half their benefits comes, the other half being provided under the financial assistance scheme), several experts recommended the abolition of this special position with regard to long-term care provision. A scientific interviewee said, this abolition would lead to a considerable proportion of the total number of those people with private contracts being on the files of the social insurance authorities. As stated by different experts, one should also consider including the self-employed and those with earnings above the ceiling, as this appears to be equitable and would additionally lead to an improvement of the financial situation in the social long-term care insurance scheme. However, some experts were of the opinion that the distinction between social insurance and private insurance was a fundamental part of the German social insurance system and, therefore, such developments in the long-term care scheme should be discussed within a wider framework.

In addition to the above, several experts mentioned the possibility of increasing the contribution rate and/or the ceiling, whereby the latter would lead to an increase in the number of persons covered by the insurance since certain employees, would then possibly no longer fulfil the income criteria for private coverage. As one expert said, considering whether to take such steps would bring up the basic question

what value does society attach to the care of the elderly in need?

Although several interviewees that commented on this declared themselves in favour of one of these ideas or a combination of both, most of the interviewees realised this would mean an increase in wage costs and would therefore be difficult to implement at the moment. Some experts doubted if it would be possible to increase the ceiling in the long-term care insurance scheme without doing the same with health insurance as both schemes currently have the same ceiling and are closely linked with each other. In contrast, other experts did not see why the close relation of these two schemes should stop the legislator from increasing the ceiling in the long-term care insurance scheme. However, an interviewee with a scientific background emphasized the necessity to keep the contributions at a reasonable level to ensure that discussions about long-term care were not exclusively about the money that goes into the scheme rather than about the efficiency of the service provided.

Finally, the interviewees were prepared to say that a purely market solution for the provision of long-term care, either on a voluntary or on a compulsory basis, does not offer an appropriate alternative to public provision. An interviewee with a practical background argued that comparatively high premiums and often non-transparent terms of a private long-term care policy keep quite a lot of people away from this market. There are different reasons leading to this situation. For instance, it is extremely difficult to calculate premiums for a largely unforeseeable risk. This is mainly due to the uncertainty regarding people's future state of health and the costs of long-term care depending on this. In the individual case, one may assume that costs for providing long-term care will be extremely high. This means that providers of long-term care policies have to establish appropriate funds out of which the costs of care can be paid in the case of need. For people who decide at a relatively advanced age to sign a private insurance contract, the remaining time for establishing such funds is often comparatively short, leading to higher premiums. It is, however, in particular the elderly who are interested in such coverage. Among younger persons where the need of long-term care appears to be far away in the future, the benefits of private long-term care insurance are often not yet regarded as significant. In addition, as the total number of policies sold so far is comparatively low, it is hardly possible to spread the risk of long-term care appropriately. Some experts would like to see the extension of private insurance on a voluntary basis in addition to the public long-term care insurance. Other experts argued that such an additional coverage would only be affordable for the better-off and not for those in greatest need.

7.6 Summary

The present Chapter has mainly discussed the following aspects of the German domiciliary long-term care scheme: the responsible institutions, the eligibility criteria, the type of service provision and the type of funding. This comprises a descriptive overview of these terms as well as an empirically-supported assessment, including proposals for reform. In addition to these main areas, different aspects of the German social protection system have been outlined and it has been shown how the long-term care insurance is integrated alongside the other social insurance sectors of pensions, health, unemployment and industrial accident. Finally, future developments were taken into consideration whereby the focus was on a proposal put forward by the German Ministry of Health to address difficulties in the provision of benefits and services from the long-term care insurance for people suffering from the various forms of dementia.

With regard to the institutions responsible for the provision of long-term care, administrative responsibility for care insurance is mainly in the hands of the managers of the newly-established long-term care funds, although their work is performed by the existing health insurance fund managers. The services in kind are predominantly provided by different private organisations, followed by five voluntary, non-profit associations (or sub-groups of these associations). As observed in the empirical analysis, because of the social insurance orientation chosen for long-term care insurance, it was efficient to give the administrative responsibility for long-tem care funds whose work is performed by the already existing health insurance funds. Another very positive element of the 'Care Insurance Act' is that it has made it easier for private providers to enter the market. This has led to a broad infrastructure on the supply side of long-term care provision. However, this increase in supply has unfortunately also led to a growth in the number of dubious service providers on the market, which makes it necessary to strengthen the quality controls by the medical services. A need for reform exists with regard to the home visits of formal providers to those people in need receiving informal care provided by relatives, friends, etc. Firstly, it seems to be advisable to extend these consultations and secondly, to transfer the responsibility from the service providers to the local authorities or to the long-term care funds.

Regarding the criteria as to whether a person is defined as disabled and therefore eligible for the benefits and services from the long-term care insurance, the scheme includes nationwide uniform eligibility criteria for domiciliary long-term care provision. Accordingly, elderly people in need are classified in three different degrees of care by considering the number and frequency of visits needed to provide help in the performance of a certain number of 'Personal Activities of Daily Life' ('P-ADLs') and 'Instrumental Activities of Daily Life' ('I-ADLs'). Furthermore, the three different degrees of disability defined are specified by additional time requirements. Assessment is the responsibility of medical services. The empirical discussion has shown that the eligibility criteria seem to be questionable, as they do not take into consideration that part of general supervision and guidance, which has nothing to do with activities of daily life. Persons with dementia are put at a disadvantage. The latest proposals on this issue by the Ministry of Health do not seem to be very helpful. It would appear appropriate to extend the existing eligibility criteria by such elements that consider the particular help required by people with dementia. An extra time value could well be allotted to the special extra care needed. Another weakness in the eligibility procedure is the difference in the results of assessment between different regions. It is therefore necessary to improve the co-ordination between the individual people working for the medical services, in particular the co-ordination when doctors perform this work.

As the discussion has illustrated, there are many benefits and services for domiciliary personal care and home-making assistance available under the long-term care insurance scheme. It is, in the main, possible to choose between services in kind (usually provided if the disabled elderly person chooses formal care) and benefits in cash (usually granted if the person is able to secure care for himself/herself from informal carers) or a combination of both. These benefits and services are paid up to a fixed limit according to the degree of care. In addition, it is also possible to apply for stand-in care, short-term care, technical aids and care aids as well as for social protection benefits for certain informal carers. The possibility to choose between different types of provision and to combine them is a very positive element of the insurance and allows those in need to opt for benefits that take account of individual circumstances. The clearly fixed amounts of provision essentially makes the scheme easier to comprehend and therefore more readily acceptable to the general public. However, the level of provision, which has remained unchanged since the long-term care insurance scheme was introduced in 1995 seems to be a problem as this failure to adjust benefits and services, e.g. to keep pace with the inflation rate, means a de facto decrease in the standard of provision. It is however clear that the insurance can only provide a partial coverage. Nevertheless, it is doubtful whether a further decline in the standard of service resulting from a refusal to increase the level of benefits and services will be acceptable to society. This failure to adjust benefits and services also increases the risk that more and more disabled elderly persons will have to apply for benefits from social assistance. Furthermore, the fact that the scheme de facto punishes the providers of good quality care which results in the person in question being re-classified in a lower degree of care and thus entitled only to a lower rate of provision, is a deplorable state of affairs that should be ended, e.g. by providing additional benefits for those providers with demonstrably good results in services.

With regard to the funding arrangements of the scheme, the main source of funding for the long-term care insurance comes from a contribution rate that is fixed at 1.7% by law. This contribution is paid up to a certain ceiling by equal contributions from employers and their employees. The ceiling for long-term care insurance is the same as for health insurance and corresponds to 75% of the ceiling in the public pension scheme. In addition, contributions to the long-term care insurance scheme come from the majority of pensioners on the basis of their income from the public pension scheme. Non-employed spouses and children of these employees are covered without paying contributions. Having in mind the difficult demographic and social changes, it seems clear that the funding of the scheme urgently needs reform. A useful option for reform seems to be an extension of the group of persons covered by social long-term care insurance (mainly self-employed persons, employees with income above the ceiling and civil servants). Further options are a higher contribution rate and a rise of the ceiling. Other funding arrangements instead of the existing 'pay-as-you-go' (e.g. purely market solutions and capital resourced insurance scheme) seem to be rather unsuitable for the near future.

8 Domiciliary long-term care in the United Kingdom

8.1 Introduction

In the United Kingdom (Great Britain and Northern Ireland) there is currently no independent scheme which covers the financial risk of domiciliary long-term care (European Commission, 2000). Rather, the scheme includes a large variety of provisions which are granted to the disabled elderly from different sectors of the social protection system. The existing diversity in service provision is also influenced by the fact that there is a range of income-related benefits in the UK that is basically available for different groups of the population and not specifically for the disabled elderly generation but for which certain elements of the criteria for eligibility are applicable to people in need of long-term care.

In order to reduce the existing complexity, at least systematically, a general overview of the main types of available sources of provision for the disabled elderly is given below in Figure 8 (See p. 186). The figure shows that a broad range of provision exists for people in need of long-term care. The figure suggests the usefulness of distinguishing between services in kind and benefits in cash. In the former group, 'Home Care' ('Home Help') and 'Meals on Wheels' are the main areas of service provision. The cash benefits include an 'Attendance Allowance' ('AA') (the only direct cash benefit to the disabled that is not income-related), an indirect benefit, the so-called 'Invalid Care Allowance' ('ICA') for informal carers, benefits that are related to income in the form of 'Income Support', a 'Social Fund', a 'Housing Benefit' and a 'Disabled Facilities Grant'. In addition to these benefits, different types of tax relief that are more or less in relation with the status of age-related-disability may be available (e.g. a reduction of the local 'Community Charge') (Tinker, McCreadie, Wright and Salvage, 1994).

However, a discussion of all such possible benefits and services goes beyond the scope of this Chapter. Therefore, in this country-report the main focus will be on 'Home Care' or 'Home Help' services, the 'Attendance Allowance' and the 'Invalid Care Allowance', which represent the most important types of long-term care provision in the UK (Compare, for example, Royal Commission on Long-term Care, 1999). The other types of benefits and services will be included in this Chapter, whenever this appears useful to complete the information. The differences which exist in the emphasis across the UK scheme with consequences in organisational and funding structures (Compare, for example, Petch, 2000) also need to be considered. To study all of these different arrangements would lead to a complexity unsuitable in this cross-national study. Therefore, the following country-report focuses primarily on long-term care arrangements in England, but differences that appear to be important will be mentioned in the course of the following discussion. However, before studying long-term care benefits and services that may be available for the disabled elderly, an overview of the UK social protection system is given (See 8.2).

Figure 8 Domiciliary long-term care benefits and services in the UK

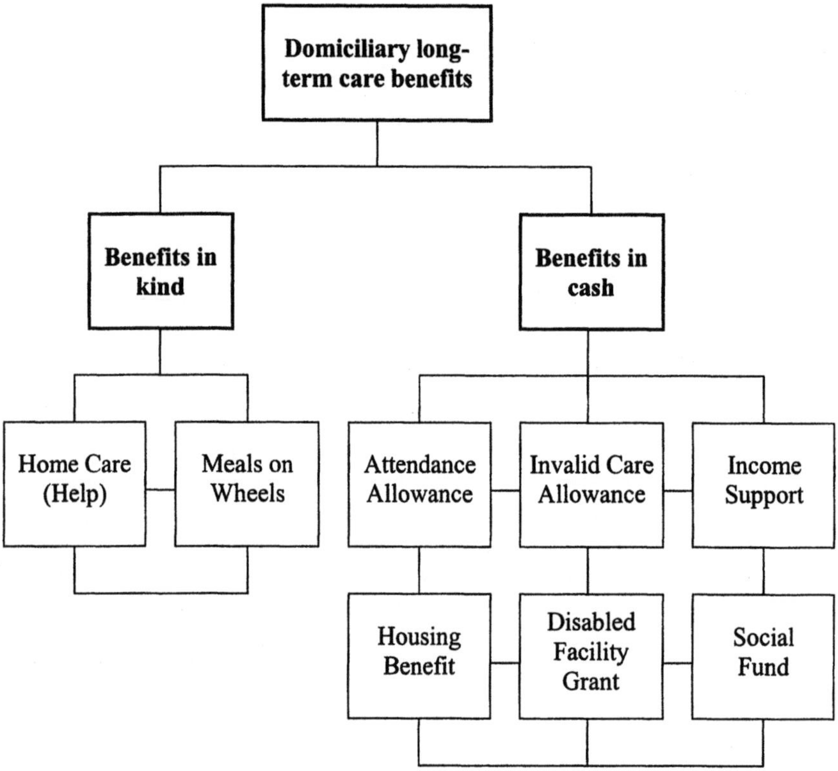

Source: References from Chapter 8

8.2 Social protection system

The social protection system, which is mainly financed by the State through national taxation, includes a variety of benefits and services. The majority of services in kind are the responsibility of the 'Department of Health' (in particular those provided by the 'National Health Service' or 'NHS'), while a second broad group of services in kind is the responsibility of the local authorities. The majority of the different types of cash benefits are provided under the authority of the 'Department of Social Security'. In this case, it is useful to distinguish between contributory cash benefits, non-contributory, non income-related cash benefits and non-contributory income-related cash benefits (Swedish National Board of Health and Welfare, 1993).

For decades, the 'NHS' has been considered the 'jewel in the crown of the Welfare State'. When established in 1948, it meant the development of comprehensive medical care. The 'NHS' provides a comprehensive public health care service that is predominantly free of charge at the point of use and mainly tax-financed. A charge however, for example, is often made for prescriptions but medicine is entirely free for certain groups of the population, such as pensioners, unemployed, children under 16 and pregnant women. In general, the 'NHS' provides comprehensive care according to people's clinical need and everyone has the right to use it, irrespectively of sex, race and class. The system's focus on primary care and the 'General Practitioner' ('GP') as the strict entry point for health care has frequently been seen as an advantage in comparison with other schemes of health care provision in the European Union. In addition to the 'GP', other health professionals provide primary care services under the 'NHS', such as dentists, opticians and pharmacies. Besides primary care, secondary care such as accident services and emergency care of elderly people and tertiary care (through specialist hospitals treating particular types of illness such as cancer) is available under the 'NHS'. Furthermore, the 'NHS' works together with the social service departments of local authorities, which are, for instance, responsible for different types of social services in kind (National Health Service Executive Communications Unit, 1996; European Parliament, 1998). Such services in kind under the responsibility of the local authorities are, for example, personal care, home-making assistance, social worker support and services for children (Rostgaard and Fridberg, 1998).

Of those cash benefits that are related to contributions, retirement pensions are obviously very important. In this matter, all employees and residents of the UK are covered by the 'Basic State Retirement Pension'. It is not possible to opt out of this scheme, but it is, of course possible to add other pensions. Every employed person pays 'National Insurance' ('NI') contributions that include payments to this 'Basic State Retirement Pension' if the person's earnings are above a certain level ('Lower Earnings Limit'). In general, the employer takes these contributions out of the wage/salary payments and also makes payments for its employees from its own earnings. Self-employed persons have to pay 'NI' contributions themselves. The eligibility criteria for receiving a full 'Basic State Retirement Pension' are based on contributions having been paid into the 'NI' scheme for a significant part of the person's working life. To receive a full pension, men currently need 44 qualifying years and women 39 years. Those who retire with less than one quarter of the qualifying years for a full pension are not eligible to receive any state pensions. Wives not working on their own may be eligible for a 'Basic State Retirement Pension' through their husband's contribution. However, the benefits for a couple where the pension depends solely on the contributions of one person are usually lower than for a couple where the woman and the man have made sufficient contributions independently of each other and, therefore, are eligible in their own right. Currently, people usually reach the basic pension age at 65 (UK Department of Social Security, 2000a).

In addition to the 'Basic State Retirement Pension', the majority of those retiring today would have either a 'State Earnings Related Pension Scheme' ('SERPS') or another type of pension. The contributions to the 'SERPS' are based on a percentage of earnings while a person is working and paying 'NI' contributions. For employees, the 'SERPS' is paid by government together with the 'Basic State Retirement Pension' (starting from the same retirement age), with the amount of payments for the 'SERPS' depending on the earnings while working. Those who are self-employed are not included into the 'SERPS'. In general, the average 'SERPS' payments are around 20% of the average earnings on which contributions have been paid. In contrast to the basic pension, a person would already be entitled to some 'SERPS' benefits if he or she has paid a certain amount of 'NI' contributions in the period of one year. As mentioned above, it is also possible to choose other types of pensions instead of the 'SERPS' during one's working-life. This is called contracting-out of 'SERPS'. Currently, it is possible to join an 'Occupational Pension' (if the employer offers one) to supplement the 'Basic State Retirement Pension' or buy a 'Personal Pension'. With respect to the future, it will also be possible to buy a 'Stakeholder Pension' (UK Department of Social Security, 2000b). However, as a study by the Swedish National Board of Health and Welfare (1993) has argued, these retirement pensions often have in common that, even in combination, they provide relatively low benefits in relation to a recipient's former earnings during his or her working life. For example, combining the 'Basic State Retirement Pension' with the 'State Earnings Related Pension Scheme', the allowances would be approximately 30 to 50% of the final salary.

Another important contributory related benefit in cash is the 'Jobseekers Allowance'. In order to receive benefits from this scheme, a person usually has to be between 18 and 64 (men) or between 18 and 59 (women), has to be out of work or working on average less than 16 hours a week, has to be registered at a labour exchange or employment agency and be actively seeking work (UK Department of Social Security, 2000c). Furthermore, for those who are employed, it may be possible to receive 'Statutory Sick Pay' for a period up to 28 weeks in one spell of sickness (UK Department of Social Security, 2000d). Finally, a 'Maternity Allowance' is also illustrative in the context of contribution-related cash benefits. For this grant, women must have been employed or self-employed for a duration of at least 26 weeks in the test period (66 weeks before the week the baby is due) and must have a weekly income of a certain amount (UK Department of Social Security, 2000e).

Turning to non-contributory cash benefits, both income-related and non income-related, it is noteworthy in both cases to begin with that there is a broad range of such benefits and it may not be useful to offer a complete overview within the limited scope of this section of the study. For several of these benefits, there are aspects of the eligibility criteria that can be met by people in need of long-term care. The most important of these types of benefits available for disabled elderly people will be discussed in later sections on the domiciliary long-term care scheme and this allows us to dispense with details at this point. However, to provide examples of the variety of such benefits, some are listed below. In the income-related non-contributory benefits group, some of the important ones are 'Income Support', 'Disabled Facilities Grant', payments from the 'Social Fund', 'Housing Benefit' and 'Disability Working Allowance'. The non-contributory benefits, which are not income-related include, for example, 'Attendance Allowance', 'War Pensions', 'Mobility Allowance', 'Disability Living Allowance' and others (See, for example, Tinker, McCreadie, Wright and Salvage, 1994; UK Department of Social Security, 1997).

8.3 Analysis of the current domiciliary long-term care scheme

8.3.1 Responsible institutions

Generally, the responsibility for the provision of domiciliary long-term care is mainly in the hands of two government departments and the local authorities. The government institutions are the 'Department of Health' and the 'Department of Social Security'. The local authorities have a broad responsibility for social service provision (including domiciliary long-term care), mainly through their 'Social Service Departments' ('SSD') (See, for example, Rostgaard and Fridberg, 1998).

The 'Department of Health' is accountable for promoting regulations within which the 'SSD' of the local authorities act (Rostgaard and Fridberg, 1998). In addition, it oversees the 'NHS'. Within the framework of the 'NHS', in general, personal care and home-making assistance are scarcely provided, but nevertheless clear points of contact exist with domiciliary long-term care tasks. For example, nursing care ('District Nursing') under the 'NHS' which is mainly provided by district nurses in special cases includes elements of personal care in addition to tasks such as taking blood pressure, exchanging catheters or giving injections (Hutten, 1996e; National Health Service Executive Communications Unit, 1996). At the same time, the 'NHS' operates in partnership with the 'SSD' of the local authorities, which have the leading role in community care[1] provision. The 'NHS' works with them to ensure the effective planning and delivery of community services. This involves, for instance, contributing to the assessment of people's needs for community care or providing support in a number of settings (National Health Service Executive Communications Unit, 1996). In this matter, the 'General Practioners' ('GP') have a decisive function in referring an elderly person to the 'SSD' of the local authorities and for supporting applications for certain types of cash allowances, e.g. the 'Attendance Allowance' ('AA') (Tinker, McCreadie, Wright and Salvage, 1994).

The 'Department of Social Security' provides different funds for long-term care through a range of cash transfers (e.g. 'AA' and 'ICA'). The administrative handling of such benefits is mainly taken over by different regional social security offices, and their local authority sub-divisions (See, for example, UK Department of Social Security, 2000f).

Through the 'National Health Service and Community Care Act in 1990', important changes occurred in domiciliary long-term care and these have only been marginally redirected by the present Labour government (Hudson, 2000). A key element of these changes has been to transfer the (financial)

---

1 The exact meaning of 'community care' has, however, varied over time from domiciliary care provision to a plan for caring by the entire 'community' (Tinker, McCreadie, Wright and Salvage, 1994). As Tinker (1984) argues, the idea of 'community care' includes a range of different elements. It encloses public awareness of the importance of care provided by the informal sector (i.e. by relatives, friends, etc.), but also awareness of the limitations of care provided on an informal basis. It comprises the idea of neighbours and friends helping but appreciates a limit to the type of care they will provide. As the content of the 'National Health Service and Community Care Act' of 1990 shows, it may also include residential care. The general guidelines for 'community care' which have been identified by an earlier report from the 'House of Commons', include a preference for domiciliary care over residential care, and a recognition of the need to enable the person concerned, as far as possible to have a 'normal life', to integrate in society, to avoid separate provision, segregation and restriction and to prefer local services to more remote ones (House of Commons Social Services Committee, 1985). Although there seems to be no uniform definition, the above statements may have offered an idea what is meant by 'community care' in the UK - basically it involves much more (e.g. types of residential care and nursing care at home) than the field of research of the present study (domiciliary long-term care).

responsibility for community care mainly from central government to the 'SSD' ('Social Work Departments' in Scotland) of the local authorities[2]. In addition to domiciliary long-term care through 'Home Care' or 'Home Help' services, a range of other community services, for example, 'Day Care', 'Community Psychiatric Nursing' and 'Social Work', are available within the framework of this local authority provision (Hutten, 1996; Davies and Fernandéz and Saunders, 1998). In this matter, the local authorities have, for example, responsibility for assessing the care needs of the population, for shaping the markets of care, for choosing between service providers, and for monitoring service performance (Knapp, Hardy and Forder, 2001).

With regard to the providers of domiciliary long-term care services, the introduction of care markets (accelerated by the 'National Health Service and Community Care Act in 1990') has led to a rapid increase in the share of publicly funded care provided privately in the 1990s. For example, in 1992 just 2% of domiciliary long-term care was provided by the private sector. Up to 1999, that share had grown to 51% (England) (Knapp, Hardy and Forder, 2001). Private sector provision in this case means that there are organisations that have concluded contracts with the 'SSD' of the local authorities for the provision of domiciliary long-term care services. In this matter it appears worth mentioning that while the Conservative government in the early 1990s encouraged the provision of services by private organisations, the present Labour government has not expressed a preference for any source, whether private, voluntary, non-profit or public authority, to provide the publicly-funded care services for elderly persons in need. It has been argued that it is not decisive who provides the care, but it is the quality of the service provision that counts (Knapp and Hardy and Forder, 2001). As stated by Laing and Saper (1999), the "community care reforms can be credited with kick-starting independent sector supply of home care services for state-funded clients" (p. 97). However, as Hardy and Wistow (1999) have found, the shares of the private sector in publicly funded provision varies extremely across the country. In this matter, the private providers of domiciliary long-term care are on the other hand scarcely concentrated in bigger organisations; a majority consists of a number of small (local) providers (Hardy and Wistow, 2000). It is noteworthy that there is a broad area of service provision for disabled elderly that is not controlled and subsidised by state authorities. In such cases, help comes mainly from private organisations that are often directly paid by the individual in need, informal carers or voluntary, non-profit organisations. However, statistical

[2] In Northern Ireland, the services otherwise usually provided by the 'SSD' of the local authorities and the health services under the 'NHS', are largely provided under the responsibility of the same community trust organisation (Glendinning, 1998).

data on the overall size of this sector is not available (Knapp, Hardy and Forder, 2001).

8.3.2 Eligibility criteria

8.3.2.1 General Description

As noted earlier, there is a range of different arrangements in the domiciliary long-term care scheme of the UK. Because of this complexity, it appears useful to study the eligibility criteria by distinguishing between services in kind and benefits in cash. In the former group, 'Home Care` and 'Home Help` are the main areas of service provision. The most important cash benefits include an 'Attendance Allowance` ('AA`) (the only direct cash benefit to the disabled that is not income-related) and an indirect benefit, the so-called 'Invalid Care Allowance` ('ICA`) for informal carers.

8.3.2.2 Eligibility criteria for services in kind

As mentioned above, 'Home Care` ('Home Help)` services are provided by local authorities. In many local authorities 'Home Help` services have been re-designated 'Home Care` services. Basically, about 70% of people in need are referred by primary health care providers (usually a 'GP`) or hospitals and the rest are mainly self-referrals. There is, however, no necessity for a formal referral. All referrals receive an assessment by a 'Local Authority Social Worker` (often called a care manager). For those eligible for publicly financed services (frequently elderly people with a low income), the 'Local Authority Social Worker` normally decides the number of hours for (publicly financed) care provision. In other cases, the number of hours will largely depend on the amount of money the elderly people in need are willing to pay. In general, only the minority of disabled elderly, i.e. those with low incomes and often with no source of informal care, receive considerable state support from local authorities (Hutten, 1996e). In this connection, there are, however, significant differences among the local authorities, as there are no nationally applicable criteria for the assessments. In practice, this means that assessments are based on locally fixed criteria, so that the question of whether a person receives publicly financed care and, if so how much, may well depend on where he or she lives. In this connection, there are also different ways of deciding whether and to what extent an elderly person is expected to contribute towards the publicly financed services. These facts are in contrast to the regulations in the sector of residential care, where people that have capital of € 25,670 (£ 16,000) or more usually have to pay the fees for care in full, while people with capital of between € 16,044 (£ 10,000) and € 25,670 (£ 16,000) are expected to make contributions to the fees and for each € 401 (£ 250) of capital an income of € 1.60 (£ 1) per week is assumed (capital of less than € 16,044 (£ 10,000) is ignored as is any income it produces). The maximum capital limit of € 25,670 (£ 16,000) means that only around 44% of single old people above the age of 75 are entitled to some public support (Royal Commission on Long-term Care, 1999). Although there are no detailed regulations, one may assume that some local authorities to some extent apply similar criteria of eligibility for domiciliary services (Royal Commission on Long-term Care, 1999).

8.3.2.3 Eligibility criteria for benefits in cash

With regard to benefits in cash, the so-called 'Attendance Allowance' ('AA') for disabled elderly persons over 65 who need help with personal care is a very important one, as it is the only benefit for the disabled elderly that is not income-related and virtually the only benefit exclusively for this group of people. Other types of benefit are normally available for a much wider group of people than just the disabled elderly, although aspects of the eligibility criteria for those benefits can be applied to people in need of long-term care. All these benefits have, however, in common that they are not related to contributions to the 'National Insurance' ('NI').

With regard to the 'AA', the criteria of eligibility depend on the question of where a person aged 65 and over lives and on the extent of the need to be looked after (residence and state of health conditions). With regard to the residence conditions, it is usually necessary for a disabled elderly person living at home to have been resident in the UK for at least 26 weeks in the 12 months immediately prior to his/her claim for benefit. With regard to state of health conditions, the situation is rather more complicated. First of all, it is usually necessary for the elderly person to fulfil the eligibility criteria for six months (qualifying period) before he or she qualifies for the benefits. For those elderly with a terminal illness, this qualifying period is not applicable. There are two different types of benefit, the lower and the higher rate. In order to receive the higher rate, the elderly person must have a frequent and continuing need of a certain amount of help with bodily functions (e.g. washing and bathing, preparing food for easy consumption, toileting, getting in and out of bed, outdoor walking, dressing, walking, standing, using stairs) or help in avoiding substantial danger (e.g. from falls or due to mental illness), both during the day and at night. Daytime care means that an elderly person needs frequent attention from another person throughout the day in connection with his/her bodily functions or continual supervision throughout the day in order to avoid substantial danger to himself/herself or others. Night-time care means that at night, an elderly person needs prolonged or repeated attention from another person in connection with his/her bodily functions. Home-making assistance is not normally included within the framework of help with bodily functions, but help with bodily functions may, for instance, involve help with laundry where this forms part of a continuous episode of attention of a personal and intimate nature in connection with a bodily function. The lower rate is granted for those elderly persons who need to be looked after by day or at night. All claims for 'AA' are decided by independent 'Adjudication Officers' on the basis of the information supplied on a completed claim form. If there is more information needed, it is possible, for example, that a 'Departmental Doctor' may examine the applicant (UK Department of Social Security, 1997; UK Department of Social Security, 2000g).

Another important benefit in cash is the so-called 'Invalid Care Allowance' ('ICA'), which is not directly available for the disabled elderly. It is usually paid to people over 16 and under 65 (age condition) who are unable to work because they are caring for a person receiving 'AA' at home on an informal basis. It is therefore not a direct, but an indirect benefit in the sector of domiciliary care. In this connection, it is worth mentioning that the 'ICA' would also be available for those looking after someone who is getting other types of benefits, e.g. the 'Disability Living Allowance' (for disabled people under the age of 65). As with the 'AA', the payment does not depend on the amount of income and capital held by the carer or the disabled elderly person, nor on 'NI' contributions. Those who are receiving 'ICA' are, however credited with 'NI' contributions. A further criterion for benefits is that the informal carer has to look after the disabled elderly person receiving 'AA' for at least 35 hours weekly. Finally, it is not possible to be paid 'ICA' if the informal carer is on a course of full-time education (21 hours weekly or above) or if he or she has a job from which he or she earns more than € 80 (£ 50) a week before tax and after the deduction of allowable expenses (i.e. free meals at workplace, accommodation provided by employers, etc.). It is not possible to receive full 'ICA' in addition to other types of social benefits, such as the 'Incapacity Benefit', the 'Severe Disablement Allowance', the 'Jobseeker's Allowance', the 'Maternity Allowance' or the 'Retirement Pension'. Those informal carers who already receive a benefit which duplicates the 'ICA' will be paid the difference. In other words, the rate of the other benefits is deducted from the 'ICA'. As in the case of the 'AA', the claims are considered by 'Adjudication Officers' whose decisions are intended to be independent of the Department of Social Security (UK Department of Social Security, 1997; UK Department of Social Security, 2000h).

8.3.3 Type and amount of provision - benefits and services

8.3.3.1 General Description

As already illustrated (Compare Figure 8, page 186), there is a range of different domiciliary long-term care benefits in the UK. As in the previous section examining eligibility criteria, the most important types of long-term care provision available to the disabled elderly will be illustrated by distinguishing between those in kind on the one hand and those in cash on the other.

8.3.3.2 Domiciliary care services in kind

With regard to 'Home Care' ('Home Help') services, which are run by 'SSD' of the local authorities, there is a large variation between the individual authorities. No national task profile exists by which different kinds of home helps (carers) perform different tasks. Recently, in many local authorities, the service of 'Home Help' has developed more into a 'Home Care' service, with greater emphasis on the provision of personal care. 'Home Care' ('Home Help') providers may help elderly people with home-making tasks (i.e. help with shopping, cooking, cleaning, laundry) and personal care (i.e. assistance with getting into and out of bed, bathing, dressing, eating and toileting) and perform social duties (e.g. talking with the disabled elderly, helping disabled elderly persons to maintain contact with friends) (Hutten, 1996e). In the early 1990s, there was a quite lively discussion as to whether the aim of 'Home Care' ('Home Help') should be to support a broad number of elderly people in need with basic home-making tasks or whether the provision should concentrate its resources on those elderly people that are in extreme need of care (Tinker, McCreadie, Wright and Salvage, 1994). It seems that most local authorities prefer to concentrate their resources on more extended care for a smaller number of elderly persons. Between 1992 and 1998 the average hours of public-funded care that entitled households have received increased from 3.2 to 5.8 weekly (England). As a result, between 1992 and 1997 the number of disabled elderly receiving such long-term care provision decreased by 11% and went down a further 6% up to 1998 (England) (Knapp and Hardy and Forder, 2001).

8.3.3.3 Domiciliary care benefits in cash

The 'Attendance Allowance' ('AA') is a non-contributory benefit and the only benefit paid to the disabled elderly which is not related to their income (capital). There are two different types of benefit. The higher rate, which is paid for those disabled elderly who need looking after both day and night, amounts to € 85.91 (£ 53.55) per week. The lower rate, which is paid to the disabled elderly who need looking after by day or by night amounts to € 57.44 (£ 35.80) per week (UK Department of Social Security, 2000g).

As with the 'AA', the 'Invalid Care Allowance' ('ICA') is a non-contributory benefit that is not income-related. It is, however, not paid to the disabled elderly, but to adults who are unable to go to work because they are caring for a disabled elderly person who is receiving 'AA' (UK Department of Social Security, 1997). As the rules for benefits depend on individual circumstances (e.g. certain other types of social benefit overlap with the 'ICA' and are therefore deducted from the maximum amount, while it is also possible to receive additional amounts, for example, on the basis of the fact that the informal carer has dependent children), it is difficult to give details of the exact amounts paid. As a basic guideline, around € 64.82 (£ 40.40) is paid on average to informal carers (UK Department of Social Security, 2000h).

8.3.4 Funding

With regard to the financing of the domiciliary long-term care scheme in the UK, it is again useful to distinguish between cash benefits and services in kind.

In most parts of the UK, domiciliary long-term care provision in kind is the responsibility of the local authorities, i.e. services such as 'Home Help' and 'Home Care' are mainly paid for by central government allocations. The other major part of the finance comes from local taxation ('Council Tax') and from charges or contributory payments from the recipients of the services. It is important to note that there is comparatively little direct government control over the detailed allocation of local authority expenditure, reflecting the local authority autonomy. The national government resources that are spent on the domiciliary long-term care commissioned by the local authorities comprise a grant that covers a range of service blocks, but the separate administrations have discretion with regard to the exact amount to be used for the individual type of local service. With regard to charges or contributory payments, it is well known that there is a wide variation between local authorities. Some local authorities charge a small flat rate for 'Home Care' ('Home Help'), some charge full costs. Some local authorities apply a variety of regulations on what income and capital persons in need may have before they will be expected to make contributory payments (Tinker, McCreadie, Wright and Salvage, 1994; Royal Commission on Long-term Care, 1999).

As regards domiciliary long-term care benefits in cash, taxation is virtually the only source of finance and provision is unrelated to contributions to the National Insurance. The 'Attendance Allowance'('AA') is also unrelated to income and capital and paid at fixed rates to the eligible elderly in need. The 'Invalid Care Allowance' ('ICA') that may be paid at fixed rates to the informal carer of a disabled elderly person is, however, not related to capital either, but a certain amount of income from employment may prevent 'ICA' benefits being payable and other types of social benefit may also reduce the amount payable. However, contributory payments by the disabled elderly are not relevant in the case of these two types of benefit. The benefits through the 'AA' and the 'ICA' are usually paid from national taxation under an overall budget that is set by the 'Department of Social Security' (Tinker, McCreadie, Wright and Salvage, 1994; UK Department of Social Security, 2000g and 2000h).

Finally, it would be useful to offer figures on the overall public costs for the sector of domiciliary long-term care. As a 'Royal Commission on Long-term Care' found out (1999), it was not possible to shed definitive light on this matter. However, to give the reader a rough idea, the current provision for long-term care in general (including the sector of domiciliary as well as the sector of residential care) is probably about € 11.4 billion (£ 7.1 billion) for the 'National Health Service' and 'Social Services' provided by the local authorities per year and about € 6.42 billion (£ 4 billion) for expenditure by private individuals. In addition, an estimated € 9.6 billion (£ 6 billion) of 'Social Security' benefits are disbursed for the disabled elderly (Royal Commission on Long-term Care, 1999). However, as the 'Royal Commission on Long-term Care' comments on this data, "the uncertainty as to the figures is in itself a cause of concern. No one really knows just how much public or private money goes to support older people in long-term care" (Para. 4.4, 1999).

8.4 Ways forward

In the 1990s, the need to introduce significant reforms in the finance and organisation of long-term care was a distinguishing feature of social policy debate in the UK. Within the framework of this discussion, the Labour Party made an Election Manifesto commitment to establish a 'Royal Commission on Long-term Care' if elected to Government. On the 1st of May 1997, the Labour Party took office and announced the establishment of the Royal Commission in December of that year (Henwood, 1999). The job of the Commission was to examine the short and long-term options for a sustainable scheme of funding for domiciliary and residential long-term care for elderly people, and to recommend how, and in what circumstances, the cost of such care should be apportioned between public funds and the disabled elderly. It appears noteworthy that besides the focus on the disabled elderly, the job of the Commission was also to look at long-term care for younger people that suffer from disability (European Commission, 2000).

In terms of the current scheme for long-term care, the Commission argues that it is failing, and in clear need of reform. "Within it there are too many flows of funds which have been designed for different purposes and what the individual does or does not get is out of their control. People have no idea what to expect. The tendency of the scheme to require impoverishment - and its proof - before it will help leads to despair which in our judgement is unacceptable. Modestly prudent people risk losing their dignity, partly as a result of their condition and partly because of how the system deals with it. People have no choice but to receive services for which all but the poorest have no further choice to pay" (Royal Commission on Long-term Care, 1999, Para. 4.50).

Based on the examination of the long-term care arrangements, the Commission recommended a new scheme of funding that should establish a clear partnership between the public spending on the one hand and the individual's responsibility on the other. In considering the more detailed regulations of a scheme, the Commission suggested splitting the costs of long-term care between living costs (food, clothing, heating amenities, etc.), housing costs (the equivalent of rent, mortgage payments and local 'Council Tax') and personal care (the additional costs of being looked after due to frailty or disability). The Commission further said that the elderly in need should be responsible for living and housing costs (both should be subject to a contributory payment according to means) and that the State should pay for personal care after assessment and according to need. The Commission justified the priority of public payments for personal care by saying that "these are the costs which unpredictably and through no fault of their own, old people have to incur when unfortunately they can no longer be looked after at home or cannot be sent home after hospital treatment. They reflect the true risk and 'catastrophic' nature of needing long-term care. In our judgement it is right for the State to exempt personal care from means testing altogether. This is our key recommendation" (Royal Commission on Long-term Care, 1999, Para. 6.32). On funding, the recommendation of the Commission is that the scheme should be paid from general taxation on a 'pay-as-you-go' system (Royal Commission on Long-term Care, 1999).

So far there has been a cautious reaction to the Commission's report, frequently explained by the fact that long-term care for the elderly is a complex issue. However, as Henwood (1999) said, "in the absence of an immediate endorsement from the Government, there is some concern that further procrastination will mean that the proposals stand little chance of being adopted prior to the next General Election, or that some of the cheaper options might be adopted which would ameliorate the situation but would not deal with the fundamental question of respective rights and responsibilities" (p. 25).

8.5 Assessment and options for reform of the current domiciliary long-term care scheme

8.5.1 General description

The following sections present an assessment of the domiciliary long-term care scheme in the UK. In addition, options for reform are discussed. The data to hand have been empirically verified and were obtained from semi-structured interviews with experts in the field (See Appendix B). These included scientific experts and experts with a practical background whereby the latter predominantly consisted of persons representing service provision and persons representing possible funders of long-term care. The main focus of this discussion is on services provided by the local authorities. In addition the most important cash benefits for the disabled elderly and their caring relatives ('Attendance Allowance' - 'AA' and 'Invalid Care Allowance' 'ICA') are included in the analysis. As in the previous descriptive part of this country-report, the established research questions set out in the 'Methodology Chapter' guide the structure of the following sections.

8.5.2 Assessment and options for reform of the responsible institutions

As explained by an interviewee with a practical background, the main responsibility for domiciliary care (See 8.3.2) services in kind is with local authorities 'Social Service Departments' ('SSD'). They have responsibility for funding and purchasing and since the mid 1990s have become less responsible for actual provision. Responsibility for this is mainly in the hands of private organisations. At the same time the health authorities have responsibility for all health care, including, for example, nursing care provided at home. A national government department, since recently the 'Department for Work and Pensions', is responsible for administering the 'AA' and the 'ICA' which are both available in cash. In addition, a disabled elderly person may be entitled to a range of income-related benefits which are likewise administered at the departmental level. Another expert noted that there is a quite considerable market of long-term care services that are directly purchased by elderly people themselves.

The existing complexity of responsible institutions for individual long-term care benefits and services has been criticised by different experts. An interviewee with a practical background declared

> *it is known that a lot of people do not claim benefits to which they are entitled because they do not know about them, because they are too proud to go through the scheme or because they just do not know how to get into it.*

Other experts argued that it is actually very difficult for those concerned to find out what types of benefits and services are available for them and who is responsible. People often find it hard to get a broad picture of the different institutions which could perhaps provide some kind of benefit or service. Furthermore, while applying for the individual types of provision, people quite often have to cope with varying bureaucratic authorities and complex application forms.

As illustrated by an expert with a practical background,

> *there are instances where an elderly person for example may be provided with 70% of personal care which is the responsibility of the local authority 'Social Service Departments' (e.g. washing and dressing) and with 30% of nursing care at home (e.g. giving injections) that is the responsibility of the 'National Health Service'. Apart from a few experimental projects, there is not necessarily very good cooperation or communication between the health and local authority personnel.*

A scientific interviewee said that elderly people often obtain help from a variety of authorities. Frequently there is no authority which co-ordinates the different types of help. This leads to scrappy provision with negative results for those concerned. As further argued, the different responsibilities in service provision make it extremely difficult to offer a service package which actually suits an elderly person's needs. Another interviewee pointed out that the overall resources provided for elderly people in need of long-term care could be used much more efficient by better co-ordination.

Another issue discussed in this connection is the assessment of an elderly person's needs. For long-term care services available at local level, assessment is usually carried out by a social worker from the 'Social Service Department'.

As explained by an interviewee with a practical background

> *elderly people, for example, are usually in need of care as soon as they are discharged from hospital. There are instances where this works well and elderly persons have their care package when they come out of hospital but experience shows that it does not work for a lot of people. There is not necessarily very good collaboration or communication between the hospital and the local authorities. It is also quite common that elderly people are living in a community and have increasing care needs and therefore want an assessment to be made by the local authorities. The good practice here is that a local authority social worker comes and assesses the personal care needs and if the social worker sees that there are needs which are not being covered they should get the health authorities involved (this means a multi-disciplinary assessment is made). Equally, if an elderly person with personal care needs goes to a local 'GP` he or she will often direct the patient to the 'SSD` but the 'GP` may also ask for a district nurse, for example to look at nursing care needs, and then there should be some co-ordination between the two. However, this does not always happen and there is very little co-ordination in some areas. In addition, there can also be a 'disaster` in that the family may have to wait a very long time for a basic care package to be arranged and this can lead to extreme hardship for the family. There is often a long waiting list for assessment, depending on the place of residence. Local authorities have levels of risks and if, for example, an elderly person is living alone he or she will usually get a quicker examination, but if a family member is caring for the person in need, local authorities quite often argue that the applicant is at a lower risk and this means that they will not come immediately (without considering what might happen with the informal carer in the meantime) and it can take months, even years, in some areas to get an assessment.*

Other experts emphasised the benefits of a single assessment which applies to domiciliary long-term care and health care services if this is carried out by a multi-disciplinary team of experts (e.g. one or more health professionals, social workers and specialists in other fields). It was argued that if there is a need for both types of help, collaboration between responsible authorities in assessing an elderly person's need should lead to more efficiency and may ensure that those concerned get a co-ordinated care package. In addition, it should be possible to prevent superfluous repetition in assessing a particular person through different authorities. It was further stated that the goal of an assessment should be to focus on the person who needs help more than on the authority who pays for the service. The experts also noted that such single assessments are currently by no means common across the country. However, different interviewees were confident that a single assessment will become the norm across the country rather than experimentally. Their optimism is chiefly based on the 'National Service Framework for Older People' that was published in 2001 and includes the single assessment process as a key guide-line for 'NHS' bodies and local authorities which has to be enforced by April 2002.

An interviewee with a practical background said it would be worth thinking about transferring cash benefits available under the responsible national department ('AA' and 'ICA') to the local authorities as the concentration of the available long-term care provision on one single authority could make things more straightforward for those concerned and could lead to savings by dispensing with one bureaucratic procedure. However, other experts contradicted this. For example, an interviewee with a practical background argued

> *the difficulty in doing that would be to ensure that the money was actually spent on the things for which it is intended. It could be very difficult to make sure that money is actually going where it supposed to, when transferring the responsibility for the 'AA' and 'ICA' to the local authorities, if it is not specifically earmarked. Although there are complications in having two parallel schemes, people at least do know that one deals with money and one deals with services and there may be some logic in keeping them separate. The main point is that there are huge risks that the money could 'evaporate' if the local authorities have unrestricted responsibility.*

Another interviewee expected that if cash benefits were to move to the control of the local authorities it is likely that central government would cut resources that are available, e.g. in the same way as with housing benefits in the 1980s. In addition, it appears possible that local authorities would use the money in different ways and this would lead to inequity among those concerned.

As an expert with a practical background said, another problem exists in connection with the fact that most of the provision of long-term care is contracted out to private organisations. This expert remarked

> *often the carers of private organisations are not well trained. Many elderly people have to cope with a lot of different carers and this lack of consistency can be particularly confusing for persons suffering from dementia.*

Another interviewee said

> *the great problem at the moment is the recruitment of care workers who are badly paid and whose social rights are very limited. Pay is especially low in the private sector and working conditions are poor. Local authorities are looking for the cheapest possible (mainly private) service provider and, elderly people usually have no choice between the providers.*

A scientific interviewee recommended the provision of domiciliary long-term care by a mixture of public, private and voluntary, non-profit providers. This quasi-market structure may help to ensure that elderly persons in need can make a choice, keep the costs of care at a reasonable level and maintain the quality of care while retaining the option to co-ordinate services.

In this matter, another scientific expert recognised favourable trends where service providers were concerned and said

> *there is some evidence that the various domiciliary care services have meanwhile developed to such an extent that they can provide quite intensive support for people in their own homes whereas 5 years ago these people had no option but to go into institution - there is some evidence that there is now a greater diversity of domiciliary care services and they are better able to cope with people with more serious disability. This would mean that older people who are much more dependent could stay at home longer.*

As explained by a scientific expert, in order to widen the choice of services and service providers for elderly persons and to be able to offer a service package according to individuals needs, special attention was given to care management, mainly under the overriding responsibility of the local authorities. There has been good experience over the years with services that are paid for from the care managers' own organisation, mainly the local authority. However, if an elderly person is in need of services that are not paid for by the local authority, e.g. nursing care at home which is funded by the 'NHS', the care manager in most cases is not able to co-ordinate the assessment procedure and the approved services. Another scientific interviewee added that only in some experimental areas has the care manager the power to make spending decisions for nursing care services at home in addition to personal care and home-making assistance services.

In the recent past there have been increasing moves by the government to deal with the difficulties arising from the unsatisfactory co-ordination of different services an elderly person may need. In the year 1999, for example, a 'Health Act' was put in effect which includes partnership arrangements to give the 'NHS' authorities and the local authorities the flexibility to be able to effectively improve service provision. These arrangements are intended to break down barriers between the health and local authorities and provide for flexibility in three ways: pooled budgets, lead commissioning and, integrated provision. Local authorities and 'Health Authorities' or 'Primary Care Trusts' may be partners in such an agreement. As explained by a scientific interviewee, pooled budgets provide the option for the participating partners to gather resources into a fund to pay for different types of health and local authority services that are a part of the fund agreement. There are no national regulations about how much money each partner puts in the pool. This is based on the local partnership arrangement and could mean, for example, that half comes from the local authority and half from the health authorities. Another expert noted that, depending on the local agreement arrived at, local administration staff might, for example, be given the authority to make decisions on the provision of nursing care if this is paid for out of the pool. With regard to commissioning from one source, this expert explained it means that a range of services which have to be specified by the local partners in the arrangement will be ordered (commissioned) from a single point. This, for instance, would enable the commissioning of personal care and nursing care to be brought together. Finally, with regard to the third possible area of coordination - integrated provision - the expert stated that there could be one institution (e.g. a local authority or a 'Primary Care Trust') that, for instance, basically provides health and domiciliary long-term care services. These integrated providers could directly deliver all services themselves or cooperate with other providers (e.g. private organisations) for contracting out certain services. As illustrated by an interviewee, at the end of the year 2001, 62 local authorities were making use of this flexibility. Of these 62, only 22 are using it for services relating to elderly people.

Several interviewees welcomed the partnership arrangements in principle. As stated by a scientific expert,

> *the advantage is of course that these arrangements offer the opportunity for collaboration between health and local authorities in a way that has not been done before. They offer sufficient flexibility and if there is a willingness to act at the local level they can lead to integration between the health authorities and those responsible for social care.*

However, the expert also drew attention to some weak points in these arrangements. He said

> *the main disadvantage is that they are non-directive and leave the decision to take action to local initiative and this is highly undesirable. The problems this brings have been clearly revealed by research. One would, therefore, hope for some form of directive which encourages action. There is too much room for interpretation. In particular there is no timetable specifying that co-ordination at the local level has to be implemented and it is left very much up to local initiatives. In one sense, this approach reflects a desire to act democratically but it also means that the problems arising from poor co-ordination are not taken as seriously as they might be if there were a directive to take action from the central government.*

Another interviewee concluded

> *the relatively low number of participating authorities shows that there are still major problems or barriers in trying to bring the 'NHS' institutions and local authorities together. For example, local authorities are looked at and judged by central government based on criteria different from those applied to health authorities. It was also said that there are differences in how and at what times these different institutions acquire resources. This makes it difficult to pool budgets. In addition, there are problems within the organisations as well, particularly in transferring staff to the integrated provider organisation, because the 'NHS' and local authorities have different conditions of service, different pension schemes and so it is difficult sometimes to persuade staff to accept a change.*

As explained by an expert representing a possible funder of long-term care, in the next stage of this development of partnership arrangements between the 'NHS' and local authorities, new organisations, so-called 'Care Trusts', are currently being considered and will enable a still closer co-ordination and integration of services. From April 2002 onwards, it will be possible to establish such a trust and, as said by an interviewee with a practical background, politicians expect to see these new organisational structures operating widely by 2005. It is most likely that the new 'Care Trusts' will be formed by a 'Primary Care Trust' and a local authority. It is the local partners who are authorized to define the individual services which will be included in the service provided by these trusts. An expert with a scientific background said that it is far from settled what services will be included in those provided by such a new 'Care Trust'. There is, for example, one administrative area where a trust will be created that provides mental health provision for elderly people and learning disability services and, in a neighbouring authority there are plans that a 'Primary Care Trust' joins with the 'SSD' of the local authority, which means that a whole range of service provision will be available.

A number of experts generally welcomed this next step of improving the integration and co-ordination of health and local authority services. There were, however, some interviewees who pointed to various uncertainties with regard to the new 'Care Trusts'. As argued by an expert with a scientific background,

> *there currently exist artificial barriers between health- and social care organisations and it makes little sense to the user of a service (the elderly person) to distinguish between health and social care. What matters is the nature and quality of the service provided. There are huge advantages in bringing together health and social care. As with collaboration between the 'NHS' and local authorities, the danger and potential disadvantage of these new organisational structures is, in particular, the fact that there is no compulsion to create a 'Care Trust'. There is an injunction to collaborate but no compulsion and I would much rather see a stronger injunction for local authorities and health services to work together to break down any potential barriers, so that there is joint training, joint initiatives and so on. One must also say that a very high degree of sensitivity is required in bringing cultures and traditions together, and that creating the necessary structures is an extremely sensitive management task. Consequently problems may arise through a lack of adequately trained managers for such partnerships. There are always difficulties in joining health and social services because the latter are part of the democratic structure whereas the health service is governed centrally. Caution must therefore be exercised in considering legitimacy and democratic accountability. These problems are not insurmountable, however, and it is essential that the health service and local authorities join together.*

An interviewee with a practical background said, on the one hand, the new 'Care Trusts' would make the scheme clearer and more coherent. On the other hand, she feared that within the framework of providing services within these new 'Care Trusts', domiciliary long-term care would play second fiddle to the concerns of health services.

One expert was in favour of transferring the domiciliary long-term care services from the control of the local authorities to the health authorities.

Others opposed this by arguing that it would be very difficult to come to such agreements at the local level. The better and more acceptable way at the local level would be to create a new organisation, i.e. a 'Care Trust', into which the health service and the local authorities each brought certain types of services.

8.5.3 Assessment and options for reform of the eligibility criteria

In contrast to the cash benefits available from a national department where very clear eligibility criteria are used to decide if an elderly person is entitled to provision, the domiciliary long-term care services available from the 'SSD' of the local authorities are normally granted without reference to any national guidelines (See 8.3.2). Several experts criticized this lack of national eligibility criteria for access to care at the local level. An interviewee with a practical background argued

> *the big difficulty currently is that there are no national eligibility criteria. I would prefer national criteria because I think the current scheme is so inequitable. People in different parts of the country with very similar needs can get very different services or indeed no service at all, depending on local criteria. There are huge variations between local authorities and it does not seem justified that people should get a different service just because they live in different places. This is often called the 'post code lottery'. There is also controversy about the extent to which eligibility criteria take account, not so much of people's needs, but of the budget that is available to the local authority.*

Another expert representing the service provision of long-term care stressed the necessity for national eligibility criteria to give those concerned a clear picture of what they may expect from the scheme and what not. It was also said there has been a noticeable tendency in many local authorities over recent years to make the eligibility criteria more stringent. This means that it is very possible that elderly people who would have been entitled to service provision five or ten years ago are now receiving nothing. Here, a practical expert stated

> *considering eligibility criteria, over the last 10 years or so, there has been a move towards focussing on people whose needs are greatest and this certainly makes sense since it is clear that people with the greatest needs should get most help. On the other hand, however, much less attention has been paid to people with a lower level of needs for whom help might, however, be important to prevent further deterioration. It is hoped the government has now recognised that*

not giving early support to such people will quite often lead to much greater need further down the road. It is hoped the government will try to change this situation and to emphasise the importance of early intervention, prevention and support but it will be very difficult to achieve this in practice.

Another interviewee with a scientific background added that it will hardly be possible to say to what extent available resources will need to go into a long-term care scheme until clear eligibility criteria have been established on a national basis.

A number of experts mentioned that the government is now pointing at different ways of establishing national eligibility criteria. The 'National Service Framework for Older People' not only includes the single assessment process as a key guide-line, it also provides local authorities with a broad framework for determining eligibility criteria to be used in this process. This, however, does not mean that there will be binding national recommendations as to what particular tools should be used for an assessment at the local level. It will remain in the hands of the local authorities to determine their criteria of eligibility within the given framework. There were experts who welcomed these trends as a step in the right direction. It was said that given the different needs elderly people have it would be less advisable to use a particular set of tools for assessing long-term care needs. It is very likely that such national criteria would not be comprehensive enough and may well lead to disregarding some specific need an elderly person has. In contrast to this opinion, other interviewees regretted that the 'National Service Framework for Older People' only includes a framework and no clear directions regarding the eligibility criteria. As put forward by an expert with a practical background

it is not satisfactory that the government has not said what criteria should be employed at the local level to arrive at an assessment. The government recommends making an assessment within a framework which allows local authorities to use whatever tools they wish. This lack of uniformity means that different answers will be arrived at in different places. I think we're quite uncertain in the UK about using assessment instruments. Certainly other countries have gone much further down that road. Of course, one needs to be cautious when attempting to establish national criteria and it will be necessary to arrive at a compromise between what is desirable and what is affordable. It is unlikely that an assessment instrument will be found that provides perfect answers, but it is certainly possible to ask the right kind of questions and indicate the kinds of activities that are relevant.

Another expert representing a service provider stated that the new framework regarding eligibility still leaves a lot of freedom for local authorities to interpret what the government is suggesting regarding eligibility criteria and this will inevitably lead to variations and inequity across the country. A lot of the people concerned would prefer a fixed standard assessment with equal rights, disregarding where the handicapped person lives.

In addition to assessing an elderly person's needs a 'means test' is applied - usually without taking into account the value of the home in which the person in need lives - in order to establish the person's entitlement to support from public funds and thus to determine what contribution the individual should make. As emphasised by an interviewee with a practical background, huge variations exist in the charging arrangements between local authorities and there are no binding national guide-lines. In some cases, the amount to be paid is fixed according to capital assets and income and in other cases is based on income alone. There are also cases where each person in need has to pay the same charge without considering his or her means. As was further said, in most instances only those disabled elderly with a very low income are entitled to extensive, publicly-funded long-term care services. In many cases, people with moderate means have to pay the costs of long-term care in full. In many local authorities people with capital above € 25,670 (£ 16,000) are not entitled to publicly-funded domiciliary long-term care services. Another problem arising from the variations in the means test was mentioned by one scientific expert. She pointed out that people often have no idea about the contribution expected from them and this contributes to uncertainty and a feeling that they are being treated unfairly.

There was very little support from the interviewees for the view that those in need should pay the whole cost of care themselves if their means were adequate, but a range of experts supported means testing in some form. As suggested by an interviewee with a practical background, if people have to make contributions for services based on their means, the amount should be determined by applying national criteria, with no possibility for local authorities to opt out of the scheme. Inequity across the country is simply not acceptable. Other experts were likewise in favour of a uniform and consistent approach to the determination of an elderly person means, but differed with regard to the ways of achieving this. Very generally, it was proposed that a means test should be devised which is more generous than the one currently applied at the local level. More concretely, it was recommended that the lowest level of private capital resources and income, below which no consideration is given to means, should be raised. As further recommended, another option would be to raise the upper limit, as applied by local authorities, above which people are not entitled to any publicly-funded care provision. Another option would be to provide people with means above a certain upper limit with a comparatively low minimum amount of publicly-funded care and make a charge for the rest of service provision so that no-one is completely excluded on the basis of a means test. The latter approach, for example, was found interesting by one scientific expert, who argued

> *a universal scheme that in principle excludes no one but includes charging for different people is very important in terms of demonstrating commitment to the values of social solidarity, and citizenship and inclusiveness for the elderly generation. There should be a scheme that includes everyone but it is unrealistic to have a universal scheme under which no-one is charged at all. The question is how the commitment to values of social solidarity and inclusiveness are to be reconciled.*

In contrast to this, other experts were prepared to dispense with the means test for domiciliary long-term care or do away with the means test for personal care, as proposed by the 'Royal Commission on Long-term Care'. These experts in general agreed with the justification of this view offered by the Commission. It was pointed out, for example, that an elderly person suffering from heart disease or cancer is provided with mainly free public provision through the 'NHS' but elderly people who suffer from dementia may be entitled to little or no public support, although having a similar need of care. As further said, there is no legitimacy in making a distinction between individual diseases when considering the provision of support from public funds. It is simply not equitable that people pay for one type of care and do not have to pay for another. One expert with a scientific background was also in favour of the commission's proposal to draw a line between the costs of personal care and health care (paid by the 'NHS') on the one hand - both of which should be available free of charge - and, on the other hand, the cost of care which does not normally have to do with the body of a dependent elderly person. In this connection, it was, for example, recommended that the cost of home-making assistance should be the responsibility of the individuals and be provided according to a means test. Other interviewees questioned this distinction between personal care and home-making assistance. In this matter, an interviewee with a scientific background urged

> *one should be very cautious in creating new and artificial boundaries between different aspects of domiciliary care. The needs of an elderly person are often complex and we need to be careful to avoid concentrating only on aspects of personal care. Elderly people often do not make a distinction between personal care needs and home-making assistance. Their conception of care needs often went beyond*

washing, bathing and toilet use, help with washing or with general supervision. The approach of the 'Commission' involves boundaries. It will involve saying something like personal care counts and other things do not. The example of people with mental health problems ('dementia') who may have other central areas of need in addition to personal care needs shows that we have to be careful in establishing what is paid for and what is not.

Some experts mentioned that Scotland decided to accept the recommendations of the Royal Commission and so will cut out the means test for personal care. However, because of difficulties in funding free personal care, it has just announced a delay in their implementation.

Finally, different interviewees commented on the fact that, in the past, local authorities quite often did not support those disabled elderly people who had a relative who cared for them. As emphasized by an expert working for an organisation which provided care

it is very unfair that elderly people who have the support of a family carer are often not considered for the receipt of publicly-funded services simply because they have a caring relative. People with caring families frequently get no support and the obvious assumption of the state that help from the family is automatically forthcoming often leads to difficult circumstances for both the carer, who may actually have no real choice, and the elderly person in need.

This point is further discussed in the following section on types of provision.

8.5.4 Assessment and options for reform of the type and amount of provision - benefits and services

With regard to benefits and services available for disabled elderly (See 8.3.3) several experts first of all pointed very generally to the low average levels of provision and restricted service options for those affected. As noted by an interviewee working for an institution that provided long-term care,

the benefits and services available do not even come close to equating with the long-term care which the individual often needs and must pay for.

Another expert with a practical background said

> *the current level of provision is completely insufficient. The level of benefits and services should be higher and should be provided more generously. In particular, the way in which services are 'rationed' has nothing to do with needs. We need to put far more into long term care at the local level than has so far been the case. The government should direct its attention to the development of home-based services in preference to residential care. If it is intended to do this effectively a lot more has to go into making the support viable because, at the moment, few people get the amount of provision that they need to be able to continue living in the community.*

The only benefit paid to the disabled elderly which is not related to their income and capital is the 'AA'. Again, different interviewees stressed the comparatively low amount of the 'AA' which at most amounts to € 85.91 (£ 53.55) a week. A scientific interviewee stressed another problem connected with this benefit by saying

> *the 'AA' itself is very ambiguous because it was always intended to be a contribution towards the extra costs (e.g. higher housing costs) of being disabled and was not necessarily intended to pay for care or attendance. In fact, many local authorities assume that the 'AA' is to go towards the costs of care so that a person who is receiving domiciliary care is frequently charged more for these services because the 'AA' is paid . . . This leads to problems for different people, for example it leads to the problems of how to meet the extra costs you might have because you are old and cannot get around so well (e.g. you have extra heating and similar costs).*

Looking at the services provided by local authorities, the very low level of publicly-funded support for most elderly people in need was again criticised by a number of experts. It was said that many people get no support at all (for example, persons with modest means) while others get little support and have to pay very high charges for the services available. Over recent years there has been an increasing public support only for some poor elderly people with very considerable needs. As remarked by an interviewee with a practical background, the absence of an adequate domiciliary service provision which would enable an elderly person to remain at home or would provide support after returning home from hospital has resulted in several cases to the person concerned being admitted to a home offering residential care although from the standpoint of the patient, it would have been much more desirable to be provided with adequate services which allowed him or her to remain at home.

One scientific expert mentioned another aspect. He argued that even relatively poor people could not be sure of receiving public support when they need it. There is no guarantee that the provision which currently exists at local level will be available when a particular individual needs it. As further pointed out, it is simply not possible for individuals to know what type of state support they can rely on and what they are expected to pay for themselves.

In order to improve the unsatisfactory situation of service provision at local level, the 'Royal Commission on Long-term Care' suggested that personal care should be free of charge and made available according to elderly persons' needs. A range of experts agreed with the Commission's proposal. As put forward by a scientific expert, this approach very clearly defines the responsibility of the state on the one hand for personal care and the responsibility, on the other hand, of the individuals for all other types of help needed. An interviewee representing a service provider said making personal care free would alleviate the situation of numbers of elderly people who live in poverty as a result of having to pay for long-term care privately and would also reduce the present complexity of charging for personal care throughout the country. Another expert with a practical background said, free personal care would do away with the inequalities and injustice currently resulting from differences in the provision of publicly-funded services nationwide.

There were, however, other interviewees who opposed the Commission's proposal. As argued by a scientific interviewee,

> *the provision of unlimited care would be wonderful in an 'ideal world'. This, however, only considers one half of the problem. It ignores the fact that it would lead to uncontrolled expenditure in a world of limited public resources.*

Another expert likewise underlined the necessity of limiting long-term care benefits and services. Free personal care according to need would be an unrealistic proposal. The goal should rather be to have clearly fixed benefits and services on a national basis which enable the individual to understand what the state is going to provide in the case of need and, therefore, to be able to make arrangements for any service which may have to be paid for from other sources. The aim here should be to arrive at a well-balanced amount of public support. This should, on the one hand, ease the financial burden to the extent that having to pay for care is no longer likely to reduce the individual concerned to poverty and, on the other hand should avoid too great a drain on the public resources which are needed to pay for long-term care as a whole.

The next expert feared that if personal care were to be provided free and other types of care charged for, this would not, in practice, be helpful in terms of providing elderly persons with an adequate care package. One can assume that it would instead lead to more boundaries and make coordination between artificially separated types of service provision (e.g. between personal care and home-making assistance) difficult. A scientific expert said one would have to be very careful in defining the type of care for which public support is, or is not, to be provided since persons with certain types of need, for example, persons with dementia, could otherwise quite easily be at a disadvantage.

Another scientific expert claimed the main beneficiaries of free personal care would be the well-off and their families, at the expense of poorer people. In addition, if the state provided free personal care for all it would probably mean that not enough resources were left to pay for other needs. Public resources should first of all be used for those with the most needs. This expert further stated that it seemed very likely that making personal care free would also lead to increased expectations of higher standards in service provision and of a broader range of services, both leading to higher expenditure for which available resources were not adequate.

The support for informal carers has been discussed as a further main aspect of service provision. Several experts firstly pointed to the 'ICA', a benefit which is not related to income and capital and which may be paid to people who are unable to go to work because they care for a disabled elderly person. In general, the interviewees were of the opinion that this type of support for informal carers is very poor. An interviewee representing the service provision of care said

> *the benefit is very low and people have to provide a minimum of care. Those, for example, providing 25 hours get nothing . . . The 'ICA' is not a benefit to the carer for providing care. It is an income replacement benefit that recognises the fact that the carer cannot work full time and that is quite a different thing.*

The interviewee further said that at local level most authorities do not offer the option for a person in need to choose benefits in cash instead of services in kind. Those who arrange or have to arrange their own care on an informal basis are generally at a disadvantage, as in most cases they get no support from the 'SSD'. Local authorities basically have the power to provide elderly people with cash benefits instead of services in kind, but only very few do so. An expert with a practical background stressed that many informal carers do not choose to take on the responsibility of looking after the disabled relative, they have no real choice. Some carers may prefer to do it but others may do it because there is no-one else to look after the mother or husband. The other point to be made is that if an elderly person has the support of an informal carer, he or she frequently does not get much support from the local authorities because there is a daughter, daughter-in-law or spouse who does the work.

Another interviewee with a practical background pointed towards social changes such as the increasing proportion of women in the labour market and the decrease of extended family structures. These aspects, in combination with demographic changes, are leading to a situation where, in the future, one will no longer be able to take it for granted that there will be an informal carer to support his or her elderly relative in need of long-term care. The expert further stated it is important to keep the balance between care provided by the family and care by formal organisations and so to maintain a choice for those concerned to choose from different options of service provision. It is therefore urgently necessary to offer public support for informal care on the same basis as for formal care. The expert further said it should be possible for those in need to arrange their care 'package` according to individual circumstances. This could for example mean that in cases where the person in need prefers to be cared for by an informal carer instead of being supported by a formal service provider and there is a relative willing to do this work, the local authority would support those concerned with cash benefits instead of paying for services carried out by a formal provider. In addition, the expert emphasised the necessity to offer social protection benefits for carers, e.g. in the sector of pensions, for informal carers who do not have regular paid employment because of their responsibility for their disabled relative. One scientific expert suggested considering the option of providing formal care in the event that the informal carer is temporarily unable to provide care, e.g. because of a holiday or illness.

Several interviewees mentioned that by April 2002, it will be mandatory for local authorities to provide 'direct payments` instead of services in kind to those who request this. As stated by an expert with a scientific background, this is a first step in the right direction since it gives more choice to those concerned. 'Direct payments` are, however, a substitute for services in kind and available according to the same means test. This indicates that only a few elderly people will be in a position to choose this option.

8.5.5 Assessment and options for reform of the funding

With regard to the funding arrangements for long-term care (See 8.3.4), the main interest during the interviews was initially on services provided by the 'SSD` of the local authorities. The local authorities pay for their long-term care services mainly from central government allocations. In addition, local taxation and charging are the two other essential sources of funding. As noted by an interviewee with a practical background,

> *with regard to the allocations from central government there are no binding guidelines which say that a certain percentage of the money has to be spent on domiciliary long-term care services. The allocations are not hypothecated, not ear-marked but are included in a grant total to be used for several services. Local authority (local politicians) have discretion if, for example, they want to spend less on elderly people and more on education.*

The expert further said that the uncertain flow of resources makes it very difficult to judge how much money is spent on long-term care at the local level. Another interviewee mentioned the fact that the resources that local authorities spend on providing services for the disabled elderly citizens vary across the country. A major problem is that poorer authorities have greater problems in raising the resources. Therefore, the amount of long-term care support provided depends on where elderly people lived.

Although it is not clear how much money goes on the provision of long-term care, not only at the local level but also at national level, where there is no evidence what benefits are really spent on the disabled elderly, a range of experts were prepared to say that the UK long-term care scheme is under-funded. It was also said that costs should be paid out of some sort of national scheme because of the problems and the inequity for those concerned as long as the responsibility for funding long-term care is in the hands of local authorities. However, there was disagreement among the interviewees as to what such a national scheme should look like.

As stated by an interviewee with a practical background, a 'capital-resourced' funding scheme ('pre-funding') would be worth considering. The entitlement in one generation would be built up years in advance through payments into a fund out of which future long-term care benefits and services would be paid for. Savings would ensure a higher profit for the scheme from the contributions paid than would be the case in a 'pay-as-you-go' scheme. In addition, it was argued that a 'capital-resourced' funding scheme would be less susceptible to the influence of demographic changes. Other experts rejected the option of establishing such a funding scheme for long-term care. A major reservation was that it would mean that one (the current) generation was paying twice. One interviewee representing a possible funder of care explained that 'pre-funding' meant that reserves would be built up for the next thirty or more years before services have to be paid for or those in need have become aware that they are entitled to the provision of long-term care. This means that to ensure the provision of care for those currently in need, people would have to spend money (e.g. through taxation) in addition to the contributions to the pre-funding scheme for thirty years or more. The same expert put forward another aspect. He said the uncertainty about people's physical and mental condition in 30 years or more, as well as the lack of clarity about the type of service provision (e.g. it is very difficult to give details about the informal care potential available in the future), make it extremely difficult to predict the amount of money that will be needed to pay for the long-term care of elderly people. This means it would also be a huge problem to fix the contribution rate for a 'pre-funded' scheme at a suitable level.

A range of interviewees were in favour of funding long-term care on a 'pay-as-you-go' basis, which could mean either that the current costs are paid from current social insurance contributions, current hypothecated taxes or current general taxes. It was stressed that this could be introduced as from today and all elderly people could be entitled to a certain amount of service provision right at the outset. Some experts were prepared to say it should be a social insurance scheme. However, as admitted by one of these experts

> *ideally the risk associated with long-term care should be spread by funding it from social insurance. However, as Britain does not have such a well-established tradition of social insurance as is found in some other EU countries, it probably makes more sense here to add it to taxation.*

Other interviewees said they were in favour of a long-term care scheme funded through hypothecated taxation. As emphasized by an expert with a practical background,

> *although people obviously do not like paying tax, they raise fewer objections if they can see the connection between what they are paying and what they are getting. There might be a greater acceptance of paying into a specific fund and knowing how much money is in the fund, rather than paying into a general pot of taxation. That is a major attraction of hypothecated tax. It is, for example, possible to say the 'extra penny' on tax goes to long-term care for the elderly. Hypothecated tax is something we haven't really gone into in this country and I think it might be worth exploring further.*

As stated by another interviewee with a practical background, it appears unlikely that the public will accept paying some extra money into a general fund where they fear that it may be used for some other type of public expenditure. If there is a scheme where people know exactly that the money they pay goes into a special fund for long-term care, then they are more prepared to accept these extra costs. The interviewee further said that to fund the provision of long-term care in an equitable way, a scheme on the one hand has to spread the risk across the whole population, meaning that everybody has to pay on a compulsory basis and, on the other hand, has to ensure that everyone is entitled to some kind of service provision in the case of need. As finally said, to meet these requirements, one could either fund long-term care through social insurance or hypothecated taxation.

An interviewee with a scientific background limited the benefits of funding the provision of long-term care from 'hypothecated taxation`. He argued

> *in principle I do not disagree with hypothecated taxation except once you start doing it then every special interest argues in favour it and it could end up with most of the tax paid being hypothecated.*

Another expert representing a potential funder of long-term care said that hypothecated taxation would lead to bureaucratic obstacles and undesirable restrictions on budget allocation. The two latter experts further suggested that general taxation best fits into the current UK system of social protection and is economical from an administrative point of view.

As a final consideration, different interviewees expressed doubts about funding the risk of long-term care through private insurance. An expert with a practical background argued that premiums in a private insurance policy would be related to different risks such as the risks associated with age and gender. This, for example, means that the premiums for those aged 60 and above would be higher than for those aged 30. In addition, women would have to pay higher premiums because of the higher risk of their needing long-term care. The expert further said that private insurance would not necessarily help the poorest people since, though not having enough money at their disposal, they generally have to pay at least the same premiums as the better off. A scientific interviewee put forward another aspect. She said the risk of being in need of benefit is far away in the future and young people are more attracted by the idea of spending their money than in covering the risk of needing long-term care. In addition, as women are in greater danger of needing long-term care, their premiums would be higher, although it is a well-known fact that they earn less than men. This means that it is not very probable that women could afford a market solution. The likelihood that the private insurance market does not offer a suitable solution for covering the risk of long-term care is also obvious when considering the slow growth of this sector. In this matter, an interviewee with a practical background concluded

> *under the current Labour government, private insurance is very unlikely to be a popular idea to pursue. People making provisions for their own long-term care needs with private insurance arrangements remain very few in number at the moment. Something like 30,000 long-term care insurance policies have been sold in this country and this total is very small. People who have the money to afford it are often not the ones who are most likely to need the care. If we would like to see this as an alternative scheme there would need to be far more incentives to adopt this course than there are at the moment. It is not a route that I would particularly favour but it is another one that could be considered. The last government, the Conservative government, was interested in private insurance and in partnership schemes. They would have liked to move towards such private insurance on a compulsory basis. Proposal were made including the incentive that every pound of whatever amount people paid into the scheme would be matched by a corresponding amount from the government. So there were real incentives but the scheme never got beyond the consultation stage.*

8.6 Summary

The present Chapter has discussed domiciliary long-term care provision in the UK, with the emphasis primarily on the arrangements in England. The main goal at first was to offer a descriptive overview of the scheme with regard to the responsible institutions, the eligibility criteria, the type of service provision and the type of funding. Based on this, an empirically supported assessment, including options for reform on these aspects was given. In addition to the main areas of interest, a descriptive outline of the UK social protections system was offered. It has been shown that the system is mainly funded from general taxation. In addition, 'National Insurance' ('NI') contributions are paid for obtaining entitlement to different cash benefits. The majority of the different cash benefits (e.g. 'Basic State Retirement Pension', 'Jobseekers Allowance', 'Income Support', 'Housing Benefit', 'War Pensions', etc.) are available under the 'Department of Social Security'. Probably the most important provision available in kind is a comprehensive public health support which is provided by the 'National Health Service' ('NHS') and is largely free of charge at the point of use. In addition, other different services administered by local authorities are available (e.g. domiciliary long-term care services, services for children, etc.). Finally, future developments have been considered, the focus of attention being on the recommendations of a 'Royal Commission on Long-term Care'. The main proposal of the Commission is that personal care should be provided free of charge according to need and be funded out of general taxation. So far, there has been a cautious reaction to this proposal from the government.

In considering the institutions responsible for the provision of domiciliary long-term care, the services available in kind are funded and purchased by the 'Social Service Departments' ('SSD') of local authorities. The main bulk of publicly-funded care is provided by private organisations. The administrative responsibility for cash transfers (i.e. 'AA' and 'ICA') is in the hands of the responsible government department. As observed in the empirical examination, the existing complexity of responsible institutions makes it difficult for the individual to find out where to go when in need. Another difficulty arises when an elderly person is in need of health services (e.g. nursing care) which are a 'NHS' responsibility in addition to domiciliary long-term care services. Frequently, the co-ordination between these two different sectors is very bad and this makes it hardly possible to tailor a service package for an elderly person which actually suits his or her needs. A further weakness appears to be the assessment process. It can be a very long time until an elderly person is assessed by the local authorities and the length of the waiting period frequently depends on a person's place of residence and social environment. In addition, the assessment process in most cases is solely carried out on the basis of the need for domiciliary care. It would appear appropriate to have a single assessment which applies to domiciliary long-term care as well as health care services. A single assessment should be carried out by a multi-disciplinary team of experts. This type of joint working in assessing an elderly persons need should lead to more efficiency and may ensure that those concerned get a co-ordinated care package. With regard to service providers, the analysis has shown that it might be useful to have a balanced mixture of public, private and voluntary, non-profit providers. Recently the Government's responses to the unsatisfactory co-ordination of different services an elderly person may need seems to be moving towards an improvement in the situation. In this matter, partnership arrangements between health and local authorities, that may include flexibility in the pooling of budget resources, lead commissioning and integrated provision, may be helpful in breaking down existing barriers between the two sectors. A disadvantage of this flexibility might seem to be that it is non-directive, that is, it is optional and dependent on local initiatives, this leaving a lot of room for interpretation. The relatively low number of local authorities participating so far may underline the fact that there are still difficulties at local level in using the flexibility as suggested by the government. As a next stage in this evolution of partnership arrangements between the 'NHS' and local authorities, a new organisation, so-called 'Care Trusts', is currently under discussion and it is hoped that this will promote a still closer co-ordination and integration of services. This proposed new organisational structure includes big difficulties which would still have to be overcome. For example, there is no suggestion that it would be compulsory. Bringing together health- and domiciliary care institutions and the bringing together of different institutional cultures and traditions, which the creation of such a new structure would mean, would require a high degree of sensitivity at local level that might be difficult to achieve. However, it seems to be the right direction to go in an attempt to improve the integration and co-ordination of health and local authority services.

With regard to the cash benefits available at the departmental level, very clear and nationwide uniform eligibility criteria are used to assess an elderly person's entitlement to provision. In contrast to this, domiciliary long-term care services available from the 'SSD' of the local authorities are normally granted without reference to national guidelines. The empirical discussion has shown that this is a questionable approach. There are enormous variations among local authorities in the ways of assessing an elderly person's needs. This has lead to a situation where people in different parts of the country with very similar needs may get very different services or indeed no service at all, depending on local criteria. The Government has recently provided local authorities with a broad framework for determining eligibility criteria. This, however, does not mean that there will be binding national recommendations of particular tools to be used for the local assessment. On the one hand, therefore, it initially leaves room for local interpretation and inequity but, on the other hand, it should offer the possibility of observing how successfully the individual eligibility criteria would be used at local level within the given framework. With the experiences gained from the local level in this way, it may be possible, in a further step, to arrive at equitable nationwide uniform eligibility criteria. In addition to the needs of an elderly person, a means test is the other major factor in assessing entitlement to publicly-funded long-term care services at local level and in determining the amount of the charge the individual has to pay. Again, there are very great variations between local authorities. The proposal of the 'Royal Commission on Long-term Care' to do away with the means test for personal care seems to be a possible option and is perhaps also justifiable, particularly when considering that health care is mainly free at the point of use. The question remains, however, whether this proposal is fundable and whether new boundaries might be created and inequity caused when personal care is provided free of charge whereas other types of care (such as home-making assistance) - which some disabled elderly people may particularly need - are not. An alternative option to this would seem to be the introduction of a more generous, nationwide uniform means test for domiciliary long-term care. This should initially exclude no one from service provision, but should include the establishment of fixed charges raised according to an elderly person's income and capital resources.

As the discussion has shown, the diversity in available long-term care benefits and services makes it difficult for those concerned to be aware of the type of provision that may be available. The most important cash benefit which is granted to disabled elderly without considering their income and capital is the 'AA'. For those who are unable to go to work, the 'ICA' may be available. Both the 'AA' and the 'ICA' have in common that they are relatively low and normally insufficient to represent adequate support for those concerned. Looking at the services available at the local authority level, the empirical analysis has made it clear that the support in general is very poor and many people get no support at all. In order to improve this unsatisfactory situation, the 'Royal Commission on Long-term Care' suggested that personal care should be available according to the elderly person's needs. Although this proposal seems to be helpful for elderly people, one has to ask how such unlimited provision could be financed. An alternative to the Commission's proposal could be to have well-balanced and limited service provision on a national basis which, on the one hand, eases the burden of payment for the individual and, on the other hand, keeps public long-term care expenditure at a fundable level. In addition to the currently low levels of service provision, a further need for reform exists with regard to those who make their own provision on an informal basis. As was shown, such persons largely get no local support at all and this means that they would be penalised by the scheme. It seems to be advisable that local authorities should in future be obliged to offer a person in need the option of choosing between benefits in cash ('Direct payments') and services in kind.

In the funding arrangements for the long-term care scheme, the different cash benefits are mainly paid out of general taxation. The local authorities particularly fund their services from central government allocations, other money largely coming from local taxation and charging. However, the central government allocations are provided as part of a total grant to be used for different services and there are no binding regulations that would oblige the local authorities to use a fixed part of the total for long-term care. As highlighted in the empirical analysis, there are very large variations in the amount of money local authorities spend on providing services for disabled elderly citizens and there is no data indicating how much public money is really spent on long-term care. Nevertheless, it seems obvious that the scheme is under-funded. As the empirical discussion of different options for bringing more money into the scheme has illustrated, some form of 'pay-as-you-go' scheme offers, on balance, the best way of funding long-term care. Funding the provision of long-term care from general taxation is an approach which would fit well in the current scheme of paying for social protection and would allow the government certain flexibility in budgeting. In addition hypothecated taxation is another option worth considering. It would enable the individual to see clearly what he or she may expect in return and may therefore lead to comparatively broad public acceptance.

9 Discussion of cross-national findings

9.1 Introduction

In Part I of this study it was shown that EU domiciliary long-term care schemes are currently confronted with common difficulties which have put pressure on the existing arrangements they were not designed to deal with. This mainly includes a combination of social, demographic, and macro-economic developments. As can be derived from the country reports of France, Germany and the United Kingdom, the common problems have lead to a range of broadly similar themes and priorities in public discussion in these countries where long-term care provision for the elderly is concerned. These are as follows:

- The boundaries and poor co-ordination between long-term care and health care provision including unsatisfactory assessment procedures and consequences for the nature of both types of benefits and services;
- The respective rules for public, private and voluntary, non-profit providers and shifts in shares of the market;
- The form that criteria to be used for assessing an elderly person's need might take and, to what extent income (and capital) of the applicant should be considered within the evaluation procedure;
- The amount of public provision, and the type of help for which benefits and services are granted;
- The forms of support for those who arrange care on an informal basis; and
- The search for the best way of funding arrangements for covering the risk of long-term care.

The countries studied have responded to these themes and priorities in public discussion with initiatives in several areas. Evidence from the country-reports suggests that in only a few these areas are similar directions being followed in dealing with common pressures. The majority of responses to similar problems among the countries are marked by diversity. For a synopsis of the main ways countries empirically studied (i.e. France, Germany and the UK) currently organise and fund their domiciliary long-term care arrangements, please see Table 24 below (p. 227-228). To some extent, the existing diversity seems explicable by differences in the countries' traditional approach to welfare state organisation which have predominantly emerged out of a mix of several contextual factors (e.g. a country's history, economic circumstances, legislative basis, violent events, cross-national influences, type of government and the relative influence of stakeholders or even cultural and religious values). On the other hand, there are several instances where the approaches adopted do not necessarily appear to be in accordance with strong traditions, but rather driven by other (e.g. financial) considerations. This suggests it is no longer automatically possible to assign the previous models of regime types (Compare Chapter 4) to current welfare state orientation where long-term care is concerned. New models appear to arise which take into account the pressures of demographic trends, social changes, macro-economic difficulties, and so on. These welfare state changes will be further discussed in Chapter 10.

However, the variety of domiciliary long-term care arrangements between individual countries in response to common pressures and themes in public policy discussion inevitably poses questions about the advantages and disadvantages of the different solutions chosen. While not ignoring welfare state traditions, this Chapter intends to explore a range of policy strategies for the future provision of long-term care by analysing and synthesizing evidence from the countries empirically studied and combining these findings with the extremely limited amount of scientific literature published. For assessing the advantages and disadvantages of long-term care arrangements, the criteria of 'efficiency' and 'equity' will serve as an evaluation framework (Compare, for more details, Chapter 5, pp. 86-87) for what is going to be testable according to the data at hand. As within the three country-reports, the present Chapter is structured systematically in applying the formulated research questions.

Table 24 Overview of long-term care arrangements in France, Germany, and the UK

Countries	France[1]	Germany	United Kingdom
Responsible institutions			
Main administrations	Regional authorities (Departments)	Long-term care funds	Local authority provision: 'Social Services Departments' ('SSD') of the local authorities; Nat. governm. provision: 'Department of Social Security'
Assessment procedure	Assessment by medico-social teams of experts (i.e. physicians and social workers) which work on behalf of the departments	Assessment by qualified nurses or physicians who work on behalf of the medical services of the health insurance funds	Local authority provision: Assessment by asocial workers (and sometimes additionally, physicians) who work on behalf of the local authorities; Nat. governm. provision: Assessment by adjudication officers who work on behalf of the national 'Department of Social Security' (and sometimes, additionally, physicians)
Main types of formal service provider	Private bodies	Private bodies	Private bodies
Eligibility criteria			
Criteria for assessing care needs	Standardised instrument ('AGGIR')	Standardised instrument ('P-ADL'- and 'I-ADL'-scale)	Local authority provision: Individually-based procedure; Nat. governm. provision: Standardised instrument
Consideration of the economic situation of the applicant	'PSD' scheme: Consideration of income and heir whose legacy exceeds € 45,735; 'APA' scheme: Consideration of income	No consideration of income and capital	Local authority provision: Consideration of income and capital (without taking into account the applicant's own house); Nat. governm. provision: No consideration of income and capital

[1] In France, in the year 2002, the so-called 'Allocation Personnallisée d'Autonomie' ('APA') scheme will replace the provision under the 'Prestation Spécifique Dépendance' ('PSD') scheme.

Table 24 cont.

Type and amount of provision - benefits and services			
Types of main benefits and services	Services provided in kind	Services provided in kind or cash or a combination of both	Local authority provision: Services mainly provided in kind; Nat. governm. provision: Benefits provided in cash ('Attendance Allowance' - 'AA')
Amount of main benefits and services	'PSD' scheme: € 518 monthly (on average); 'APA' scheme: Care degree I: Up to € 1,067 monthly, Care degree II: Up to € 915 monthly, Care degree III: Up to € 686 monthly, Care degree IV: Up to € 457 monthly	Care degree 1: € 383 (kind) or € 205 (cash) monthly, Care degree 2: € 920 (kind) or € 409 (cash) monthly, Care degree 3: € 1,432 (kind) or € 665 (cash) monthly	Local authority provision: 5.8 hours weekly (on average); Nat. governm. provision: Higher rate: € 85.91 weekly, Lower rate: € 57.44 weekly
Additional support for informal care	No support for informal care	Pension insurance contributions and accident insurance cover, substitute care, if the informal carer is on holiday or ill for up to 4 weeks, day- or night care	Local authority provision: Predominantly no support for informal care; Nat. governm. provision: 'Invalid Care Allowance' ('ICA'): € 35.80 weekly (on average)
Funding			
Main source of funding	Taxation	Equal contributions by employers and employees	Taxation
Co-payments (Charges)	'PSD' scheme: No (direct) co-payments but public provision usually does not represent a sufficient coverage; 'APA' scheme: Co-payments between 0 and 80% according to income	No co-payments but public provision often does not represent a full cove-rage	Local authority provision: Different amount of charges depending on the individual authorities; Nat. governm. provision: No co-payments

Source: References of Chapters 6, 7 and 8

9.2 Discussion of the responsible institutions

Irrespective of the existing diversity of administrative responsibility in the countries studied empirically, a common feature is that the provision of domiciliary long-term care in each scheme is the responsibility of institutions other than those providing health care. Evidence shows that this separation between long-term care and health care provision (e.g. nursing care at home and rehabilitation) is likely to lead to serious problems and inefficient use of resources. This is mainly owing to the fact that many elderly people have complex problems which frequently means they are in need of both types of provision and these are often poorly co-ordinated.

Evidence shows that even in Germany where there is quite a close relationship between health and long-term care funds, serious difficulties arise in providing elderly people with adequate and co-ordinated services. For example, an important problem is that institutions responsible for assessing an elderly person's need of long-term care benefits and services, often do not give adequate attention to the question of rehabilitation (paid for out of the health care scheme). In addition, as Schmähl (1999) has said, German health insurance funds which are actually responsible for paying for rehabilitation as well, often do not meet their obligations in such cases. As the advantages of rehabilitation could initially be more beneficial to the long-term care funds (which, if the rehabilitation is successful, may well have to pay lower benefits and services) than to the health care funds, it appears likely that this tendency to do nothing is based on the fear of cost-shifting. Data at hand from France and the UK likewise emphasises that existing differences in assessment procedures and accountability for individual services are leading to serious problems of co-ordination and joint working between the different institutions involved in service provision. As already realised in an earlier cross-national study on domiciliary long-term care schemes by Jamieson (1991), the boundaries and poor co-ordination between health and long-term care services often lead to gaps in the forms of help provided for elderly people. In addition, it may also lead to the building up of 'double-structures'. Another study dealing with the improvement of efficiency in the provision of social protection for elderly people by Davies (1994) carried out for the OECD has found that individual services a disabled elderly person may require are too inflexible in their responses to the complexity of needs, often do not focus on the real needs of individuals and those who care for them and failure to co-ordinate different services makes the whole system inefficient. As explained within a WHO study on health care reform by Saltman and Figueras (1997), the motivation behind the separation between different services a disabled elderly person may need often is based on cost-pressures. While health care provision is mainly free of charge, domiciliary long-term care services are often subject to some kind of cost sharing and thus become a case of the replacement of public provision by private market or family sector finance.

Although it is possible to understand the motivation (i.e. in particular to relieve financial pressure on health care administrations by shifting the responsibility to provide personal care and home-making assistance to other institutions) (Compare Glendinning, 1998) behind such policies leading to a division of the responsibilities for providing health care on the one hand and domiciliary long-term care on the other, it is equally possible to see the difficulties that emerge out of such arrangements in terms of providing co-ordinated and therefore efficient services for elderly people in need. Given the above-illustrated problems at hand leading to inefficient use of public resources, it is also possible to argue that the need for better co-ordination, or even integration of different services an elderly person may need and therefore using available resources more efficiently is obvious. It seems, however, that in the recent past, different countries have paid increased attention to improving this unsatisfactory situation. A study by Glendinning (1998) compared new developments in long-term care for elderly people on a cross-national basis and found that the move to develop integrated budgets is obvious, for example, in Denmark and Finland. Here, the budgets of local authorities cover both primary health care, nursing care at home and domiciliary long-term care provision. As experience from these countries shows, this in turn has facilitated the development of an improved co-ordination of different services for elderly people. Other countries, however, (e.g. Australia and the Netherlands), have also initiated approaches to overcoming the problems at hand (Glendinning, 1998). Likewise, in the countries empirically studied, there meanwhile has been an increasing attempt to improve efficiency in service provision.

The recent initiatives in the UK in particular, appear to offer a range of strategies for overcoming existing barriers between health and local authorities and therefore for improving efficiency in service provision for disabled elderly people. One measure has been the creation of partnership arrangements, mainly requiring three forms of flexibility that are likely to offer certain possibilities for the institutions involved. Firstly, pooled budgets give the chance of gathering resources into a fund to pay for certain services (e.g. personal care, nursing care at home and rehabilitation) that are part of the agreement. Secondly, the local partners may commission a range of services from a single point and thirdly, with integrated provision, it is possible that one institution provides a range of services, e.g. personal care and nursing care. The detailed implementation of these flexible arrangements depends on the local partners and, so far, only a relatively small number of local authorities are adopting these arrangements. This slowness in the implementation of suitable measures suggests that it is likely that the problems arising from poor co-ordination will be better dealt with if there is more direction and there is a timetable from central government behind such partnership arrangements.

Nevertheless, first experiences with these partnership arrangements in the UK suggest that if there is a concerted local effort to take action, the available flexible arrangements are likely to overcome problems arising from poor co-ordination and improve efficiency. For example, evidence indicates that the new flexible arrangements enable and motivate the responsible authorities to use the available resources for services much more efficiently. On the one hand, administrations are able to offer a well co-ordinated 'service package' which suits the elderly person's needs, on the other hand it remains hardly feasible to shift responsibilities for individual types of services between different budgets (costs), commissioners and providers. This also means the new programme seems useful in terms of limiting the risks of overlapping and superfluous services, gaps in service provision and disagreements between health and local authorities about controversial borderline cases. In addition, experience suggests that there could be huge benefits in terms of dealing with changes in an elderly person's need if the responsibility for commissioning and providing is in the hand of one leading authority.

A further step in the evolution of partnership arrangements currently planned in the UK to overcome the failure to co-ordinate and the resulting inefficiency, will be the option of introducing a new organisational structure (a so-called 'Care Trust'). Here, it will again be the local partners who are entitled to define what services are to be included in a 'Care Trust'. By offering the possibility of integrating health and local authority (e.g. domiciliary long-term care) services, it is expected that the introduction of 'Care Trusts' will facilitate an even closer co-ordination and integration of the different services an elderly person may need. In a report by the scrutiny panel guiding the development of one out of four national 'Care Trust' demonstrator sites for mental health in the UK (London Borough of Camden, 2002), it is argued that the new organisational structure would allow more efficient performance management of services provided for disabled elderly. Another key advantage would be that the establishment of a single point of entry for people in need should lead to continuing improvement in services provision. This should also prevent people in need from falling through the net between different sectors and services. In addition, it is hoped that the new organisation will promote the provision of better tailored and integrated care for people in need and will allow managers to take a more flexible approach to users of different kinds of services.

However, although the introduction of such a new organisational structure as intended in the UK seems to offer a range of opportunities to use available public resources more efficiently, the approach of integrating different health and local authority services in general appears to represent a big challenge for countries that are willing to do this. Evidence from the countries empirically studied suggests that it is generally difficult for agreement to be reached between health and local authorities. A very high degree of sensitivity is needed to bring together two separate authorities. If, as in the UK, no compulsion exists and there is no timetable and no binding framework provided by the national government for the creation of such integrated organisations, it appears even more difficult to break down the existing barriers. In addition, taking into account the history of the relationship between long-term care and health care services in different countries, one will need to be careful that long-term care services do not take a back seat to the concerns of the health services when provision is the responsibility of a new integrated trust (Compare Jamieson, 1991). Nevertheless, if there is commitment on the part of local partners, it appears possible to get the potential risks under control and therefore to benefit from the possibilities of integrated health and long-term care services.

There are, however, schemes (i.e. countries with social insurance-based sickness arrangements) in which it does not appear practicable to create partnership arrangements as well as integrated health and local (regional) authority services as illustrated above. Therefore, other approaches to improve efficiency in terms of service co-ordination are required is such countries. For example, in France, domiciliary long-term care services are currently the responsibility of regional institutions. In contrast, health care services are administered within the framework of social insurance. As noted above, there are significant problems in terms of co-ordinating 'mixed' provision from both types of institutions. The joint working between health authorities and regional administrations responsible for long-term care services in general is characterised by inefficient proceedings and there is an obvious need to improve this unsatisfactory situation. However, overcoming the existing barriers by, for instance, pooled budgets, lead commissioning and integrated provision, as suggested for countries with tax-funded sickness schemes, scarcely appears possible. People covered by insurance-based health care schemes usually have to pay contributions and on this basis, they acquire entitlement to certain types of benefits and services. In contrast, domiciliary long-term care services are the responsibility of regional administrations and are mainly funded from different types of taxation. This means that domiciliary long-term care and health care services are organised (funded) by two schemes with fundamental differences and this, for instance, makes it hardly possible to pool budgets. Based on empirical evidence from France and Germany, in countries with a social insurance based welfare state tradition, instead of arranging the provision of domiciliary long-term care at the local (regional) public authority level, administering long-term care provision within the existing framework of insurance-based schemes (e.g. for health care and pensions) would seem to be the more beneficial approach in terms of improving the co-ordination of the different types of services.

As long-term care is mainly required following illness, one obvious approach to the provision of insurance-based long-term care benefits and services is to include these in health insurance. Another option, as adopted in Germany, is to introduce separate long-term care funds alongside other sectors, but with the work of such funds being carried out by the health funds which at the same time act as health insurance funds and long-term care funds. Both approaches have in common that they would seem to support the efficient use of resources both in terms of administering the provision of long-term care and collecting contributions, since no new bureaucratic measures have to be implemented. In contrast to the first approach, the latter means that long-term care benefits and services would be provided quasi within an independent scheme, therefore, making it possible to determine exactly the relationship between the amount and type of care provided (output) on the one hand and the level of expenditure on the scheme (input) on the other. This in turn would make it easier to ascertain and to control expenditure on long-term care provision. In addition, either approach would help to eliminate the inefficiencies arising from poor co-ordination of the different services an elderly person may need, even though empirical evidence from Germany indicates that integrated health- and long-term care provision is likely to bring some advantages, compared with separate long-term care funds, in that it would limit the risks involved in simply transferring the responsibility from one sector to the other. However, data from both France and Germany shows that existing health insurance funds are currently experiencing serious financial difficulties. Therefore, an integrated approach includes the risk that contributions actually intended to cover the risk of long-term care are used to pay for health care services. In addition, from a service provision point of view as well as from a funding point of view, there is further justification for introducing a separate long-term care scheme instead of including the provision in an existing health care scheme. For example, an important factor in controlling costs for separate German long-term care insurance is that the contribution rate is fixed by law. It would have been difficult to organise this if the contribution for long-term care insurance had been included in general health insurance, the rate of contributions for which varies among the individual funds. On balance, introducing a separate long-term care insurance scheme alongside other forms of social insurance currently appears more advisable. However, if there was an improvement in countries with a long-established social insurance tradition of controlling health expenditure, joining the health and long-term care sectors could be considered in the future.

Partnership arrangements, integrated organisations and long-term care funds alongside other social schemes may all offer certain possibilities in terms of improving efficiency while co-ordinating domiciliary long-term care and health care services. These approaches alone, however, appear to be insufficient. As noted above, a further field in which efforts appear to be necessary is the procedure for assessing elderly persons' care needs. As the empirical experience obtained in the country studies indicates, there are too many instances in which assessments are limited to personal care and home-making assistance needs without taking into consideration any other types of help needed that are closely connected. For example, evidence shows that although the disabled elderly quite often require complex types of help, including an obvious need for rehabilitation, nursing care and encouragement in fighting against their disability, long-term care need assessments frequently do not consider this. There are instances where the needs for help required in addition to personal care and home-making assistance, are separately assessed by the responsible administrative body, but there are also cases in which, for example, the need for rehabilitation is simply not assessed at all nor is help with rehabilitation provided.

In the light of the above, the need for a single assessment approach that applies to both domiciliary long-term care and health services is obvious and, as experience from single pilot projects in the countries studied shows, the benefits could be enormous. In particular, it could lead to more efficiency in the use of administrative resources and would, as one may assume, obviate unnecessary repetition in the assessment of a particular person by different institutions. As an additional aspect, it appears advisable for the assessment to be made by a multi-disciplinary team of experts. Depending on the individual case, this team could include one or more health professionals, a social worker, and specialists in other fields. As Evers (1998) has found, the fact that doctors hold such a strong position in the assessing of an elderly person's entitlement to benefits and services from the German long-term care scheme and social workers have no role at all, contributes in general to the condition that needs such as general supervision and guidance are given only limited consideration within the 'service package' an elderly person receives. There can be no objections to a single assessment in terms of a country's welfare state orientation. A single assessment, which, for instance, has recently been introduced in the Netherlands (Rostgaard and Fridberg, 1998), appears to be a useful approach where tax-funded and social insurance schemes are concerned.

A further common priority in public discussion in the countries which have been involved in the empirical investigations of this study, is the type of service providers. Evidence from the country reports suggests that the global tendency is that private (in some areas voluntary, non-profit) providers have increasingly assumed the dominant role, as opposed to public (in some regions voluntary, non-profit) authorities, in the provision of domiciliary long-term care services and relatively competitive care markets have developed in several regions of the countries studied. Responsibility for regulating those markets is mainly in the hands of the public authorities (long-term care funds in Germany). As Glendinning (1998) has found, market mechanisms increase the opportunities for maximising the quantity or quality of output for a certain amount of expenditure, or for driving down the costs of achieving a given amount of output. As evidence from Germany shows, the development of competitive care markets also has a useful impact on old traditions where support for elderly people is concerned. Traditional service providers, who in the past scarcely had to cope with competition, are now being forced to make improvements, for example, in terms of economic efficiency. Another aspect is that market mechanisms that are working well at a national level are likely to counteract (especially horizontal) inequities since elderly people with the same needs may then have equal access to different providers spread over wider geographical areas, irrespective of where they live. In particular, experience from France shows some consequences of a restricted market. Here, disabled elderly people in different regions are not able to choose as only one provider is available. In the worst case, frequently in rural regions, there is sometimes simply no formal provider at all. This means that access to service providers in such cases is highly influenced by the place of residence. A useful approach to increasing the supply for those in need would be to simplify the regulations governing contracts for providers of publicly financed services and to establish transparent and reasonable reimbursement agreements so that more potential carers (organisations) are encouraged to enter the market. Knapp and Hardy and Forder (2001) who studied domiciliary long-term care markets in England argued the challenge for responsible administrations is to arrive at the right kind of competition between providers in order to generate improvement in quality, increase freedom of choice and to reduce prices. In other words, the goal should be to prevent a situation arising in which service provision is in the hands of only a few organisations which fulfil acceptance requirements and, given the existing purchasing arrangements, acquire the resources to sustain quality.

In contrast to the above-illustrated opportunities, a relatively competitive domiciliary long-term care market also involves certain risks, however, which may undermine equity. In Germany, for example, where by law preference is given to private and voluntary, non-profit providers as against public providers, the development of a 'quasi' market in many regions has unfortunately led to a situation where increasingly dubious service providers (particularly private organisations) have entered the care sector. Problems with such providers are also illustrated in the UK report. As evidence from both countries suggests, the carers in the organisations concerned are often not well trained and many elderly people have to cope with many different carers. This lack of consistency might in particular confuse people who suffer from dementia. In addition, as Whitehead (1994) has found, market approaches include the risk that providers who place particular emphasis on financial gain may give less attention to or phase out elderly people who need services that are less profitable. This is likely to lead to (in particular, vertical) inequities among elderly persons in need. Glendinning (1998) emphasised that 'quasi' markets in long-term care increase the difficulties with the coherence and co-ordination of services. In particular, problems of co-ordinating different services and risks of fragmentation in a market approach have, for instance, in Denmark and in the Netherlands lead to the exercise of considerable caution in developing 'mixed economies' of domiciliary long-term care. In addition, contracting out of certain types of help while others are carried out by public providers has also been opposed as this is likely to limit the possibilities of responding adequately and promptly to changes in an elderly person's needs. Therefore, in these countries, private and voluntary, non-profit organisations have been encouraged only to a very limited extent to enter into competition with public providers (Glendinning, 1998). In addition, experience from the countries empirically studied suggests that when elderly people have complex needs leading to the necessity of co-ordinating different types of provision, the situation is in general more complicated if private organisations are involved.

It is, indeed, not easy to find a balance between possibilities and limitations of a 'quasi' market in providing domiciliary long-term care and to reach the most efficient and equitable approaches. A useful way appears the one chosen in Australia. Here, domiciliary long-term care is traditionally provided by a balanced mix of private, voluntary, non-profit and public organisation, without giving preference to any of the three possibilities (Fine, 1998). This mix appears a useful way of generating improvements in efficiency in dealing with care markets as well as guaranteeing an elderly person's right to choose between different suppliers and preventing a standard care procedure being implemented without the possibility of exercising choice and, on the other hand, of limiting problems in the co-ordination of the different services an elderly person may receive, such problems being more likely to occur if private organisations are involved in the provision alongside public institutions. In addition as the evidence of market mechanisms in Germany shows, there needs to be a national framework of regulation and quality standards, as well as supervision of the services by the institutions responsible for administering the long-term care scheme. Public authorities should not award contracts to those service providers who do not fulfil the necessary requirements. As Knapp, Hardy and Forder (2001) have argued, it is however necessary to ensure that resources needed just for supervising and keeping such 'quasi' long-term care markets working do not exceed the benefit they bring.

9.3 Discussion of the eligibility criteria

The question that first emerges when considering the criteria used for looking at an elderly person's needs and, based on these, making decisions about the provision of benefits and services, is whether equity is better served if each elderly person's eligibility for care provision is based on an individual examination or on a national set of standardised criteria. As the empirical investigation has revealed there are, of course, justifications for both approaches.

A major argument for looking at each person in need individually is that because of the different kinds of needs an elderly person can have, it hardly appears possible to have a particular set of tools on the basis of which long-term requirements can be assessed and adequate care provided. In other words, any set of fixed national criteria incorporates the risk of not being comprehensive enough, of overlooking a specific need an elderly person may have and would therefore lead to inequity. Another important argument is that leaving the assessment decision at the local level enables the responsible administrations to consider local circumstances during this procedure.

However, experience with individually based assessments are by no means convincing. In contrast, evidence of local authority provision in the UK, where available provision is usually limited, shows that the lack of national eligibility criteria is leading to huge vertical and, in particular horizontal, inequities across the country. Services for persons with very similar needs often differ from one region to another or there is perhaps no service at all, depending on local criteria. There are also indications that in some areas the orientation of eligibility criteria is not predominantly based on people's needs, but is strongly influenced by the budget available to the local authority. This means the provision available largely depends on where the person in need lives.

The advocates of standardised eligibility criteria argue that a well-balanced and uniform national instrument counteracts the inequities referred to above. Individually based assessments would only be a real alternative in schemes where provision is available to a large proportion of the elderly population according to need and is not restricted by budget considerations. Scharf and Wenger (1995) who examined perspectives for domiciliary long-term care by looking at different countries, argued that, faced by increasingly difficult tensions between growing long-term care needs and available public resources, it is necessary to define clearly the goals and entitlements which can be met and the priorities which should be accorded to them. It was further said that if the provision of long-term care benefits and services has to be in accordance with certain priorities and therefore has to be limited, it is necessary to identify these priorities clearly. Standardised criteria on a national basis appear to be the most suitable instrument for fixing and guaranteeing such priorities.

However, empirical evidence of the use of national instruments in France and Germany suggests that it is quite difficult to arrive at criteria which are well-balanced and useful for the improvement of equity in the provision of long-term care. The instrument used in the French scheme ('AGGIR') is criticised mainly because while it certainly provides detailed information about elderly persons' state of health, it does not help in establishing the kind and/or extent of help they need. A further main weak point of the instrument is that it is a quite complicated scale which leads to incomprehensible assessment procedures for those concerned. The main weak point of the instrument used in Germany is that it predominantly focuses on the care an elderly person requires in the areas of bodily cleaning activities, nourishment-related activities, mobility-related activities and home-making activities. That type of general supervision, looking after and guiding the person, which is connected with the above-mentioned activities is also considered within the scheme, but that part of general supervision and care which has nothing to do with these activities and might be particularly important for disabled persons with dementia has remained disregarded thus far. As experience from Germany shows, the predominant orientation towards physically-related needs in the eligibility criteria leads to obvious (vertical) inequities where dealing with persons suffering from various types of dementia. As a consequence, there are people with dementia who are not entitled to any benefits at all, as they do not even fulfil the criteria for the lowest degree of care, whereas some who are in fact entitled to provision have to cope with considerable inequities regarding the extent of the provision. As argued by the Joseph Rowntree Foundation (1996) which was looking at options for covering the costs of long-term care in the UK, fixing standardised assessment tools at a national level is not a straightforward task and one has to be sensitive to the needs of different individuals.

Taking into consideration the limited public resources available in EU countries it is clear, however, that a domiciliary long-term care scheme cannot have eligibility criteria which cover almost all individual needs. In addition, a very comprehensive instrument is likely to come into conflict with other objectives such as transparency and efficiency. Therefore, the main goal when establishing national criteria that offer a basis for equal access for equal needs and unequal amounts of care for unequal needs should be to avoid obvious disadvantages for elderly people with certain conditions and to arrive at a balance between what is desirable and affordable. It is unlikely that an assessment instrument that provides perfect answers will be found but it should be possible to ask the right kind of questions and indicate the kind of task where help is required. Difficulties experienced with national instruments both in France and Germany show the need for further research in this field. The starting point for such studies could be the approach put forward in the German country report which is to extend the existing eligibility criteria by elements that consider the particular help required by people with dementia. This could be implemented by giving the need for general supervision and attention certain extra daily time values in addition to the help required in performing activities of daily life. One may then consider this extra time value within the framework of assessing disability and classifying those concerned within different degrees of care. In addition, the findings of a scientific commission that is currently reviewing the instrument used in France should also be considered in further research. Finally, experience in the UK at local level within the recently provided broad national framework should be useful in gathering further information on how successfully different eligibility criteria are being used in practice.

In addition to the aim of ensuring equity, the criteria that are used for looking at an elderly person's need are also relevant in terms of achieving efficiency. Here, evidence from the country studies again points to the advantages of a uniform approach. In particular, standardised criteria seem to be useful for providing a clear idea of what may be available from a long-term care scheme. This not only seems helpful indeed for those concerned, but also supports responsible bodies in calculating the resources needed for a long-term care scheme and keeping expenditure under control. On balance, standardised eligibility criteria on a national basis seem to be the preferable approach both in terms of improving equity and using resources more efficiently.

In addition to assessing an elderly person's needs, the other major question often comes up when assessing entitlement to publicly-funded long-term care benefits and services is whether the applicant's income and capital have to be taken into account. However, there is broad diversity in the ways this is dealt with. For example, as the Royal Commission on Long-term Care (1999) in the UK argued, long-term care, like health care provision, is the right of every citizen. It should therefore be allocated based on need not on wealth. As argued within a study carried out for the OECD (1996a), the existing order of priorities in some countries in providing some degree of income protection during illness appears questionable, particularly when taking into account the potentially catastrophic consequences of long-term care costs for the individuals concerned. In contrast, Eisen (1993) who studied alternative options for the provision of long-term care within a research project focusing on EU countries said that it appears inequitable to provide benefits and services irrespective of the assets of those concerned as such allocation could be regarded as perverse. Österle (1999), who gave consideration to different definitions of the term 'equity' to be used in the comparative analysis of long-term care schemes, likewise suggests means testing as a possible variable to accompany the principle of need.

Not only in existing literature, but also in the EU countries themselves (Compare European Commission, 2000), there is considerable diversity in dealing with means testing. In Germany, where social insurance covers long-term care risks, benefits and services are provided without considering the means of the disabled elderly. In the new French scheme ('APA`), people will no longer be completely excluded on grounds of income, but the scheme includes a co-payment to be made by a beneficiary. This variesbetween 0 and 80% and will be fixed according to the elderly person's income. In the UK, cash benefits available at national level are provided without considering the means of those concerned, but the domiciliary long-term care services available from the local authorities are granted after a means test (usually without taking into account the value of the home in which the person in need lives). Although there are considerable variations among local authorities in applying this test, it can be said in general to be very stringent and excludes many elderly people completely from service provision.

When reviewing evidence from the empirical investigation, several arguments emerge to the effect that a society should shoulder the cost of the provision of long-term care for its elderly inhabitants without taking into consideration an elderly person's means. The major justification for this approach is the difficulty of understanding why, in contrast to elderly people who need medical care and mainly get this type of help free of charge in the countries studied, many of those who require long-term care do not get adequate public support for their needs. It simply seems inequitable when some elderly people have to pay for one type of care while others receive another type of care that is mainly free of charge. For example, experience from the countries studied supplies evidence that many disabled elderly people who suffer from Alzheimer's disease are not entitled to any, or only to very limited, publicly-funded care while those elderly persons with a heart condition or cancer usually get the main bulk of care free. This suggests that a better balance between different types of support is desirable and that long-term care benefits and services should be provided without assessing the means of those in need.

However, taking into account the effects of allocation and in particular the reality of limited public resources in EU countries (Compare European Commission, 2001), one may also argue that it seems questionable or even unrealistic to disregard an elderly person's means when deciding the amount of public support he or she is entitled to. There is more justification for this when one sees that in the EU countries other areas of social protection, e.g. some types of health care provision, are also not entirely free at the point of use for many people. Nevertheless, in schemes which are based on social insurance (e.g. in Germany) where entitlement to benefits and services is mainly acquired by contributions paid into the scheme, the introduction of a general means test would not be a very realistic measure. In contrast, in countries where the provision of domiciliary long-term care is mainly tax-funded (e.g. in the UK), means testing appears to be an option worth considering.

When discussing the use of means testing in allocating domiciliary long-term care provision, this inevitably means that the equity objective which in terms of provision was basically defined as equal access for equal needs, is now accompanied by an economic variable. It is important to note that such an economic variable as the means test should not be looked at in isolation from the needs-related approach; the two items have to be considered in combination (Compare Österle, 1999). If, for example, a scheme exclusively provides benefits and services to those people in need whose assets are below a certain level, this would completely counteract the needs-related equity objective. Evidence from the countries studied suggests that even if means testing is incorporated the long-term care scheme should remain universal and application of the means test should not lead to the complete exclusion of any disabled elderly person from provision simply on the grounds of his or her income and/or capital resources. The non-exclusion of disabled elderly people with higher incomes (and capital) seems useful for ensuring that the needs of all disabled elderly persons are assessed, irrespective of the question whether they should only get reduced benefits and services because of their means. An appropriate plan of care could then be drawn up for them. Another main lesson to be learnt from experience in the countries empirically studied is that when applying a means test, it should be done by using national criteria for charging. This means there should be no possibility for responsible administrative authorities at local or regional level to opt out of the scheme. Inequities observed between local authority provision in the UK and in the French 'PSD' scheme appear to be simply unacceptable. Experience from both countries indicates that the absence of binding national guidelines inevitably leads to variations between different authorities in charging arrangements. This may well result in cases where persons with similar means get very different benefits and services depending on their place of residence.

An additional aspect of means testing which needs to be taken into account is how the individual's financial situation is considered. When deciding on contributions (co-payments) he or she has to make, there may well be inequity. This, for instance, can be seen in the new French long-term care scheme ('APA') where only the income of those in need (without taking non-earning capital into consideration) is considered. Having a means test exclusively based on the income of those in need and not taking into account their capital seems to be a questionable approach as it encourages elderly people to transform some part of their regular income into capital. Therefore, it appears advisable to assess an elderly person's entitlement to public support by using a means test that includes taking account of capital in addition to income. As in the UK, this should, however, be made without taking into account the value of the home in which the person in need lives, as otherwise the basis for domiciliary care would be taken away.

9.4 Discussion of the type and amount of provision - benefits and services

With regard to the provision available for elderly people in need of long-term care, empirical evidence from France, Germany and the UK shows that there is considerable variety among these countries in the exact amount and type of benefits and services. Looking at the EU as a whole, provision in general can be said to be marked by huge differences (Compare European Commission, 2000). Another noticeable aspect is that the amounts and types of benefits and services not only vary among different countries, they may also vary in the country itself. For example, evidence from the French 'PSD' scheme shows that if there are no national guidelines in terms of service provision, and each responsible regional institution has only broad terms of reference for determining publicly-funded long-term care, this may lead to enormous variations in the exact amount of provision granted to a disabled elderly person. There are instances in which some wealthier regions where care for elderly people is very high on the political agenda offer comparatively high levels of support, while others provide only comparatively little help. This means that the absence of national standards is likely to lead to huge horizontal and vertical inequities in terms of the provision a disabled elderly person receives.

In spite of the existing variety in the ways countries provide long-term care benefits and services, a common feature among several EU schemes is that they usually only provide limited coverage and not full provision (Compare European Commission, 2000). In Germany, benefits and services are granted according to standardised rates and on average are the highest among the countries empirically studied, but in most instances are still insufficient to meet the full costs of care. In the UK scheme, national cash benefits are provided on the basis of fixed and limited rates and services available from the local authorities, which vary among the areas, are on average low and many people get no support at all. In France, the new scheme ('APA') that will be in force from 2002 will offer expanded provision compared with the former scheme, but the limited amount of public support is still insufficient to meet the care needs of a disabled elderly person. Particularly those disabled elderly who receive reduced payments following the income test in the new provision have to make high contributions to meet the costs of care.

In terms of the amount of provision, it could, of course, from a disabled elderly person's point of view, first be desirable to have access to unlimited domiciliary long-term care provision on a national basis according to his or her needs. The availability of free provision on a national basis according to need, for example, was suggested for the UK by the Royal Commission on Long-term Care for the area of personal care. In contrast to the Commission's proposal, Joffe and Lipsey (1999) argued that such an approach, however, seems doomed to failure, as it would lead to uncontrollable expenditure and the inefficient use of resources. It was further said that free personal care for those who qualify would bind public resources for a selected area of provision in a way which would make it unlikely that other types of need could be funded. Eisen (1993) found that unlimited public support according to need is more likely to lead to uncontrollable expenditure, instead of minimising the cost of achieving a specified level of care provision. He said that unlimited care would influence the cost of long-term care provision in different cases. For example, it would encourage people to choose more comprehensive (expensive) models of care and promote an increasing overall use of services. In addition, it was argued that unlimited care might well lead to the inequitable allocation of public provision.

As evidence from the country reports suggests, a more suitable approach would seem to be to arrive at a well-balanced amount of clearly fixed national and limited benefits and services. This should on the one hand be useful to ease the burden, for those concerned, of paying for care as well as prevent huge inequities inside a country and on the other hand should facilitate the creation of a cost-control mechanism for public long-term care expenditure. If it is clear what the individual is entitled to from the state, he or she can see what needs to be paid for from other sources. In addition, providing fixed amounts of benefits and services is useful in terms of transparency, a condition that again is likely to promote equity in service provision.

In trying to decide on an appropriate level of public provision, one should also consider carefully the degree of disability for which such support is made available. As experience from the countries studied shows, it is likely that doing nothing in the early stages means that elderly people will in the future be in greater need than would be the case if help were provided earlier. In addition, doing nothing at an early stage may well lead to higher total care costs in the end. This suggests that maximising the quantity and quality of output (care) for a given level of expenditure could best be achieved by providing public support not only for elderly people in extreme need of care, but also for those with less pressing needs.

As noted above, there exists diversity among EU countries not only in the amount of provision, but also in the type of help for which benefits and services are provided. Apart from these differences and priorities in the exact definition of the type of need within the individual schemes, support in several EU countries looked at as a whole is said very generally to focus mainly on the areas of personal care and home-making assistance (Compare Rostgaard and Fridberg 1998; European Commission, 2000). In some countries (e.g. Finland and the Netherlands), the policy has been to encourage better-off elderly people to pay for home-making assistance tasks out of private means (Rostgaard and Fridberg, 1998). In the UK, local authority provision in many areas has in general developed into a personal care service. This tendency seems in accordance with the recommendation by the Royal Commission on Long-term Care (1999) for future arrangements that personal care should be provided free of charge and based on a person's need. In addition to this, it was suggested that all other types of help needed (e.g. home-making assistance) should be the responsibility of the individual. In Germany, provision is mainly orientated towards help in the areas of personal hygiene, feeding, mobility and home-making. General supervision and guidance belong to the help considered within the scheme as far as these aspects are connected with the above activities. In contrast, that part of general supervision and guidance which has nothing to do with these activities has remained disregarded thus far. As evidence from Germany shows, the latter might be particularly important for disabled elderly persons with dementia. Therefore, the limited amount of help available for this type of disability means that the scheme contains considerable inequity for persons with such syndromes. General experience from the countries studied also indicates that the care needs of elderly persons may be very complex. Many elderly people need home-making assistance, general supervision and personal care, among other things, whereas there are many elderly people who need less personal care but, instead, more home-making assistance, general supervision or guidance.

All this suggests that one has to be very careful in defining the type of care for which public resources are provided. Glendinning (1998) noted that cost sharing by focusing on personal care and excluding further types of care from public support fails to fulfil the equity criterion. It generally puts at a disadvantage those disabled elderly who need help which is not publicly provided (e.g. home-making assistance) and, particularly those people who cannot afford other types of help from private means. A study focusing on the relationship between cost-sharing and health status by Rubin and Mendelson (1995) put forward comparable objections about the effects on equity when paying for one particular type of need (e.g. personal care) from public resources. Here, a key finding is that cost sharing between the state and the individual puts the most needy at a disproportionate disadvantage. In addition, Joffe and Lipsey

(1999) fear that free personal care would inevitably lead to increasing demands for this type of support and therefore impose additional long-term care costs on top of those resulting from demographic and social changes.

It is, however, impossible to take into consideration every separate need an elderly person has, but having in mind the importance of general supervision and guidance for the increasing number of people with dementia, in order to avoid such obvious inequities as are present in Germany, it appears necessary to include these types of help in addition to personal care and home-making. This seems even more advisable when looking at the alternatives. If a long-term care scheme excludes one of these types of help from provision, the required service is often not provided at all or comes from another source. However, even the latter approach does not seem to provide a very useful solution. Having in mind the problems of poor co-ordination arising from the separation of health and long-term care services it appears likely that an additional sub-division, while drawing attention to different aspects of long-term care would itself reinforce such inefficient proceedings.

A further leading theme in public discussion in the countries studied is the support for informal care arrangements. Again, there is considerable variety in the ways such arrangements are dealt with by different long-term care schemes. For example, in the UK, an income replacement benefit ('Invalid Care Allowance') is provided for carers by the national government. At local level, the responsible institutions have the power to provide elderly people with cash benefits instead of services in kind, but only very few administrations do so. In Germany, long-term care insurance offers different options for informal care provision. For example, if elderly people in need are themselves able to arrange for adequate personal care and home-making assistance to be provided by family carers, it is possible to opt for (lower) cash benefits as an alternative to (higher) services in kind. In some EU countries, however, long-term care schemes provide virtually no support for informal care (Compare European Commission, 2000). This seems to be based on a complex set of reasons. Empirical evidence, for example, suggests that the usual exclusion from public provision in the French 'PSD' scheme for those who have a spouse or partner who, at least theoretically, is able to look after them, is based on the notion of the family's moral maintenance obligation. The spouse or partner is obliged to provide maintenance without any payment. A completely different view as compared with the French position, however, is held, for example, in Denmark, Finland, Sweden and the Netherlands. Here, the state regards it as its duty to offer public long-term care provision of such a kind as to ensure that the disabled elderly are able to cope without support from their families and relatives who are not required to contribute to the costs of care (Rostgaard and Fridberg, 1998).

There is much empirical evidence suggesting that a long-term care scheme undermines the principle of equity if it puts disabled elderly persons at a disadvantage, simply because there is, for example, a daughter, daughter-in-law, or spouse who could care for them. Those who provide care on an informal basis often do not choose to take on the responsibility of looking after the disabled relative. In contrast, they often have no real choice. There are, on the one hand, instances where relatives prefer to care for disabled elderly people, but on the other hand, there are informal carers who provide support because there is no one else to do it. In addition, as argued within a study dealing with directions in care for elderly people by the OECD (1994b), the willingness of many disabled elderly persons to live with their relatives and to receive care from them appears to be less than the readiness of relatives to provide a place to stay and long-term care. Another major aspect that has to be considered while analysing provision for informal care is the reality of social change. This particularly includes the increasing proportion of women in the labour market and the decrease in extended family structures that can be observed in most parts of the Union. Both factors strongly influence the informal care potential and, in combination with demographic developments, it is expected that these changes will lead to a situation where, in the future, one will no longer be able to take it for granted that there is an informal carer who can provide long-term care (Compare European Commission, 2001). Given this decreasing informal care potential, it appears even more advisable to support and encourage, for example, daughters, daughters-in-law, or spouses who are willing to do this work and give them a real chance.

The main conclusion to be drawn from the above evidence is that long-term care schemes should provide an option for those concerned to receive benefits in cash to arrange their own care, if they wish, rather than be provided with formal services. In other words, the State should provide help and support for those who choose to provide care on an informal basis as well as for those who prefer to be cared by a formal organisation (Compare Joseph Rowntree Foundation, 1996). This approach seems useful for arriving at an appropriate form of social contract and a suitable balance between care provided by the family and care provided by formal organisations (Compare OECD, 1996a). The option of choosing informal care provision instead of formal support is not only important for those who provide the services, it also enables people in need to arrange their care ´package` according to individual circumstances.

As noted above, there is a great diversity in supporting family care across the Union and some long-term care schemes still provide little, or no help at all (Compare European Commission, 2000). However, in the recent past, several countries have given special attention to support for informal care. For example, evidence from the UK shows the endeavour, at national level, to encourage informal care. By April 2002, it will be mandatory for local authorities to provide 'direct payments' instead of services in kind to those who request this. In Germany, the new long-term care insurance offers a range of options to support care provided by the family. Here, an entitled disabled elderly person who prefers to be cared for by an informal carer who is willing to this may opt for cash benefits instead of receiving support by a formal provider. Another alternative is to combine formal with informal care. In addition, in the event that an informal carer is temporarily unable to provide support, for example because of illness or holiday, the scheme covers this eventuality by providing formal care for a certain period. Finally, as informal carers do not usually have regular paid employment because of their responsibility for their disabled relative, the German insurance provides social protection benefits, e.g. for the public pension sector. In the search for options to support the sector of informal care, international attention has also been drawn to labour market regulations in Sweden. Here, it is possible that family carers receive up to thirty days of paid care leave, and for this period can be employed by a local administration as paid workers (Scharf and Wenger, 1995). Another interesting approach has been implemented in Denmark, where for a certain time it is possible to leave a job in order to care for a terminally ill relative (Rostgaard and Fridberg, 1998). In Sweden and Denmark, the amount of payments for family carers on such occasions is approximately in accordance with that of formal carers (Scharf and Wenger, 1995).

A final factor which has emerged from the country studies is that regulations concerning public support frequently virtually inhibit a possible improvement in an elderly person's status in terms of the need of help by providing lower levels of support. The German experience is an interesting illustration of this dilemma. Here, if an elderly person's state of health improves because of good care, it is possible that this person's level of need will be downgraded, for example, from care degree 3 to the lower care degree 2. As a consequence, he or she would only be entitled to lower benefits and when care was provided by a formal organisation, this organisation would likewise receive lower payments from the insurance institution for its services. One way of improving this unsatisfactory and inefficient situation would be to make benchmarks between the individual providers within which the changes in the health of their clients are compared. Those providers comparing favourably with others could then be entitled to additional public payments. Such an approach, for example, has been adopted in Japan where long-term care insurance which has been in force since the year 2000 provides additional incentives for service providers if the disabled elderly person's degree of disability improves (Anonymous, 2001). However, the problem described here not only emerges in the sector of long-term care, but is also a general weak spot in most health care schemes in industrial countries. Therefore, there is an urgent need for research into the dilemma that an improvement in a person's health status is hardly recognized, but rather leads to the inefficient situation where the provider of services is put at a financial disadvantage when the client has a lower need of help.

9.5 Discussion of the funding

There are at least the following four broad options for funding domiciliary long-term care (Compare Wittenberg, Sandhu and Knapp, 2002):

- Family-based funding out of individuals` income and capital (savings);
- Private market-sourced insurance funding;
- Private market-sourced insurance funding with public sector support; and
- Public sector funding.

Looking at the last option of public sector funding independently, this approach itself comprises several further possibilities for covering the costs of long-term care. The basic question to be dealt with there would be whether a public scheme should be based on ′capital-resourced` funding (′Pre-funding`) or on ′pay-as-you-go` funding. A next necessary step would be deciding whether a public sector approach should operate on a local/regional or on a national basis. Finally, it would be necessary to take into account whether the scheme chosen so far has been based either on social insurance contributions, hypothecated taxation, or general taxation.

Starting with the first approach noted above, which is that individuals or families pay for domiciliary long-term care out of their own income and/or capital when such costs occur, there is far-reaching agreement in international literature (See, for example, Royal Commission on Long-term Care, 1999; Wittenberg, Sandhu and Knapp, 2002) that this option fails to achieve efficiency. To be able to pay the often huge and unforeseeable costs of potential long-term care needs out of private means, people would have to save huge amounts of capital during their lifetime. However, even if individuals have certain amounts of capital for this purpose at their disposal, it appears likely that during the process of care, many elderly people nevertheless would become unable to pay these costs. Another aspect is that saving large amounts of money in order to be able to pay for long-term care means that those resources could not be used for other purposes. As only a certain percentage of elderly people require long-term care provision, those who do not need it, would still have saved to counter the risk of age-related disability and would therefore have been prevented from using that money for other things. Therefore, to cover increasing long-term care needs by some sort of risk pooling appears much more efficient than to expect those elderly people unlucky enough to require care at the end of their life to pay for themselves out of their income and/or capital (Wittenberg, Sandhu and Knapp, 2002).

In addition to the inefficiency of this method, paying for the costs of long-term care out of income and capital does not seem to ensure equal resources for equal needs. It would mean that those with greater care needs would usually have to pay for more care out of their private means than those with lower needs (the more healthy). Moreover, it also does not equitably redistribute costs between rich and poor people. Another aspect of inequity is that women, who on average have a higher life expectancy than men and are at higher risk of needing long-term care, would need to save more capital than men (Wittenberg, Sandhu and Knapp, 2002).

In contrast to funding long-term care through individual's income and capital, private market sector insurance (voluntary or compulsory) is a form of risk pooling and therefore would be a more efficient approach (Royal Commission on Long-term Care, 1999). In addition, private insurance would also ensure some kind of shifting of costs from those with fewer care needs to those with greater care needs (Wittenberg, Sandhu and Knapp, 2002). However, one still has to ask why, in contrast to the sector of health care in the EU where there is a considerable market for private insurance, private policies are by no means common in the sector of long-term care. For example, in the UK only about 30,000 long-term care insurance policies have been sold so far and therefore, inadequate pooling is a serious problem. Taking into consideration evidence from the country reports, it however becomes clear that private cover against the risk of needing long-term care fails to ensure equity in a number of respects.

An initial difficulty is that premiums in a private insurance policy are related to gender. Women, who on average have a higher life expectancy than men and are at higher risk of needing long-term care, have to pay higher premiums for a private insurance policy. This contrasts with the fact that women on average earn less than men and means that it is not very probable that women could afford a market solution. Moreover, private insurance premiums are not raised progressively or proportionally with income and those with lower incomes usually have to pay exactly the same premiums as the more affluent. This puts those with lower means at a disadvantage, as they have to pay the same contribution from smaller financial resources.

In addition, premiums for private insurance policies are usually not related to income, but are based on the estimated risk of the individual needing long-term care. This means that two individuals with the same income and capital may have to pay different contributions. Empirical evidence suggests that private companies are very discriminating in assessing the risk of age-related disability.

This may mean that either only healthy people will get insurance policies or that those exposed to some special kind of risk have to pay very high premiums. Another important argument why private policies may not offer reasonable cover is that premiums are also related to age. For example, premiums for those, say, aged 65 and above are normally higher than for those, say, aged 30. However, it is the elderly in particular who are interested in such cover. Among younger people, the risk of being in need of long-term care appears to be far away in the future and long-term care benefits are often not yet regarded as important. Therefore, younger people may be more attracted by the idea of spending their money than in insuring themselves against such risks.

To sum up, the above purely market sector solutions mitigate against vertical equity and do not offer an appropriate solution in terms of unequal treatment for unequals. On the contrary, it appears that private long-term care insurance arrangements are regressive in that affluent people would pay proportionally less than those who are poorer. In addition, market approaches fail to support horizontal equity as people with the same income and wealth may well not pay the same risk-related premium.

A further option for funding the risk of domiciliary long-term care would be to subsidise and therefore to promote the development of the private insurance market from public resources, often described as a voluntary 'partnership approach' (Compare Royal Commission on Long-term Care, 1999). This normally could be done by directly subsidising the premiums. Tax relief, for example on long-term care premiums, would be another possibility. Evidence from the United States of America where such schemes have been tried on a voluntary basis show that they have not lead to marked expansion of the private long-term care insurance market and therefore, have kept the market insurance small with serious problems in terms of pooling. One main reason for the relative lack of success of this approach is that younger and middle-aged people have not been willing to take out policies. Another problem with such 'partnerships' is that they are also not likely to prevent people of the same income and capital normally having to pay different premiums since unfavourable selection (e.g. based on health and sex) would usually remain under such a system of promoting private long-term care insurance (Cadette, 2000).

In addition to the above approach which would be on a voluntary basis, another option would be to require people to buy long-term care policies which are supported by the public sector. However, opinions differ as to whether requiring people to buy long-term care insurance policies on a compulsory basis is a legitimate use of the power of the state. A compulsory scheme raises the question how it could be made affordable for those of low and moderate means (Cadette, 2000). Another aspect is that if private insurance were compulsory and people had to buy insurance policies early in their life, this would probably only limit the age-related element of risk selection and not those of sex and health. To solve these problems it might be possible to create a scheme in which the public sector subsidizes the premiums according to the income and capital of the insured and additionally compels private companies to accept all people on standard terms without risk selection based on age, gender and health (Wittenberg, Sandhu and Knapp, 2002). It appears, however, questionable whether such a compulsory private sector scheme with far-reaching public sector influence is preferable to a scheme paid for out of some sort of public sector approach.

As evidence from the country studies shows, there are several ways of funding public long-term care support. The basic question to be dealt with initially is whether a public scheme should be based on 'capital-resourced' funding ('Pre-funding') or on 'pay-as-you-go' funding. 'Pre-funding' would mean that entitlements in one generation are built up years in advance through payments into a fund out of which future services are paid for. Advocates of such an approach argue that savings ensure a higher profit for the scheme from the contributions paid than would be the case in a 'pay-as-you-go' scheme and therefore it would be the more efficient way of funding in the long-term. Another major argument put forward is that a 'capital-resourced' funding scheme would be less susceptible to the influence of an ageing population than a 'pay-as-you-go' scheme (See, for example, Schmähl, 1992). However, Eisen (1993) found that funding insurance against the risk of age-related disability by a 'capital-resourced' scheme would not lead to 'immunisation' against the effects of demographic change, as the yield of the contributions paid is an endogenous variable which goes down as the population decreases.

The main criticism of 'pre-funding', however, is that reserves would have to be built up for the next, say, thirty or more years before services have to be paid for, or those in need have become aware that they are entitled to the provision of long-term care. As a consequence, in order to cater for those elderly people who are currently in need of long-term care, resources would be necessary (e.g. raised through taxation) for thirty years or more in addition to the contributions to the 'pre-funding' scheme. In other words, introducing a 'pre-funded' long-term care scheme means that one (the current) generation has to pay twice (See, for example, Royal Commission on Long-term Care, 1999). Therefore, it appears likely that the amount of the contributions could depend more on the age than the financial status of the population which means that such a scheme would fail to ensure equity. To avoid this inequity between generations, Schmähl (1992) discusses the option of a public compensation payment or subsidies on contributions for the current generation. It was said, however, that such payments would lead to the situation that this (borrowed) money was not available for funding other purposes. Therefore, it appears doubtful that a 'pre-funded' scheme with compensation payments for the current generation would be more efficient than a 'pay-as-you-go' scheme (Compare, Breyer, 1989). In addition, as evidence from the country-reports suggests, there are also other problems in terms of efficiency with 'pre-funding' long-term care arrangements. Different factors make it extremely difficult to predict the amount of money that will be needed to pay for the long-term care of elderly people. In addition to the uncertainty about people's physical and mental condition in 30 or more years' time, making it hardly possible to arrive at reasonable figures, another unclear area is the inability to make predictions about developments in the types of service provision and the informal care potential. These uncertainties mean it would be extremely difficult to fix the contribution rate for a 'pre-funded' scheme at a suitable level and in the most efficient way.

Considering the difficulties with 'pre-funding', particularly the inequities which would arise from the double burden that the current generation would have to bear, it appears advisable to consider the option of funding a public long-term care scheme on a 'pay-as-you-go' basis. For example, the Royal Commission on Long-term Care (1999) also analysed both major approaches to funding a public sector long-term care scheme and recommended that, given the problems with 'pre-funding', provision in the UK should on principle be paid for on a 'pay-as-you go' basis. It was argued that a major attraction of a 'pay-as-you go' scheme is that in contrast to 'pre-funding', it can be introduced as from today and all disabled elderly people can be entitled to a certain amount of service provision right from the outset. In Germany, before the introduction of the long-term care insurance in 1994, the subject provoked quite a controversy. However, in terms of the funding method, the two main political groups, the Christian Democrats and the Social Democrats, agreed on the adoption of a 'pay-as-you-go' scheme. Here, a major argument in favour of a 'pay-as-you-go' scheme instead of a 'pre-funded' scheme was that it improved the possibility of using public resources more equitably.

Another necessary step would be deciding whether a 'pay-as-you-go' (or 'pre-funded') scheme should operate on a local/regional or on a national basis. Local or regional money to be used for funding a long-term care scheme could, for example, come through local (regional) taxation or allocations from central government. Wider-ranging literature (See, for example, Mossialos and Dixon, 2002) suggests different arguments in favour of this approach. An argument often put forward is that this represents the more democratic approach, as each individual authority would be separately able to decide how much money will go to the funding of long-term care according to the local or regional needs. Another justification for local or regional funding is that it would increase transparency concerning the link between the amount of money available at local or regional level and the amount to be spent on a certain type of social protection (e.g. long-term care) as opposed to funding by the national government when the available budget is usually used for a much wider range of purposes. Finally, the exact type of long-term care spending can be adjusted directly to local or regional needs.

However, empirical evidence from France and the UK where local or regional money is used to pay for providing long-term care supports a range of counter-arguments. First, there are some administrative areas with a comparatively low number of inhabitants. This means that in terms of efficient risk pooling, putting the funding on such a narrow basis would appear to be a questionable approach. In addition, poorer authorities simply have greater difficulties in raising the resources and, there are authorities with a comparatively very high proportion of elderly people. This means that the demand for long-term care services and the strain on financial resources required in such areas is likely to be higher than in administrations with a younger population. Another aspect is that policy orientation varies among the authorities, meaning that some institutions spend less on elderly and more on younger people. The consequence of this unequal starting-point among the authorities is that the amount of long-term care provision an elderly person receives may depend on his or her place of residence. Another problem could be that different rates of local or regional tax are applied in different authorities. In general, this means that it would be extremely difficult to achieve horizontal equity if the responsibility of paying for benefits and services were in the hands of different local or regional administrations. In order to avoid these problems when funding long-term care at local or regional level, it would be necessary to built up a complicated scheme of re-allocating resources to the different authorities. This however, is done neither in France nor in the UK and scarcely seems conceivable.

Given the inequities for those concerned, as long as the responsibility for funding long-term care is in the hands of local or regional authorities, this approach appears to be an unacceptable answer to the problem of funding the costs of long-term care. It would appear to be much more equitable to devise some sort of national scheme in order to spread the risk across the whole population. From an administrative view, the cost of collecting money on a national basis would be lower than if it were done at regional or local level. As the Royal Commission on Long-term Care (1999) has argued, it would seem desirable to have a scheme into which on the one hand everyone has to pay and, on the other hand, one out of which everyone is entitled to some kind of provision in the case of need. It seems possible to achieve this by funding long-term care benefits and services from a national 'pay-as-you-go' scheme that is either based on social insurance contributions, hypothecated taxation or general taxation.

Funding long-term care through social insurance means that the current costs are paid out of present social contributions which usually come from employees and employers (See, for example, Saltman and Figueras, 1997). As evidence form the country-reports suggest, a major argument in favour of a social insurance-based scheme is that, for example, in contrast to a scheme which is funded by general taxation, people can be aware of the connection between what they are paying for insuring themselves against the risk of age-related disability on the one hand and, what they may get in return for their contribution in the case of need on the other. One may also assume that people will pay their contributions more willingly if they know what their money will be spent on, rather than paying into a general fund where one has to fear that the money may well be used for other types of public expenditure. In addition, in countries with a long-established tradition of social insurance (e.g. France and Germany), a contribution-based long-term care provision fits well within the framework of the already existing insurance-based schemes (e.g. the schemes for health care and old-age). As a study carried out for the Joseph Rowntree Foundation (1996) has found, in cases where it is possible to implement a scheme within the existing framework of social protection, this provides a basis for a low-cost and efficient mechanism for collecting contributions.

Unfortunately, as Mossialos and Dixon (2002) have found, social insurance schemes do not necessarily contribute to vertical equity in funding terms. It was argued that contributions to be paid are generally not progressive, but proportional to income. Moreover, social insurance can even be more regressive as contributions in the 'traditional' way are usually only raised on earned income. Income from other sources (e.g. investments and rents) is normally excluded when calculating contributions although such income is on average higher among more affluent. In addition to the above, when taking into account that among those with the same overall assets, different parts of their overall income, depending on its source, are excluded from consideration, there may also be horizontal inequity.

Despite the debatable effects on the principle of equity when funding a social insurance scheme mainly from contributions calculated on the basis of earned income, it appears questionable whether such a 'traditional' insurance based scheme will remain fundable in the future without far-reaching reform. The case of Germany provides an interesting example of this dilemma. Here, empirical evidence shows that the social insurance based long-term care scheme mainly funded from contributions by employers and employees is expected to get into serious financial difficulty in the future. Already now, the scheme does not allow an adequate response to additional demands placed on it, such as, for example, the need to provide care for people with dementia. The difficulties with the German scheme spring first from the increasing need for long-term care because of the growth in the number of elderly people (who are the main recipients of long-term care provision). In connection with this increase, the number of people of working age who predominantly pay for the scheme is decreasing. This leads to a reduction in the total amount of money that is flowing into the scheme, while at the same time the need is continuing to increase. Another aspect is the tendency towards a decreasing informal care potential which is necessarily leading to an increasing demand for services in kind that are usually more expensive than informal provision. Furthermore, other factors such as the currently high unemployment rate in social insurance-based countries are aggravating the situation. Overall, these difficulties, which are not only a German phenomenon but also influence the provision in other EU countries, for example France (See, for example, European Commission, 2001), raise doubts that social insurance mainly funded by the working population (as traditionally designed) will remain efficient in the future without introducing reforms.

In light of the difficulties arising from the 'traditional` way of paying for long-term care on a social insurance-basis, evidence from France suggests the interesting approach of giving the funding a broader basis. Here, in addition to social insurance contributions from employees and employers, benefits in some sectors of social insurance (e.g. entitlements arising from time spent bringing up children under the pension scheme) are funded by ear-marked taxation. In France, this special, ear-marked tax or charge is raised proportionally with a fixed rate for different types of income, e.g. rental income. Overall, the experience acquired in France shows that this approach could be useful for coping with the above-mentioned challenges in 'traditional` social insurance schemes. In addition, it would also be useful in terms of limiting the inequities illustrated above. It therefore appears worth considering this approach for social insurance-based schemes in other countries with similar problems. This, for example, has already been done in Luxembourg, where a social long-term care insurance partly based on the German model was introduced in 1998. The funding of this scheme was put on a broader basis by raising contributions based on all types of income, including salaries and wages, capital gains, and interest on capital as well as rental income (Luxembourg Ministry of Social Security, 1998).

In addition to the above, the empirical investigation identified a probably even greater difficulty in terms of achieving vertical equity which may arise in a social insurance- based scheme. As evidence from Germany shows, different groups of people (mainly self-employed persons, employees with income above a certain ceiling and civil servants) can opt out of the social (long-term care) insurance, combined with taking out a compulsory private insurance policy. In contrast to other sectors of social insurance (where private insurance provision in general appears to be more efficient), it is determined by law that benefits and services available under a private insurance plan for long-term care have to be equivalent to those provided by the social insurance. However, the contributions that have to be paid by those insured differ between the two schemes and although this has to be considered for each individual case, the tendency that the majority of people who opt for a private insurance pay lower contributions is obvious. The vertical inequity may be particularly clear when considering that an employee whose income reaches the ceiling that allows him to change to private insurance may freely decide whether to take this step or remain covered by statutory social insurance. In addition, comparing the financial situation of the privately insured with those paying social insurance, the privately insured person is significantly better off. This is mainly because the proportion of younger people and people earning higher salaries is much higher in the private sector. Another aspect is that social insurance covers more elderly people (and also many socially weak people) than the private sector and the proportion of those receiving long-term care provision is about twice as high as in the private sector. In France (where long-term care provision is not at present covered by social insurance), with a social insurance scheme that covers most of the population (e.g. employees and their families), a range of special schemes (e.g. for civil servants) and also independent schemes (e.g. for self-employed persons), there is an organisational structure for social insurance which is similar to that in Germany. This means that a social insurance-based long-term care coverage would have to cope with similar inequities.

It appears, however, hardly conceivable that a national long-term care scheme can work if certain groups within society (mainly the wealthier), such as the self-employed and civil servants do not have to participate. This would strongly work against the achievement of vertical equity and increase the tendency for the scheme to be regressive. Under a universal scheme there would be no special entitlement for certain groups within the population. Such a scheme would ease the financial burden on the statutory social insurance system and would generally help to achieve vertical equity. Consequently, in countries like Germany and France, it appears advisable to consider incorporating the individual schemes within the framework of social insurance. However, as the distinction between social insurance and other forms of insurance is a fundamental part of the system in general, a discussion of such developments cannot be limited to long-term care provision and it has to be considered within a wider framework. This is, however, an extremely complicated issue and a desirable change would seem difficult to achieve in the near future. Those countries that are considering providing long-term care on a social insurance basis seem, meanwhile, to be forced to incorporate the provision of long-term care within the existing complexity of different types of insurance. One way of dealing with the present situation of huge vertical inequities would be to implement a long-term care scheme with equal contributions and compensation payments between social- and compulsory private long-term care insurance funds.

However, a social insurance-based long-term care provision only seems a suitable approach for countries with a well-established insurance tradition. In those countries which do not have such a welfare state orientation, but a tradition of taxation-funded provision (e.g. the UK), a social long-term care insurance would not fit in the existing framework. It appears likely that it would operate in isolation from other sectors of social protection and therefore not in the most efficient way. In addition, there has been no reference so far to recent justified reflections in such countries about social insurance approaches. It would therefore make sense to consider further funding approaches (e.g. general taxation and hypothecated taxation).

A major attraction of general taxation is that it would best fit into the existing schemes in countries with a tax-based tradition of social protection (e.g. the UK) and is therefore likely to be put into practice efficiently. In addition, funding the provision of long-term care from general taxation allows pooling the risk of the enormous costs associated with age-related disability across the whole population in a very efficient way. When general taxation is the major source of funding long-term care for the elderly, its effects on equity are frequently not distinguishable from the effect on the equity of other types of social protection as the money normally used is derived from a general pot (Compare Mossialos and Dixon, 2002). However, Wagstaff, Van Doorslaer and Van der Burg (1999) have found that direct taxes which are raised on a national basis are progressive in all countries whereas indirect taxes which are usually raised as a percentage on goods and services are normally regressive. These findings are in accordance with an earlier study by Gottschalk, Wolfe and Haveman (1989) who compared the funding mechanism of health care schemes in the Netherlands, the UK and the United States of America. A major conclusion reached was that the UK offers the most progressive method of paying for health care, mainly because the scheme makes use of the highest proportion of funds from general taxation (90%) among the countries examined. The Royal Commission on Long-term Care (1999) also advocated the approach of funding long-term care from general taxation by arguing that it is largely progressive and money would be spent in an efficient way. In addition, as shown, for example, by experience in Denmark and Sweden, collecting and spending taxes on a local or regional basis with no national scheme of redistribution may mean that there are geographical variations and this increases horizontal inequity across the country. In contrast, taxation on a national basis will usually reduce such diversity (Van Doorslaer, Wagstaff and Van der Burg, 1999).

An alternative approach to general taxation would be to fund the provision of long-term care by 'hypothecated' (or ear-marked) taxation. This, for example, could mean that an extra tax is raised on all types of income that is used to pay for the costs of long-term care for elderly people. Vertical equity in terms of 'hypothecated' taxation largely depends on whether it is raised progressively or proportionally. Both types are possible. If 'hypothecated' (or ear-marked) tax is raised on a national basis, it would not have an adverse effect on horizontal equity. As evidence from the county-reports suggests, as in the case of social insurance, the major attraction of 'hypothecated taxation' is that people are able to see the connection between what they are paying into the scheme and what they will get from it in the case of need. This appears likely to lead to greater acceptability of taxation than paying into a general pot. Against the approach of 'hypothecated taxation', empirical evidence suggests that it limits flexibility in the fixing of public budgets. Another problem found is that once this method of paying for the provision of long-term care is adopted, a range of special interests groups would argue in favour of hypothecation and this could end up with many taxes paid on a hypothecated basis. This would result in bureaucratic obstacles and restrictions on budget allocation. Therefore, from an administrative point of view, general taxation appears to be more efficient, particularly as it better fits into the existing schemes of funding social protection in countries with tax-based schemes (e.g. the UK). On the other hand, there has been hardly any practical experience of 'hypothecated taxation' so far, but this idea seems worth further consideration and scientific research in this field could be profitable.

9.6 Summary

By using the criteria of 'efficiency' and 'equity' as a framework for the evaluation procedure this Chapter has analysed and brought together empirical evidence in the country reports from France, Germany and the UK and combined these findings with available literature. This has thrown light on the advantages and disadvantages of different approaches to domiciliary long-term care arrangements with regard to responsible institutions, eligibility criteria, benefits and services, as well as funding arrangements. In addition the Chapter has indicated a range of policy strategies for the future provision of long-term care. The individual findings are illustrated below.

With regard to the institutions responsible for providing long-term care, their separation from administrations responsible for general health care has been identified as a problem common to all the countries studied. This is mainly owing to the fact that elderly people often have complex problems and need help from both sectors. These different types of help, however, are quite often poorly co-ordinated and this leads to obviously inefficient proceedings. It was shown that different attempts are at present being made in the countries studied to cope with these problems. Based on empirical evidence, in countries with a taxation-funded health care scheme, it appears possible to break down existing barriers between the two sectors by implementing partnership arrangements. A further and, of course, much more far-reaching step to overcome this failure to co-ordinate and the resulting inefficiency would be the creation of a new organisational structure which offers the possibility of integrating health and long-term care services. In countries with an insurance tradition, introducing a separate long-term care insurance scheme (with the work of long-term care funds being undertaken by the health funds, which then act as both health insurance funds and long-term care funds) alongside other forms of social insurance currently appears the most efficient approach. Another common difficulty in the countries studied is that the assessment of people with long-term care needs often does not include many other needs which are closely related (e.g. rehabilitation). The discussion has brought to light a range of arguments that point to the benefits of a single assessment procedure that includes long-term care as well as general health needs. In particular, this is likely to improve the co-ordination of different services and lead to greater efficiency. As a further aspect, the tendency in different long-term care schemes to give private (and voluntary, non-profit) organisations increasingly the dominant role in service provision has been analysed. Experience obtained in countries studied, however, rather suggests that where efficiency and equity are concerned it would be more advisable if long-term care came from a well-balanced mix of public-, private as well as voluntary, non-profit providers without giving preference to any of the three possibilities.

The question that first emerged while considering the criteria used for looking at an elderly person's needs was whether equity is better served if each elderly person's eligibility for care provision is based on an individual examination or on a national set of standardised criteria. While advocating the option of looking at each person individually one could, for instance, argue that because of the different needs an elderly person may have, it hardly appears possible to have a particular set of tools on the basis of which long-term requirements can be accurately assessed and adequate care provided. However, available evidence from countries with such an approach shows that individually-based assessments are likely leading to great (in particular, horizontal) inequity among those concerned, for example arising from geographical variations. Standardised criteria appear to be the best approach for counteracting such inequity. In addition, standardised criteria offer some advantages compared with individual based assessments in terms of efficiency. It would therefore seem, on balance, advisable to have a national set of eligibility criteria instead of looking at each disabled elderly person individually. However, arriving at standardised criteria which appear equitable is a difficult undertaking and caution is advisable when deciding on such tools. As the discussion has shown, the goal when establishing standardised criteria that offer a basis for equitable access to care should be to avoid obvious disadvantages for elderly people with certain conditions and to arrive at a balance between what is desirable and affordable. In addition to the needs a disabled elderly person has, the other major question to be dealt with here is whether the income and capital of those in need should be considered. As emerged from the country studies, the ways in which countries deal with this aspect varies widely. Evidence at hand suggests different arguments for providing long-term care without a means test. In particular, it simply appears inequitable when some elderly people have to pay for one type of care (i.e. domiciliary long-term care) while others receive another type of care (i.e. health care) free of charge. The other side of this is that, having in mind the effects of allocation and the limited public resources in EU countries, it also seems possible to justify a means test (based on income and capital, but without taking into account the value of the home in which the elderly person in need lives). Evidence, however, suggests that even if means testing is incorporated the long-term care scheme should remain universal and its application should not lead to the complete exclusion of any disabled elderly person from provision simply on the grounds of income and capital. The latter approach appears to be worth considering in particular in schemes where the provision is not based on contributions.

Although there are big differences in the amounts and types of benefits and services available, most EU long-term care schemes have in common that they usually do not offer a full provision. This, on the one hand, is understandable because of the limitation of public resources and, on the other hand, as the analysis has shown that unlimited provision might well lead to the inequitable allocation of public provision and inefficient use of resources. As evidence from the country reports suggests, a more suitable approach would seem to be to arrive at a well-balanced amount of clearly fixed national and limited benefits and services. This should be useful to ease the burden of paying for care for those concerned, as well as prevent huge inequities and should facilitate the creation of a cost-control mechanism for public long-term care expenditure. Looking at the type of help for which support should be granted and given the variety of possible syndromes, it would seem useful to provide benefits and services for personal care, home-making as well as on general supervision and guidance, according to a disabled elderly person's particular needs. Evidence shows that when a long-term care scheme excludes one of these types of help, there is inequity among elderly people and, in addition, the boundaries between the different forms of provision become even more marked, co-ordination becomes more difficult and procedures more inefficient. Another theme discussed is the support for informal care. Here, evidence from the empirical investigation suggests, it is simply not equitable that a long-term care scheme puts those elderly people at a disadvantage who arrange their own care on an informal basis. Adequate support could comprise cash benefits, social protection benefits for the carers and cover for eventualities for which the informal carer is unable to provide care. Finally, the section on benefits and services has analysed the dilemma that long-term care schemes often virtually inhibit possible improvement in an elderly person's status of health by providing lower levels of support. A possible option to counteract such inefficient proceedings would be to make benchmarks between the individual providers of care and to reward those who perform best.

As the discussion on funding arrangements used to pay for long-term care has shown, family-based funding out of individuals' income and capital as well as private insurance policies, with or without public sector support, appears to be an unsuitable alternative for funding long-term care, both in terms of equity and efficiency. This suggests that long-term care costs should be paid out of some sort of public scheme. Here, a 'pay-as-you-go' scheme appears to be more appropriate than a scheme based on 'pre-funding' which would be likely to lead to inequity, in particular as one generation (the current one) would have to pay twice. The other basic decision to be made when looking at the options for a public scheme is whether it should be funded on a national or local (regional) basis. Experience from the countries studies suggests the usefulness (both in terms of efficiency and equity) of spreading the risk across the whole population by having a national scheme across the country instead of giving the responsibility for paying to the local or regional institutions. In countries with an established tradition of social insurance, it seems useful to implement a national 'pay-as-you-go' scheme alongside this existing framework. However, owing to the inequity (in particular, vertical inequity) arising from the 'traditional' way of funding social insurance by contributions from employees and employers, it seems advisable to expand this established funding approach by a special, ear-marked tax which could be raised on different types of income. In addition, it appears desirable that insurance-based schemes should no longer entitle certain groups (e.g. self-employed people and civil servants) to opt out of the general social scheme. In contrast, in countries with a well-established tradition of taxation-funded health care services, evidence suggests that the most efficient and equitable approach to funding long-term care would be to do this from general taxation. In addition, 'hypothecated taxation' seems to be a possible alternative when more experience of such an approach has been gathered.

10 The development of state welfare in EU countries

10.1 Introduction

In the final section of Part I of the present study, the goal was to look at the relationship between EU domiciliary long-term care arrangements and traditional models of welfare state regimes that have been useful as a basis for the analysis of social protection schemes. These models also seem to have covered the various forms a domiciliary long-term care scheme could take and have taken over recent years, i.e. the classification illustrated by Esping-Anderson ('The Three Worlds of Welfare Capitalism', 1990) and the division into welfare states of the Bismarck and Beveridge type. There is some indication that at the turn of the millennium, in contrast to previous times, traditional models of welfare state regimes no longer necessarily cover the various forms a long-term care scheme could take. This knowledge, however, is derived from limited available literature in this area as well as being based on the descriptive overview of domiciliary long-term care arrangements in the Union in this study (Compare Chapter 4). As referred to in Part I, much more detailed analysis and empirical evidence is required before it is possible to draw reliable conclusions with regard to this very complex issue.

As the empirical investigation revealed, the EU countries studied have responded to common problems (i.e. mainly a combination of social, demographic and macro-economic developments) which have put pressure on the schemes they were not designed to deal with, by a range of initiatives in terms of both organising and funding long-term care. In the previous Chapter 9 it has already been suggested that some of these initiatives on the one hand appear to be in accordance with each country's traditional approach to welfare state orientation. On the other hand, the empirical analysis has identified several areas which do not seem to accord with welfare traditions. This would mean that evidence from the countries studied appears to support the assumption based on Part I of this study, that traditional models of welfare state regimes do not necessarily cover the various forms current long-term care schemes could take.

The aim of the present Chapter is to analyse in some detail the relationship between the French, German and UK long-term care schemes and the Esping-Anderson, Bismarck/Beveridge models of welfare state regimes. As discussed in Chapter 4, both models are based on a mix of public, market and family provision of social protection. In addition to this, the second section of this Chapter aims to draw conclusions from the preceding analysis and, based on this, to identify broad trends and developments in terms of how the three basic principles (i.e. family, market and public sector) theoretically underlying the provision of social protection services are applied in EU long-term care arrangements.

10.2 Relationship between domiciliary long-term care schemes and models of state welfare regimes

In France, provision of social protection is, traditionally, mainly based on the 'Bismarck' model of the welfare state. This means that, for example, health care and pensions are usually managed within social insurance schemes and the main source of funding is contributions, often paid by employees and/or employers. The administrative responsibility for provision is normally in the hands of non-state bodies (Compare p. 65). Bearing this tradition in mind, it appears astonishing that the new autonomous long-term care scheme in France ('APA') is not based on an insurance model and thus implemented alongside other forms of social protection but is the responsibility of the regional (public) authorities. Subsequently, funding for the costs of long-term care is not derived from contributions, but comes from taxation. These arrangements, however, mean that key elements of the new French long-term care scheme ('APA') do not accord with the 'Bismarck' model of the welfare state.

In addition to its orientation towards the 'Bismarck' model, social protection arrangements in France have frequently served as an example of what Esping-Anderson has described as the 'conservative' type of welfare state regime (Compare p. 61). A key element of this model is that the allocation effects are very limited and this means that status differential is all-important. If one looks at the new 'APA' scheme, it is clear that this, in fact, includes a redistribution between well-off and poor people, particularly in the provision of services. As the co-payments which the individuals have to make according to their income can represent up to 80% of the total provision, the scheme may in the individual case even lead to a comparatively clear redistribution. Another striking feature of the 'conservative' model of welfare state is the influence of voluntary, non-profit and in particular church organisations (market elements are usually negligible). This also takes into account the obligation to preserve the traditional role of the family in the provision of social protection. In practice, this means that the state frequently only acts when the family is no longer able to look after its members. In addition, social protection is particularly related to earned income. The above-noted obligation of the family to look after its members before the state provides support is still marked in the French 'PSD' long-term care scheme. Here, the complete exclusion of the spouse or partner from provision is based on the notion that the individuals concerned are considered to be obliged to provide maintenance without payment. However, under the new 'APA' scheme which will replace the 'PSD' scheme in 2002, those disabled elderly persons who have a spouse or partner who is able to look after them will no longer necessarily be excluded from public provision. In other words, the new French long-term care scheme may also provide services although the family, at least theoretically, is able to look after its disabled elderly member. In addition, provision under the 'APA' scheme is not particularly related to earned income but is basically available for the whole population. Finally, private providers increasingly play a dominant role in service provision. All this suggests that the new French long-term care arrangements not only largely fail to accord with the 'Bismarck' model, but also differ in key elements from Esping-Andersons' 'conservative' welfare state regime.

A similar welfare state tradition to that in France can be found in the next country empirically studied, Germany. Here, there is also a long-established tradition that the main schemes of social protection are frequently in line with the 'Bismarck' approach and indeed the German domiciliary long-term care provision in the first place appears to be a manifestation of this insurance-based model of welfare state, funded by contributions from employers and employees. However, a more detailed comparison between the long-term care scheme and traditional sectors of social insurance (e.g. the health care scheme) shows that there are differences. For example, in contrast to the sector of health care where the main services are provided free at the point of use, long-term care provision usually does not represent a full service, but is granted in the form of a fixed and limited allowance that depends on the degree of disability. That care which is needed in addition to the publicly-funded provision has mainly to be paid out of private means. The intention with long-term care insurance was, from the start, to avoid setting up a comprehensive scheme covering all the needs of disabled elderly persons. This is recognisable in the fact that while in the sector of health care the rate of contributions for the scheme not only varies between individual funds but has also increased on average over recent years, the contribution rate for the long-term care insurance has, since 1996, been fixed at 1.7% of so-called 'insurable income' for all funds and this rate has not changed since then. This fixed contribution rate, which is a key element for controlling the costs of long-term care provision means that the amount of benefits and services is limited, in principle, by a certain budget. Another new feature of long-term care insurance, one not found in traditional health care insurance in Germany, is the option for disabled elderly people to obtain cash benefits and arrange family care, if they wish, instead of receiving services in kind from a formal organisation. Finally, in contrast to the traditional provision of social insurance funded-services mainly by public and voluntary, non-profit organisation, private bodies are now the largest group of publicly funded domiciliary long-term care providers.

In addition, Germany, like France, is not only a country which usually manages its schemes of social protection based on the 'Bismarck' model, but is also a typical example of a 'conservative' welfare state according to Esping-Anderson. As, for example, Jamieson (1991) in her internationally recognised study found, the German domiciliary long-term care arrangements at the beginning of the 1990s were also predominantly oriented towards the 'conservative' welfare state model. Looking at the present long-term care provision, there is some indication that it is in accordance with 'conservative' welfare traditions as the former arrangements were. One is encouraged to come to this conclusion, in particular, by the fact that the new scheme does not distinguish between poor and well-off people in the provision of benefits and services. However, looking more closely at present German long-term care arrangements, it becomes clear that the scheme differs from other significant features of the 'conservative' model. For instance, in contrast to a typical 'conservative' scheme, long-term care insurance provides benefits and services not only when the help of the family is exhausted, but already at the very start of an elderly person's neediness according to the scheme's definitions of disability. In addition, the above-noted tendency of long-term care services to be increasingly provided by private organisations is also inconsistent with the traditional model of the 'conservative' welfare state which is more based on public (voluntary, non-profit) service provision.

Looking at the UK, the country is known for its tradition of mainly basing its schemes of social protection on the 'Beveridge' model of the welfare state (Compare p 65). A key feature of this model is its universal coverage, with all residents being basically covered by the scheme's provision. This, however, does not necessarily mean that benefits and services offered will be of a consistently high standard. Another key element of the 'Beveridge' model is that provision is mainly financed from taxation and services are usually provided by public authorities. Where domiciliary long-term care is concerned, benefits and services in the UK are of a comparatively low standard and provision is theoretically available to the whole population, although many disabled elderly people are, finally, excluded from local authority provision, mainly following a usually strict means test. In addition, as is to be expected for a scheme based on the 'Beveridge' model, long-term care arrangements in the UK are mainly paid out of taxation. However, although the effects of the 'Beveridge' model on long-term care provision are unmistakeable, there are some tendencies which are not necessarily in line with the UK's traditional welfare orientation. In particular, the rapid increase in the proportion of publicly-funded care provided by private organisations in the 1990s (at the turn of the millennium more than half of total provision comes from the private sector) is not at all in line with the original 'Beveridge' model of the welfare state which is actually based on a strong orientation towards services provided by the public sector.

Where the Esping-Anderson classification of welfare state regimes is concerned, current local authority long-term care arrangements, just as several other areas of social protection in the UK, seem to fit well into the 'liberal' model of the welfare state (Compare p. 61). Services, on average, leave something to be desired and are predominantly provided for people of low-income, usually working class, who are dependent on state assistance. Another characteristic feature of the traditional 'liberal' model is that the state encourages the market, either passively by guaranteeing only a minimum of public support, or actively by subsidising private schemes of social protection. Indeed, during the 1990s the Conservative government in the UK was interested in encouraging the private long-term care insurance market and private-public partnership schemes. However, given the inequity and inefficiency often found in private market long-term care arrangements (Compare Chapter 9), it is not surprising that the scheme never got beyond the consultation stage. In addition, since the end of the 1990s, there is increasing public discussion and criticism of the long-term care scheme in general and suggested proposals for reform are largely not in accordance with the traditions of the 'liberal' welfare state model. Probably, the most important research which has provided impetus for reform is the report by a Royal Commission on long-term care (1999). The Commission's key proposal is that personal care should be available, after assessment, for everyone according to need and without taking into account the individual's income and capital. Bearing in mind the 'liberal' model of the welfare state which is based on a level of service that tends to be low and is particularly provided for those in low income groups, the proposal clearly intends to break with tradition. Although it is questionable whether the Labour Government will take action based on these recommendations, the initiative of the Commission in any case shows that serious thought is being given to the possibility of the country's relinquishing its position as a 'liberal' welfare state where domiciliary long-term care for the elderly is concerned.

10.3 The role of family, market and public sector in domiciliary long-term care provision

To conclude, the above analysis should have clearly demonstrated that the traditional models of welfare state regimes as proposed by Esping-Anderson and the division into the Bismarck/Beveridge types can, as originally planned, no longer cover all the forms that the present arrangements for disabled elderly people in the countries studied take. This applies both to the relationship between long-term care arrangements and the models on which social protection in the countries has traditionally been based, as well as to the relationship between long-term care and the other possible models of traditional welfare arrangements. It is obvious that reform over recent years in the domiciliary long-term care schemes of the countries studied have involved a reconsideration of long-established welfare traditions. These findings accord with conclusions that could be drawn from the descriptive data in Part I of this study. Since the descriptive findings are not specifically based on evidence from the countries studied but from the EU as a whole, and certain factors (i.e. mainly a combination of social, demographic and macro-economic developments) which seem to have predominantly contributed to the shifts in the welfare mix of the countries empirically studied are an EU-wide phenomena, it also appears likely that traditional models of welfare state regimes no longer necessarily cover the various forms a long-term care scheme in other EU countries might take.

It is, of course, impossible to identify new welfare state models based on the evidence of domiciliary long-term care schemes obtained in the course of this study. However, it is possible to identify broad trends and developments in the way in which the three basic principles underlying the provision of social protection services are applied in current EU long-term care arrangements. Taking into account that countries empirically studied have adopted different approaches in their response to common themes and priorities in public discussion of long-term care provision, one may assume that there are likewise variations from the wider welfare state point of view. However, as Glendinning (1998), in comparing new developments in long-term care for elderly people on a cross-national basis found, there appear to be similar welfare developments in different countries in the response to new long-term care challenges. An interesting finding of this study was that different EU countries intended to keep long-term care expenditure within limits by shifting some public responsibility for funding or providing age-related long-term care benefits and services to the family sector while developing new programmes. The evidence from the welfare state orientation in the countries empirically studied seems to verify these findings.

For example, Glendinning argued that in recent reforms in the UK and Germany, relatives are intended to play a major role in caring for disabled elderly people. In both countries, new arrangements contain incentives to encourage families to play a more active role. As the present study shows, the possibility of opting for cash benefits instead of services in kind is, in particular, contributing to a shift in the care provided from formal organisations to the informal sector. In addition, Glendinning stressed that charges are a key instrument in shifting responsibility for paying the costs of long-term care from the public to the family sector. As the empirical evidence shows, charging not only is a significant feature of local authority provision in the UK, but will also be an important element in the new French 'APA' scheme. Although the German long-term care insurance scheme does not include direct charges for service users, many individuals frequently have to make contributory payments, owing to the fact that provision is usually limited, though generous (i.e. the costs to cover the extent of a disabled elderly person's needs are usually higher than public provision). Moreover, public long-term care provision in the countries studied is restricted to certain types of care. In Germany and France, provision is mainly orientated towards help in the areas of personal care and home-making. In the UK, local authority provision in many areas has in general developed into a personal care service. This means that other types of help an elderly person needs are excluded from public provision, for example, general supervision, guidance and home-making, and therefore have to be paid for from other sources, mainly by the individuals in need themselves. While looking at the role of the market in the mix of welfare principles, it is useful to distinguish between the responsibility for financing and providing long-term care. As shown in the empirical analysis, private insurance policies, with or without public sector support, appear to be an unsuitable alternative to public approaches for funding long-term care. Market solutions, however, seem to be playing an increasingly dominant role, as opposed to mainly public (voluntary, non-profit) authorities, in the provision of services. Evidence from several regions in France, Germany and the UK shows the common reality that private providers are by now the largest provider of domiciliary long-term care services and relatively competitive care markets have developed.

Looking at the developments in empirically studied domiciliary long-term care schemes from a very broad schematic point of view, it is possible to argue that the responsibility for domiciliary long-term care arrangements is increasingly moving to 'the centre' of the Evers' (1990) 'welfare triangle' which is based on three principles (i.e. family, market and public sector) (Compare Chapter 4, p. 57). This is illustrated in the figure below (p. 270).

Figure 9 Domiciliary long-term care and the 'welfare triangle'

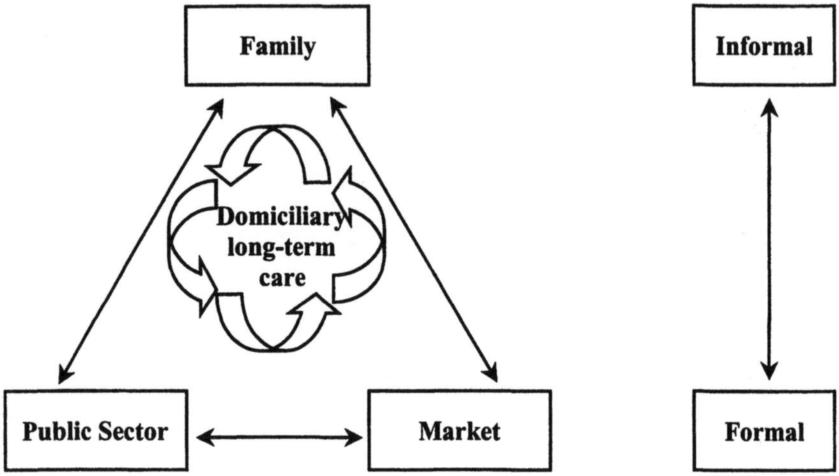

Source: Modification of Evers, 1990

Given the EU-wide dimension of the problems (i.e. mainly a combination of social, demographic and macro-economic developments) which have largely led to the fact that the empirically studied countries are in a process of redefining their long-term care policies, it seems likely that the illustrated tendency to move towards the centre of the 'welfare triangle' while defining new arrangements will also be found in the schemes of other countries. However, despite similar tendencies in general welfare state orientation, one should bear in mind that the exact balance between public, family and market arrangements is still considerably influenced by the context in which policies are formulated and the reforms that are being considered are in detail specific to the countries concerned. As empirical evidence indicates, in particular covering contextual factors such as political institutions, a country's history, legislative basis, etc. appear to impose restrictions upon the extent of such changes in welfare traditions. Compared to the factors noted above, political change appear to be of lesser importance in some countries. For example, despite significant political changes after the 1996 election in Germany, the existing schemes of social protection (including the long-term care scheme), did not deviate in principle from previous years, although there seems to be a necessity for further-reaching reform. However, further research which is required to identify new models of state welfare, based, for example, on individual long-term arrangements, despite similarities, needs to be sensitive to such country-specific features.

10.4 Summary

This Chapter has first analysed, in some detail, the relationship between the French, German and UK domiciliary long-term care schemes and the Esping-Anderson, Bismarck/Beveridge models of welfare state regimes. By using evidence from the empirical investigation, key differences and similarities in this relationship have been highlighted. In general, the analysis has clearly shown that whereas traditional models of welfare state regimes seemed to have covered virtually all the forms an EU long-term care scheme could take and have until recently taken, they no longer necessarily cover the various forms long-term care schemes could now take. These conclusions accord with the earlier indications in Part I of this study which are based on descriptive data.

Based on these findings, it was possible to identify broad trends and developments in the roles played by the three basic sources of support (public, market and family) with regard to current EU long-term care arrangements. Here, a key finding is that all countries studied intend to control public expenditure by shifting considerable responsibility for funding and providing long-term care to the family sector. Private market approaches do not seem to be a very suitable alternative for funding the costs of long-term care, but in fact are increasingly assuming a dominant role in the provision of formal services. In general, there appear to be many similarities in the welfare developments taking place in response to new long-term care challenges. From a very broad point of view, it even seems possible to argue that the responsibility for domiciliary long-term care arrangements is tending to shift towards the centre of the 'welfare triangle' formed by the three welfare principles. Given the EU-wide dimension of the problems at hand, making it necessary that countries redefine their long-term care arrangements, it appears likely that this not only applies to the countries empirically studied, but also to other long-term care schemes.

11 General policy reflections

In order to compare and evaluate alternative public policy responses to the need for financing and organising long-term care for the elderly, this study has carried out a range of descriptive and empirically-based research from which broad reflections have emerged. These reflections may serve as a basis for policy strategies in the individual EU countries and are summarised below. In the interests of clarity, each reflection is related to the findings of the study.

Responsible institutions

The following general policy reflections have been derived from an analysis of the institutions responsible for the provision of domiciliary long-term care:

1. In countries with a tradition of tax-funded financing of health care, the creation of partnership arrangements between health and long-term care administrations is likely to offer certain possibilities for reducing existing inefficiency arising from the boundaries between these two institutions involved in the support of disabled elderly people and the poor co-ordination of their services. As was discussed on pages 230-231 this, however, requires commitment on the part of the local partners.
2. Integrated health- and long-term care provision may facilitate an even closer co-ordination and integration of the different health and long-term care services a disabled elderly person may need and therefore be helpful in using available public resources more efficiently in countries with established taxation-funded health care schemes. This point is clearly illustrated in the discussion presented on pages 231-232.
3. As indicated on pages 232-233, in countries with social insurance-based health care arrangements, introducing a separate long-term care insurance alongside other forms of social insurance, but with the administration of such an insurance being carried out by the health funds - which at the same time act as health and long-term care funds - appears to be the best approach for achieving efficiency in the administration of long-term care.
4. A single assessment approach that applies to both long-term care and health services and which is made by a multi-disciplinary team of experts is likely to increase the possibilities for using public resources more efficiently as pointed out on page 234.
5. The provision of long-term care by a well-balanced mix of private, voluntary, non-profit and public bodies, without giving preference to any of the three, seems a useful way of generating improvements in efficiency in dealing with care markets as well as limiting problems in the co-ordination of the different services. This may also enhance choice, thus limiting the risks of horizontal and vertical inequity, as set out on pages 234-236.
6. A national framework of regulations and quality standards, as well as supervision of the services by the institutions responsible for administering

the long-term care scheme would be valuable for ensuring that care markets are 'working' and in counteracting inequity (in particular, vertical inequity) among elderly persons in need (See page 236).

Eligibility criteria

Major factors have been reviewed with regard to the criteria to be used for looking at an elderly person's needs and, based on these, for making decisions about the provision of domiciliary long-term care. The following are the policy reflections which have emerged from this discussion:

7. As discussed on page 237, assessments in which each person in need is looked at individually are likely to lead to vertical and, in particular horizontal, inequities. These are likely to be acceptable only in schemes where long-term care provision is not restricted by budget considerations, but available to a large proportion of elderly people according to need.
8. As stated on pages 237-238, well-balanced, standardised eligibility criteria on a national basis seem to be desirable to counteract inequity in a long-term care scheme.
9. The main goal when fixing such standardised assessment tools at a national level should be to avoid obvious disadvantages for disabled elderly with certain complaints and to arrive at a balance between what is desirable and what is affordable (See page 238).
10. From the point of view of efficiency, standardised criteria on a national basis likewise seem to be the preferable approach compared with an individually based assessment. This aspect has been clearly emphasised on page 239.
11. With respect to equity (as detailed on pages 239-240) in an ideal situation it is reasonable to expect that long-term care benefits and services should be provided without reference to the elderly person's means, in particular, when one remembers that some individuals would otherwise have to pay for one type of care (i.e. domiciliary long-term care) while others receive another type of care (i.e. general health care) that is mainly free of charge.
12. Taking into account the reality of limited public resources and the effects of allocation, it is, however, possible to construct a reasoned argument that, particularly with tax-funded long-term care schemes, it is questionable to disregard an elderly person's means when assessing entitlements to long-term care support. This is discussed in detail on pages 239-241.
13. On page 241, it is stressed that means testing, if applied, should not be considered in isolation from the need-related equity objective when assessing an elderly person's entitlement. Therefore, it is important that the application of means testing does not lead to a complete exclusion of elderly persons from benefits and services simply on the grounds of income and capital.

14. National criteria for charging to be used in a means test approach are useful to counteract inequity, as stated on page 241.
15. From an equity point of view, it appears advisable to consider capital (without taking into account the value of the home in which the elderly person lives) in addition to income when using a means test (See pages 241-242).

Type and amount of provision - benefits and services

With regard to domiciliary long-term care provision available for those in need, a number of different approaches in terms of the amount and type of benefits and services have been analysed. The following policy reflections can be based on this:

16. The provision of unlimited long-term care benefits and services according to need is likely to lead to inefficient use of public resources and inequitable allocation of provision. This point is clearly made in the analysis presented on page 243.
17. A well-balanced number of clearly-fixed, national and limited long-term care benefits and services would seem useful for reducing the risk of inequity and should facilitate the creation of a mechanism for controlling expenditure, as pointed out on page 243.
18. The point was made on page 243 that providing benefits and services not only for those elderly people in extreme need of long-term care, but also for those with less pressing needs (e.g. at the beginning of disability) would improve efficiency in service provision.
19. As stated on pages 244-245, those long-term care schemes which provide benefits and services exclusively for one particular type of need, for example personal care, and exclude further types of care from support (e.g. home-making), undermine the principle of equity (in particular, vertical equity) and are likely to make service provision proceedings more inefficient.
20. From an equity point of view, as made clear on page 245, it would appear desirable to provide benefits and services for personal care, home-making assistance as well as general supervision and guidance.
21. The argument on pages 245-246 makes the important point that long-term care schemes fail to fulfil the criterion of equitable allocation of provision if they put elderly persons at a disadvantage, simply because there is a relative who could care for them.
22. It is suggested on pages 246-247 that in order to improve the possibilities for equitable allocation of provision, long-term care schemes should offer help and support for those who choose to be looked after by a formal provider as well as for those who prefer to be cared for on an informal basis.
23. In order to counteract the inefficient situation in service provision which arises if a long-term care scheme provides lower payments after an elderly

person's health has improved because of good care, there should be additional incentives to reward the work of such providers whose clients therefore have less need of help, as argued on pages 247-248.

Funding

By analysing different options for funding the provision of domiciliary long-term care, it was found that:

24. As described on pages 248-249, family-based funding of long-term care out of individuals' income and capital fails to achieve efficiency and contributes to inequity.
25. The analysis on page 249 explains that private market-sourced insurance funding is a form of risk pooling but still may not offer an efficient solution if the market for such products is comparatively negligible.
26. As argued on pages 249-250, private market-sourced insurance funding detracts from vertical equity and probably fails to achieve horizontal equity.
27. Private market-sourced insurance funding with public sector support on a voluntary basis does not seem very useful in terms of expanding the insurance market for long-term care policies and is therefore likely to do little to cope with the problems of inefficient pooling. This point is clearly illustrated in the discussion presented on page 250.
28. Private market-sourced insurance funding with public sector support on a voluntary basis also does not appear to be useful for counteracting horizontal and vertical equity (See page 250).
29. On pages 250-251, the argument is put forward that private market-sourced insurance funding with public sector support on a compulsory basis would be useful in terms of risk pooling but there would need to be far-reaching and complex public sector influence and binding guidelines for policies as well as subsidies for premiums, according to individual assets, in order to counteract inequity.
30. As pointed out on pages 251-252, it appears very doubtful whether a ′pre-funded` public long-term care scheme would provide a more suitable approach in terms of efficiency than a scheme based on a ′pay-as-you-go` mechanism.
31. Where equity is concerned, the discussion on pages 251-252 has shown that funding the provision of long-term care on a ′pay-as-you-go` basis seems to be the preferable approach compared with ′pre-funding`.
32. As argued on pages 252-254, from the point of view of both efficiency and equity, it appears advisable to spread the risk of funding the costs of long-term care across the whole population by some sort of national scheme instead of a scheme that operates on a local or regional basis.
33. On pages 254-255 it is argued that in countries with an established tradition of social health insurance, where efficiency is concerned, it would be more profitable also to cover the risk of long-term care by an insurance-

based scheme instead of applying another funding mechanism (e.g. general taxation). It remains, however, questionable whether such a social insurance based scheme, will be able to work in the most efficient way if it keeps its traditional structure with funding mainly derived from contributions on earned income.

34. Funding schemes based on social insurance, which include the possibility for different groups of people (e.g. self-employed, employees with income above a certain ceiling and civil servants) to opt out of the unified public insurance are likely to increase the possibility of serious vertical inequity since they could lead to a situation in which well-off people pay proportionally less than people who are not so well-off. This is made clear on pages 255-256.
35. In addition to inequity (in particular, vertical inequity) which could arise in social insurance-based funding schemes, when there is a possibility for certain groups of people to opt out, the method of raising contributions in several of such schemes based solely on earned income is moreover increasing the likelihood of vertical inequity and may also promote horizontal inequity, as set out on page 254.
36. On pages 255-257 it is suggested that in order to improve equity in a social insurance-based long-term care scheme, it would be desirable to incorporate special individual schemes with no entitlement for certain groups (e.g. self-employed people and civil servants) to opt out of the general scheme and to expand the established funding approach (i.e. contributions from employees and employers) by introducing a special, ear-marked tax (charge) which could be raised on different types of income. This would not only be useful from an equity point of view, but would also improve efficiency in funding long-term care.
37. In countries with a tradition of funding the financing of health care from tax revenues, it would seem desirable, where both efficiency and equity are concerned, to pay for the costs of long-term care out of general taxation, as indicated on pages 257-258.
38. The point is made on page 258 that in countries with a tradition of funding the financing of health care from tax revenues, the option of 'hypothecated taxation' also seems to be a possible alternative to general taxation when more experience of such an approach has been gathered.

In addition, the study has shown that current welfare state orientation, where domiciliary long-term care provision for the elderly is concerned, can no longer be assigned to previous models of regime types. There is, rather, a tendency that welfare states are in a process of re-defining their ideologies and developing new models and partnerships between family, market and public sector provision that take account of macro-economic, social and demographic developments in EU countries.

12 Future Work

- This study has given consideration to the inefficiency arising from the boundaries between health care administrations responsible for nursing care, rehabilitation, etc. and institutions administering domiciliary long-term care provision (e.g. personal care and home-making), which are both involved in the support of disabled elderly people living at home, and from the poor co-ordination of their services. Evidence at hand shows that another area in which major problems of co-ordination in several EU countries exist is the boundary between hospital and domiciliary long-term care services. Further research is needed to analyse this boundary in service provision and based on this to establish ways of improving the co-ordination between the two areas.
- An overall objective of most long-term care policies in EU countries is that disabled elderly people should, wherever possible, be cared for in their own homes and this is also the most widespread wish of elderly people themselves. Keeping elderly people in their own homes not only requires the provision of adequate domiciliary long-term care, to which the present study has drawn attention, but also requires suitable housing conditions. Evidence from this study and elsewhere suggest that a full investigation should be carried out which looks at appropriate forms of aid and possibilities of further-reaching housing adaptations that would enable disabled elderly to stay in their own homes longer. This research should also include giving thought to public support for such home modifications and reflections on how such measures could be better co-ordinated (or even integrated) with the provision of domiciliary long-term care and health care services. In addition, such work may also consider new and innovative forms of housing for disabled elderly people.
- One of the policy recommendations of this study was that nationally standardised eligibility criteria should be applied instead of relying on an individually based assessment. However, difficulties experienced with a national instrument in different countries show the need for future research to be carried out in order to gather additional information on how successfully different eligibility criteria are being used in practice. This may enable eligibility criteria to be formulated which are well-balanced and useful for the improvement of equity in the provision of long-term care. The starting point for such research could be the approach put forward in this study for improving the German long-term care scheme. In addition, the findings of a scientific commission which is currently reviewing the instrument used in France should also be included in such research. Finally, experience in the UK at local level within the recently provided broad national framework should also be considered in this work.

- This study found that long-term care schemes are likely to reduce provision after an elderly person's health has improved because of good care. In other words, an improvement in a person's health is hardly recognized, but rather leads to the inefficient situation where the provider of services is put at a financial disadvantage when the client has less need of help. Research should be carried out to determining ways of improving this unsatisfactory and inefficient situation. As the problem described here emerges not only in the sector of long-term care, but is also a general weak spot in most health care schemes in industrial countries, such research could range more widely.
- In this study, the focus has been on public policy responses to the financing and organisation of long-term care. Another key aspect in long-term care is the quality of services. Evidence from the countries studied suggests that existing regulations frequently do not guarantee a sufficiently high standard of service and thus research which may provide the impetus for reform is needed.
- This study on domiciliary long-term care is one of the first of its kind and the countries included in the empirical analysis (i.e. France, Germany and the UK) have been selected on the basis of three main considerations, namely, the extent to which countries represent different types of long-term care schemes, the importance of long-term care reforms and to make a comparison between countries with a comparable number of inhabitants and similar levels of affluence. There appear to be other criteria which may justify the selection of different countries and there is an urgent need for more reliable and uniformly defined cross-national research on domiciliary long-term care schemes in general. In this connection, there should be empirically-supported research which looks at countries wishing to join the EU.
- The present study has shown that the EU domiciliary long-term care schemes can no longer be assigned to the previous models of regime types. Bearing in mind the fact that domiciliary long-term care provision is not isolated from other services, but is usually embedded in a country's social protection system and that the current difficulties largely common to all EU countries (e.g. ageing of the population, mass unemployment) also influence other sectors, it seems that the EU welfare states in general are currently being compelled to re-define old ideologies and to develop new programmes. This means that it is likely that new models of state welfare will continue to appear. Research is required to identify such new models of the welfare state which would in turn be useful as a basis for further studies on social protection schemes.

References

Abel-Smith, Brian and Titmuss, Kay (1987): *Selected Writings of Richard M. Titmuss: The Philosophy of Welfare*, London: Allen and Unwin Limited.

Alber, Jens (1993): *Older People in Europe: Social and Economic Policies: The 1993 Report of the European Observatory: Health and Social Services*, Brussels: Commission of the European Communities.

Alford, Robert (1969): *Bureaucracy and Participation: Political Culture in four Wisconsin Cities*, Chicago: Rand McNally & Co.

Allen, Isobel and Perkins, Elisabeth (1995): *The Future of Family Care for Older People*, London: HMSO.

Anonymous (1998): A Survey of Social Insurance: Privatising Peace of Mind, *The Economist*, 24th October 1998.

Anonymous (2000): Die Häusliche Pflege boomt weiterhin, *Häusliche Pflege*, 9 (4): pp. 22-24.

Anonymous (2001): Japanische Pflegeversicherung nach deutschem Vorbild, *Häusliche Pflege*, 10 (2): p. 9.

Antonnen, Anneli and Sipilä, Jorma (1996): European Social Care Services: Is it possible to identify Models?, *Journal of European Social Policy*, 6 (2): pp. 87-100.

AOK - Die Gesundheitskasse (2000): *Praxis Aktuell*: Beiträge, Essen.

Arvidson, Göran (1995): Regulation of Planned Markets in Health Care, in: Saltman, Richard B. and von Otter, C.: *Implementing Planned Markets in Health Care*, Buckingham: Open University Press.

Austrian Federal Ministry of Labour and Social Affairs, (1995): *Provision for Long-term Care in Austria*, Vienna: Federal Ministry of Labour and Social Affairs.

Baldwin, Peter (1990): *The Politics of Social Solidarity*, Cambridge: University Press.

Bayer, Ronald and Caplan Arthur L. and Daniels, Norman (1983): *In Search of Equity, Health Needs and the Health Care System*, New York: The Hasting Centre Series in Ethics.

Belge Assurance des Mututalités Chrétiennes (1992): *De Aangepaste Katz-schaal*, Brussels.

Belgium Ministry of Finance and Budget (1994): *Begroting Gezondheidsinstellingen, Welzijn en Gezin*, Brussels.

Blair, Tony and Schröder, Gerhard (1999): *The Way Forward for Europe's Social Democrats*, Berlin: German Social Democratic Party.

Blondeau, Jacques and Dubois, David (1997): Financing Old-age Dependency in Europe: Towards Overall Management of Old Age, *The Geneva Papers on Risk and Insurance*, 22 (82): pp. 46-59.

Boerma, Wienke G.W. and De Jong, Frans A.J.M. and Mulder, Peter H. (1993): *Health Care and general Practice across Europe*, Utrecht: Nivel.

Bräutigam, Martin and Schmid, Josef (1996): Pflege im modernen Wohlfahrtstaat. Der deutsche Fall in vergleichender Perspektive, *Staatswissenschaften und Staatspraxis: Rechts-, wirschafts- und sozialwissenschaftliche Beiträge zum sozialen Handeln*, 7 (2): pp. 261-284.

Breyer, F. (1989): On the Intergenerational Pareto-Efficiency of Pay-as-go Financed Pension Systems, *Journal of Institutional and Theoretical Economics*, 145: pp. 653-658.

Cadette, Walter M. (2000): *Financing Long-term Care: Options for Policy*, New York: The Jerome Levy Economics Institute.

Cass, B. (1990): Gender and Social Citizenship, *Paper presented at the 24th annual Social Policy Association Conference*, University of Bath.

Centre for Policy on Ageing (1993): *Older People in the Community*, London.

Chapman, Tom and Johnson, Alan (1995): *Growing old and needing Care: An Audit of the Health and Social Care Needs of the Elderly*, Aldershot: Avebury.

Caullychurn, Silvie (1997): Personnes Agées: Des Aides pour, *Protection Sociale* (902): pp. 20-30.

Clasen, Jochen (1997): *Social Insurance in Europe*, Bristol: The Policy Press.

Cologne Reinsurance Company (1995): *Long-term Care Insurance: International Perspective and Acturial Considerations*, Cologne.

Culyer, A.J. and Wagstaff, Adam (1994): *Reforming Health Care Systems*, Cheltenham: Edward Elgar Publishing Limited.

Danish Ministry of Social Affairs (1995): *Social Policy in Denmark: Social Pensions*, Copenhagen.

Danish National Institute of Social Research (1994): *Ist das Gras beim Nachbarn grüner? Deutsche und dänische Sozialpolitik in der Praxis*, Copenhagen.

Davies, Bleddyn (1994): Improving the Case Management Process, in: OECD: *Social Policy Studies No. 14: Caring for Frail Elderly People: New Directions in Care*, Paris.

Davies, Bleddyn (1995): The Reform of Community and Long-term Care of Elderly Persons: An international Perspective, in: Scharf, Thomas and Wenger, G. Clare: *International Perspectives on Community Care for Older People*, Aldershot: Avebury.

Davies, Bleddyn and Férnandez, José and Saunders, Robin (1998): *Community Care in England and France: Reforms and the Improvement of Equity and Efficiency*, Aldershot: Ashgate Publishing Limited.

De Roo, Aad A. (1995): Contracting and Solidarity: Market-orientated Changes in Dutch Health Insurance Schemes, in: Saltman, Richard B. and von Otter, C.: *Implementing Planned Markets in Health Care*, Buckingham: Open University Press.

Dutch National Association of Home Care (1997): *Home Care in the Netherlands*, Bunnik.

Edvartsen, Trond O. (1996): *Possibilities and Problems in Cross-national Comparative Analysis of Long-Term Care Systems*, Frankfurt am Main: Johann Wolfgang Goethe-University (Faculty of Economics).

Eisen, Roland (1993): *Alternative Sicherungsmöglichkeiten bei Pflegebedürftigkeit*, Frankfurt am Main: Johann Wolfgang Goethe-University (Faculty of Economics).

Eisen, Roland (1995): *An international Comparison of Securing Long-term Care Systems*, Frankfurt am Main: Johann Wolfgang Goethe-University (Faculty of Economics).

Eisen, Roland and Sloan, Frank A. (1996): *Long-term care: Economic Issues and Policy Solutions*, Norwell (Massachusetts): Kluwer Academic Publishers.

Esping-Anderson, Gosta (1990): *The three Worlds of Welfare Capitalism*, Cambridge: Polity Press.

European Commission (1997): *EC Economic Data Pocket Book*, No 8-9, Luxembourg.

European Commission (1998): *Social Protection in Europe: Modernising Social Protection and Adapting Systems to Change*, Brussels.

European Commission (1999): *Sozialschutz bei Pflegebedürftigkeit im Alter in den 15 EU-Mitgliedsstaaten und in Norwegen*, Brussels.

European Commission (2000): *Sicherung bei Pflegebedürftigkeit*, Brussels.

European Commission (2001): *Beschreibung der sozialen Lage in Europa*, Brussels.

European Parliament (1998): *Health Care Systems in the EU - A Comparative Study*, Luxembourg.

Eurostat data bank (1998): *Female and Male Life Expectancy*, Luxembourg.

Eurostat data bank (2002a): *Population Statistics*, Luxembourg.

Eurostat data bank (2002b): *Population Projections*, Luxembourg.

Eurostat data bank (2002c): *Unemployment Figures*, Luxembourg.

Eurostat data bank (2002d): *Female and Male Life Expectancy at Age 65*, Luxembourg.

Eurostat data bank (2002e): *Statistical Portrait of Women and Men in all Stages of Life*, Luxembourg.

Eurostat data bank (2002f): *Erwerbstätige Frauen*, Luxembourg.

Eurostat data bank (2002g): *Nominal GDP and GDP per Head*, Luxembourg.

Eurostat data bank (2002h): *Social Protection Expenditure per Head*, Luxembourg.

Evers, Adalbert (1990): Shifts in the Welfare Mix - Introducing a new Approach for the Study of Transformations in Welfare and Social Policy, in: Winterberger, Helmut: *Shifts in the*

Welfare Mix. Their Impact on Work, Social Services and Welfare Policies, Boulder (Colorado): Westview Press.

Evers, Adalbert and Pijl, Marja and Ungerson, Clare (1994): *Payments for Care: A Comparative Overview*, Aldershot: Avebury.

Evers, Adalbert and Leichsenring, Kai and Strümpel, Charlotte (1995): *Klientenrechte: Sozialpolitische Steuerung der Qualität von Hilfe und Pflege im Alter*, Wien: Austrian Ministry of Labour and Social Affairs.

Evers, Adalbert (1998): The new Long-term Care Insurance Program in Germany, *Journal of Aging and Social Policy*, 10 (1): pp. 77-98.

Faessel, Alfred (2001): *'Private Correspondence`*, Strasbourg.

Ferlie, Ewan and Challis, David and Davies, Bleddyn (1989): *Efficiency-improving Innovations in Social Care of the Elderly*, University of Kent at Canterbury: Personal Social Services Research Unit.

Fieber, Andreas (1997): *Pflegeversicherung im Vereinigten Königreich*, Frankfurt am Main: Johann Wolfgang Goethe-University (Faculty of Economics).

Fieber, Andreas (1999): *Pflegeversicherungssysteme im Vereinigten Königreich und in der Republik Irland*, Idstein: Schulz-Kirchner Verlag.

Fine, Michael (1998): Acute and Continuing Care for Older People in Australia: Contesting new Balances of Care, in: Glendinning, Caroline: Rights and Realities: *Comparing new Developments in Long-term Care for Older People*, Bristol: The Policy Press.

Fischer, Ingo (1992): *Staatliche Einkommenssicherung und Niedrigeinkommenshaushalte: Ein institutioneller und empirischer Vergleich für die USA, Großbritannien und die Bundesrepublik Deutschland*, Frankfurt: Campus Verlag.

French Decree No. 97-426 (2000): *Relatif aux Conditions et aux Modalités d'Attribution de la Prestation Spécifique Dépendance Instituée par la Loi n° 97-60 du 24 Janvier 1997.*

French Decree No. 97-427 (2000): *Fixant le Guide de l`Evaluation de la Personne Agée Dépendante.*

French Law No. 97-60 (2000): *Prestation Spécifique Dépendance (PSD).*

French Law No. 2001-647 (2001): *Allocation Personalisée d`Autonomie (APA).*

French Ministry of Employment and Solidarity (2001a): *Allocation Personnalisée d`Autonomie*, Paris.

French Ministry of Employment and Solidarity (2001b): *La Prestation Spécifique Dépendance au 31 mars 2001*, Paris.

French Ministry of Employment and Solidarity (2001c): *L`Allocation Personnalisée a l`Autonomie*, Paris.

French Ministry of Employment and Solidarity (2001d): *Vieillir en France Dignement: Un noveau Droit ouvert à Tous*, Paris.

French Ministry of Labour and Solidarity (1998): La Presentation Spécifique Dépendance, *Bimestrel d'Information Juridique du Ministère de L'Emploi et de la Solidarité*, No. 12, 01-02/1998, Paris.

Fries, J. (1980): Ageing, Natural Death and the Compression of Morbidity, *New England Journal of Medicine*, Vol. 303: pp. 130-135.

Gabanyi, Monika and May, Stefan and Schneider, Markus (1992): *Absicherung des Pflegerisikos am Beispiel ausgewählter Länder*, Bonn: German Ministry of Labour and Social Affairs.

Gabanyi, Monika (1995): *Die politische Willensbildung und der Aspekt der Qualitätssicherung in der ambulanten Pflege*, Augsburg (Thesis).

Garber, Alan M. (1996): To Comfort Always: The Prospects of Expanded Social Responsibility for Long-term Care, in: Fuchs, V.R.: *Individual and Social Responsibility*, Chicago: University Press.

Garg, Heinrich (1995): *Pflegebedürftigkeit als Gegenstand ökonomischer Sicherungspolitik*, Frankfurt am Main: Verlag Peter Lang.

German Care Insurance Act (2000): *Soziale Pflegeversicherung - SGB XI.*

German Federal Social Assistance Law (2000): *Bundessozialhilfegesetz - BSHG.*

German Ministry of Health (2000): *Fünf Jahre Pflegeversicherung - eine Zwischenbilanz*, Berlin.

German Ministry of Health (2001): *Entwurf eines Gesetzes zur Verbesserung für Pflegebedürftige mit erheblichem allgmeinem Betreuungsbedarf*, Berlin.

German Ministry of Health (2002a): *Leistungsempfänger der sozialen Pflegeversicherung am Jahresende nach Altersgruppen*, Berlin.

German Ministry of Health (2002b): *Leistungsempfänger der sozialen Pflegeversicherung*, Berlin.

German Ministry of Health (2002c): *Die Finanzentwicklung der sozialen Pflegeversicherung*, Berlin.

German Ministry of Labour and Social Affairs (1996): Long-term Care Insurance, *Social Policy Information*, Volume Z8473, Bonn.

German Ministry of Labour and Social Affairs (2000): *Sozialhilfe in Deutschland: Entwicklung und Strukturen*, Berlin.

German Pension Insurance Act (2000): *Gesetzliche Rentenversicherung - SGB VI.*

German Social Welfare Legislation - General Part (2000): *Sozialgesetzbuch – Allgemeiner Teil - SGB I.*

Gershuny, Jonathan (1983): *Social Innovation and the Division of Labour*, Oxford: Oxford University Press.

Giaoutzi, M (1991): Greece, in: Nijkamp, P. and Pacolet, J. and Spinnewyn, A. and Vollering, C. and Wilderom, S. and Winters, S.: *Services for the Elderly in Europe: A Cross-national Comparative Study*, Leuven: Higher Institute of Labour Studies.

Glendinning, Caroline (1998): *Rights and Realities: Comparing new Developments in Long-term Care for Older People*, Bristol: The Policy Press.

Gottschalk, P. and Wolfe, B. and Haveman, R. (1989): Health Care Financing in the USA, UK and Netherlands: Distributional Consequences, *Changes in Revenue Structures. Proceedings of the 42nd Congress of the International Institute of Public Finance* (1989), Athens.

Gottschalk, P. (1995): Housing and Supportive Services for Frail Elders in Denmark, in: Pynoos, Jon and Liebig Phoebe S.: *Housing Frail Elders. International Policies, Perspectives and Prospects*, London: John Hopkins University Press.

Grignon, Michel (2001): *'Private Correspondence`*, Strasbourg.

Gruenberg, E. (1977): The Failures of Success, in: *Milbank Memorial Fund Q55*: pp. 3-24.

Ham, Chris (1997): *Health Care Reform: Learning from International Experience*, Buckingham: Open University Press.

Hardy, B. and Wistow, G. (1999): The Development of Domiciliary Care: Mission Accomplished?, *Policy and Politics*, 27: pp. 173-186.

Hardy, B. and Wistow, G. (2000): Changes in the Private Sector, in: Hudson, Bob: *The changing Role of Social Care*, London: Jessica Kingsbey Publishers.

Hauser, Richard (1991): Probleme der vergleichenden Analyse von Systemen sozialer Sicherung - Drei Beispiele aus dem Bereich von Alterssicherung, *Theoretische Grundlagen der Sozialpolitik II*, Berlin.

Henrard, J.C. (2001): *'Private Correspondence`*, Strasbourg.

Henwood, Melanie (1999): *Home and Away: Reflections on Long-term Care in the UK and Australia*, University of New South Wales: Social Policy Research Centre.

Héritier, Adrienne (1996): The Accommodation of Diversity in European Policy-making and its Outcomes: Regulatory Policy as a Patchwork, *Journal of European public policy*, 3 (2): pp. 149-167.

Holt, Robert T. and Tarner, John E. (1970): *The Methodology of Comparative Research*, New York: Free Press.

House of Commons Social Services Committee (1985): *Community Care: With special Reference to Adult Mentally Ill and Mentally Handicapped People*, London: HMSO.

Hudson, Bob (2000): Conclusion: Modernising Social Services - a Blueprint for the new Millennium?, in: Hudson, Bob: *The changing Role of Social Care*, London: Jessica Kingsley Publishers.

Hugman, Richard (1994): *Ageing and the Care of Older People in Europe*, New York: St. Martin's Press.

Hurst, Jeremy (1994): The NHS Reforms in an International Context, in: Culyer, A.J. and Wagstaff, Adam: *Reforming Health Care Systems*, Cheltenham: Edward Elgar Publishing Limited.

Hutten, Jack B.F (1996a): Home Care in Finland, in: Hutten, Jack B.F. and Kerkstra, Ada: *Home Care in Europe: A Country-specific Guide to its Organisation and Financing*, Aldershot: Ashgate Publishing Limited.

Hutten, Jack B.F (1996b): Home Care in Italy, in: Hutten, Jack B.F. and Kerkstra, Ada: *Home Care in Europe: A Country-specific Guide to its Organisation and Financing*, Aldershot: Ashgate Publishing Limited.

Hutten, Jack B.F (1996c): Home Care in Portugal, in: Hutten, Jack B.F. and Kerkstra, Ada: *Home Care in Europe: A Country-specific Guide to its Organisation and Financing*, Aldershot: Ashgate Publishing Limited.

Hutten, Jack B.F (1996d): Home Care in Belgium, in: Hutten, Jack B.F. and Kerkstra, Ada: *Home Care in Europe: A Country-specific Guide to its Organisation and Financing*, Aldershot: Ashgate Publishing Limited.

Hutten, Jack B.F (1996e): Home Care in the United Kingdom, in: Hutten, Jack B.F. and Kerkstra, Ada: *Home Care in Europe: A Country-specific Guide to its Organisation and Financing*, Aldershot: Ashgate Publishing Limited.

Hutten, Jack B.F. and Kerkstra, Ada (1996): *Home Care in Europe: A Country-specific Guide to its Organisation and Financing*, Aldershot: Ashgate Publishing Limited.

Igl, Gerhard and Stadelmann, Falk (1998): Die Pflegeversicherung in Deutschland, in Sieveking, Klaus: *Soziale Sicherung bei Pflegebedürftigkeit in der Europäischen Union*, Baden-Baden: Nomos Verlagsgesellschaft.

Jamieson, Anne (1991): *Home Care for Older People in Europe: A Comparison of Policies and Practices*, Oxford: Oxford University Press.

Jani-Le Bris, Hannelore (1993): *Family Care of Older People in the European Community*, Dublin: European Foundation for the Improvement of Living and Working Conditions.

Johnson, P. and Falkingham, J. (1992): *Ageing and Economic Welfare*, London: Sage.

Joffe, Joel and Lipsey, David (1999): Note of Dissent, in: Royal Commission on Long-term Care: *With Respect to Old Age: Long-term Care - Rights and Responsibilities*, London: HMSO.

Jordan, Erwin (2000): *Die Situation von dementiell Erkrankten - Perspektiven der Pflegeversicherung*, Berlin: German Ministry of Health.

Joseph Rowntree Foundation (1996): *Meeting the Costs of Continuing Care: Report and Recommendations*, York.

Katz, S and Ford, A.B. and Moskowitz, R.W. and Jackson, B.A. and Jaffe, M.W. (1963): Studies of Illness in the Aged: The Index of ADL: A Standardised Measure of Biological and Psychosocial Function, *Journal of the American Medical Association*, 185, pp. 914-919.

Kaufmann, Otto (1997): Frankreichs solidarische Sécurité Sociale in der Krise, in: von Maydell, Bernd: Die Krise des Sozialstaats in internationals Perspektive - Denkanstöße für Deuschland -, *Sozialer Fortschritt*, 46 (1, 2): pp. 4-8.

Kemeny, Jim (1995): Theories of Power in the three Worlds of Welfare Capitalism, *Journal of European Social Policy*, 5 (2): pp. 88-105.

Kerschen, Nicole (1998): Die neue spezifische Pflegeleistung in Frankreich, in Sieveking, Klaus: *Soziale Sicherung bei Pflegebedürftigkeit in der Europäischen Union*, Baden-Baden: Nomos Verlagsgesellschaft.

King, Anna (1993): *Older People across the EC: Similarities and Differences*, London: Centre for Policy on Ageing.

Knapp, Martin (1984): *The Economics of Social Care*, London: Macmillan Publishers Limited.

Knapp, Martin and Hardy, Brian and Forder, Julien (2001): Commissioning for Quality: Ten Years of Social Care Markets in England, *Journal of Social Policy*, 30 (2): pp. 283-306.

Knauth, B. (1993): *Statistical Portrait of Older People, in: Social Europe 1/93*, Commission of the European Communities, Brussels.

Köhler, Gabriele (1992): Methodik und Problematik einer mehrstufigen Expertenbefragung, in: Hoffmeyer-Zlotnik, Jürgen H.P.: *Analyse verbaler Daten. Über den Umgang mit qualitativen Daten*, Opladen: Westdeutscher Verlag.

Köstler, Ursula (1996a): *Nach deutschem Vorbild? Die geplante Pflegeversicherung in Luxemburg,* Frankfurt am Main: Johann Wolfgang Goethe-University (Faculty of Economics).

Köstler, Ursula, (1996b): Frankreich verschiebt die Einführung einer Pflegebeihilfe für ältere Menschen auf 1997, *Unabhängige Zeitschrift für Sozialpolitik*, 45 (6): pp. 145-150.

Köstler, Ursula, (1996c): Frankreich diskutiert die Einführung einer Pflegebeihilfe für alte Menschen, *Soziale Sicherheit*, 45 (3): pp 109-111.

Köstler, Ursula (1997a): Luxemburg wird 1998 eine soziale Pflegeversicherung einführen, *Unabhängige Zeitschrift für Sozialpolitik*, 46 (9, 10): pp. 238-240.

Köstler, Ursula (1997b): *Pflegeversicherung in Frankreich*, Frankfurt am Main: Johann Wolfgang Goethe-University (Faculty of Economics).

Kokot, Stefan (1997): *Probleme der sozialen Sicherungssysteme im Europäischen Integrationsprozeß*, Frankfurt am Main: Johann Wolfgang Goethe-University (Faculty of Economics).

Korpi, Walter (1983): *The Democratic Class Struggle*, London: Routledge & Kegan Paul.

Kratz, Charlotte R. and Simpson, H. Marjorie (1980): *Care of the Long-term Sick in the Community*, Edinburgh: Churchill Livingstone.

Laing, William and Saper, Paul (1999): Promoting the Development of a Flourishing Independent Sector alongside Good Quality Public Services, in: Royal Commission on Long-term Care: *With Respect to Old Age: Long-term Care - Rights and Responsibilities, Research Volume 3*, London: HMSO.

Lamnek, Siegfried (1989): *Qualitative Sozialforschung (BD. 2): Methoden und Techniken*, München: Psychologie Verlags Union.

Leibfried, S. (1993): Towards a European Welfare State?, in: Jones, C.: *New Perspectives on the Welfare State in Europe*, London: Routledge.

Leichter, Howard M. (1979): *A Comparative Approach to Policy Analysis: Health Care Policy in four Nations*, Cambridge: University Press.

London Borough of Camden (2002): *The Development of a Mental Health and Social Care Trust for Camden and Islington: The Report of the Mental Health and Social Care Trust Scrutiny Panel*, Camden.

Lund Pederson, Lone (1998): Health and Social Care for Older People in Denmark: A Public Solution and Threat?, in: Glendinning, Caroline: *Rights and Realities: Comparing new Developments in Long-term Care for Older People*, Bristol: The Policy Press.

Luxembourg Ministry of Social Security (1995): *La Dépandance au Luxembourg, Analyse de l'Existant et Concept pour l'Avenir*, Luxembourg.

Luxembourg Ministry of Social Security (1998): *Long-term Care Insurance*, Luxembourg.

Lynch, Fergal (1998): Health Funding and Expenditure in Ireland, in: McAuliffe, E. and Joyce, L.: *A healthier Future? Managing Health Care in Ireland*, Dublin: IPA.

Mahoney, F.I. and Barthel, D.W. (1965): Functional Evaluation: The Barthel Index, *Maryland State Medical Journal*, 14: pp. 61-65.

Manton, K.G. (1982): Changing Concepts of Morbidity and Mortality in the Elderly Population, *Milbank Memorial Fund Q60*: pp. 133-224.

Martin, Claude (2001): *National Profile: The 'Specific Dependency Benefit` and its Effects on Women Carers*, University of Rennes: CNRS Unit.

Maynard, Alan (1975): *Health Care in the European Community*, London: Croom Helm.

McDowell, I. and Newell, C. (1987): *Measuring Health: A guide to rating Scales and Questionnaires*, New York: Oxford University Press.

McKie, John and Richardson, Jeff and Singer, Peter and Kuhse, Helga (1998): *The Allocation of Health Care Resources*, Aldershot: Dartmouth.

Meier, Volker (1995): *Conflicts on Care for the Elderly, Long-term Care Insurance, and Bequests*, University of Halle: Department of Economics.

Meinolf, Dierkes and Weiler, Hans N. and Antal, Ariane Berthoin (1987): *Comparative Policy Research: Learning from Experience*, Aldershot: Gower.

Merton, Robert K. and Fiske, Marjorie and Kendall, Patricia L. (1956): *The Focussed Interview: A Manual of Problems and Procedures*, Glencoe: The Free Press.

Meuser, Michael and Nagel, Ulrike (1997): Das ExpertInneninterview - Wissenssoziologische Voraussetzungen und methodische Durchführung, in: Fiebertshäuser, Barbara and Prengel Annedore: *Handbuch Qualitativer Forschungsmethoden in der Erziehungswissenschaft*, Weinheim: Fiebertshäuser and Prengel.

Mishra, Ramesh (1990): *The Welfare State in Capitalist Society: Policies of Retrenchment and Maintenance in Europe, North America and Australia*, London: Harvester Wheatsheaf.

Mossialos, Elias and Dixon, Anna and Figueras, Josep and Kutzin, Joe (2002): *Funding Health Care: Options for Europe*, Buckingham: Open University Press.

Mossialos, Elias and Dixon, Anna (2002): Funding Health Care in Europe: Weighing up the Options, in: Mossialos, Elias and Dixon, Anna and Figueras, Josep and Kutzin, Joe: *Funding Health Care: Options for Europe*, Buckingham: Open University Press.

National Health Service Executive Communications Unit (1996): *A guide to the National Health Service*, London.

Nijkamp, Peter and Pacolet, Jozef and Spinnewyn, Hilde and Vollering, Ans and Wilderom, Celeste and Winters, Sien (1991): *Services for the Elderly in Europe: A Cross-national Comparative Study*, Leuven: Higher Institute of Labour Studies.

O'Connor, J.S. (1993): Gender, Class and Citizenship in the Comparative Analyses of Welfare State Regimes: The Theoretical and Methodological Issues, *The British Journal of Sociology* 44 (3): pp. 501-518.

OECD (1988): *Social Policy Studies: Ageing Populations: The Social Policy Implications*, Paris.

OECD (1994a): *Social Policy Studies No. 12: New Orientations for Social Policy*, Paris.

OECD (1994b): *Social Policy Studies No. 14: Caring for Frail Elderly People: New Directions in Care*, Paris.

OECD (1996a): *Social Policy Studies No. 19: Caring for Frail Elderly People: Policies in Evolution*, Paris.

OECD (1996b): *Social Policy Studies No. 20: Ageing in OECD Countries: A critical Policy Challenge*, Paris.

OECD (1998): *Social and Health Policies in OECD Countries: A Survey of current Programmes and recent Developments*, Paris.

Österle, August (1999): *Equity and Long-term Care Policies: A Framework for the Comparative Analysis*, Florence: European University Institute.

Orloff, A. S. (1993): Gender and the Social Rights of Citizenship: The Comparative Analyses of Gender Relations and Welfare States, *American Sociological Review*, 58 (3): pp. 303-328.

O'Sullivan, Tim (1998): Changing Relationships and the Voluntary and Statutory Sectors, in: McAuliffe, E. and Joyce, L.: *A healthier Future? Managing Health Care in Ireland*, Dublin: IPA.

Pacolet, Jozef and Wilderom, Celeste (1991): *The Economics of Care of the Elderly*, Aldershot: Avebury.

Parker, G. (1992): Counting Care: Numbers and Types of Informal Carers, in: Twigg, Julia: *Carers: Research and Practice*, London: HMSO.

Pauly, Marc V. (1996): Almost Optimal Social Insurance for Long-term Care, in: Eisen, Roland and Sloan, Frank A.: *Long-term Care: Economic Issues and Policy Solutions*, Norwell (Massachusetts): Kluwer Academic Publishers.

Petch, A (2000): The Changing Role of Social Care: UK Variations, in: Hudson, Bob: *The Changing Role of Social Care*, London: Jessica Kingsley Publishers.

Pfaff and Nagel (1994): Health Care Systems in Countries of the European Community, *Das Gesundheitswesen*, 56 (2): pp. 57-116.

Pijl, Marja (1998): A Report from France, in: Weekers, Sykvia and Pijl Marja: *Home Care and Care Allowances in the European Union*, Utrecht: NIZW.

Plute, Gerhard (1996): Das Risiko der Pflegebedürftigkeit: Europäische Modelle,: *AOK-Bundesverband*, (8).

Ritter, Ulrich Peter (1995): *Some Basic Considerations and Methodological Decisions in Comparative Research*, Frankfurt am Main: Johann Wolfgang Goethe-University (Faculty of Economics).

Ritter, Ulrich (1997): *Vergleichende Volkswirtschaftslehre*, München: R. Oldenbourg Verlag.

Rivlin, A.M. and Wiener, J.M. (1988): *Caring for the Disabled Elderly*, Washington (D.C.): The Brooking Institution.

Rose, Richard (1985): *The States Contribution to the Welfare Mix*, University of Strathclyde: Studies in Public Policy No. 140.

Rostgaard, Tine and Fridberg, Torben (1998): *Caring for Children and Older People: A Comparison of European Policies and Practices*, Copenhagen: The Danish National Institute of Social Research.

Royal Commission on Long-term Care (1999): *With Respect to Old Age: Long-term Care - Rights and Responsibilities*, London: HMSO.

Rubin, R. and Mendelson, D. (1995): A Framework for Cost Sharing Policy Analysis, in: Mattison, N.: *Sharing the Costs of Health: A Multi-country Perspective*, Basel: Pharmaceutical Partners for Better Healthcare.

Saltman, Richard B. and Figueras, Josep (1997): *European Health Care Reform: Analysis of current Strategies*, Copenhagen: WHO Regional Publications.

Saltman, Richard B. and Figueras, Josep and Sakellaridis, Constantino (1998): *Critical Challenges for Health Care Reform in Europe*, Buckingham: Open University Press.

Salvage, Ann V. (1995): *Who will care? Future Prospects for Family Care of Older People in the European Union*, Shankill: European Foundation for the Improvement of Living and Working Conditions.

Scharf, Thomas and Wenger, G. Clare (1995): *International Perspectives on Community Care for Older People*, Aldershot: Avebury.

Schmähl, Winfried (1992): *Zum Vergleich von Umlageverfahren und kapitalfundierten Verfahren zur Finanzierung einer Pflegeversicherung in der Bundesrepublik Deutschland*, Stuttgart: Verlag W. Kohlhammer.

Schmähl, Winfried (1999): *Pflegeversicherung in Deutschland: Finanzbedarf und Finanzverflechtung. Empirische Befunde und offene Fragen*, University of Bremen: Social Policy Unit.

Schmidt, Michael (1995): *Guter Rat zur Pflegeversicherung*, München: Verlag C.H. Beck.

Schneider, M. and Dennerlein, R.K.H. and Köse, A. and Scholtes, L. (1992): Health Care in the EC Member States: Health Policy special issue, *Health Policy*, (1,2): pp. 113-123.

Schneider, Ulrike (1999): Die soziale Pflegeversicherung in Deutschland: Gestaltung, Implementierung und erste Bewertung, *Internationale Revue für Soziale Sicherheit*, (2): pp. 37-89.

Schrijvers, A.J.P. (1997): *Health and Health Care in the Netherlands*, Utrecht: De Tijdstroom.

Schütze, Fritz (1977): *Die Technik des Narrativen Interviews in Interaktionsfeldstudien - dargestellt an einem Projekt zur Erforschung von kommunalen Machtstrukturen*, University of Bielefeld: Faculty of Sociology.

Schulze, Hans-Joachim and Wirth, Wolfgang (1996): *Who cares? Social Service Organisations and their Users*, London: Cassell.

Schumacher, Christoph (1998): Pflegeversicherung und Leistungsexport - Gemeinschaftsrechtliche Zuordnung, in: Sieveking, Klaus: *Soziale Sicherung bei Pflegebedürftigkeit in der Europäischen Union*, Baden-Baden: Nomos Verlagsgesellschaft.

Spynnewin, Hilde (1991): France, in: Nijkamp, P. et al.: *Proceedings of a Seminar on national Diversity and European Trends in Services for the Elderly*, Leuven: Higher Institute of Labour Studies.

Stake, Robert E. (1995): The Art of Case Study Research, *London: Sage Publications Limited.*

Swedish National Board of Health and Welfare (1993): *Health Care and Social Services in seven European Countries*, Stockholm.

Swiss Federal Office of Social Insurance (1997): *Sicherung und Finanzierung von Pflege- und Betreuungsleistungen bei Pflegebedürftigkeit*, Bern.

Taylor-Gooby, Peter (1991): Welfare State Regimes and Welfare Citizenship, *Journal of European Social Policy*, 1 (2): pp. 93-105.

Tinker, Anthea (1984): *Staying at Home: Helping elderly People*, London.

Tinker, Anthea and McCreadie, Claudine and Wright, Fay and Salvage, Ann V. (1994): *The Care of Frail Elderly People in the United Kingdom*, London: HMSO.

Titmuss, Richard M. (1958): *Essays on the Welfare State*, London: Allen and Unwin Limited.

Titmuss, Richard M. (1964): *Commitment to Welfare*, London: Allen and Unwin Limited.

Titmuss, Richard M. (1970): *The Gift Relationship: From Human Blood to Social Policy*, London: Allen and Unwin Limited.

UK Department of Social Security (1997): *Non-contributory Benefits for Disabled People*, London.

UK Department of Social Security (2000a): *The Basic State Retirement Pension*, London.

UK Department of Social Security (2000b): *The State Earnings Related Pension Scheme*, London.

UK Department of Social Security (2000c): *Jobseeker's Allowance*, London.

UK Department of Social Security (2000d): *Statutory Sick Pay*, London.

UK Department of Social Security (2000e): *Maternity Allowance*, London.

UK Department of Social Security (2000f): *Benefits Agency Regions*, London.

UK Department of Social Security (2000g): *Attendance Allowance*, London.

UK Department of Social Security (2000h): *Invalid Care Allowance*, London.

Van der Linden, B.A. and van Dam, Y. (1997): Home Care, in: Schrijvers, A.J.P: *Health and Health Care in the Netherlands*, Utrecht: *De Tijdstroom*.

Verheij, Robert A (1996): Home Care in France, in: Hutten, Jack B.F. and Kerkstra, Ada: *Home Care in Europe: A Country-specific Guide to its Organisation and Financing*, Aldershot: Ashgate Publishing Limited.

Vollering, J.M.C. (1991): *Care Services for the Elderly in the Netherlands: the Package Model*, Amsterdam: Tinbergen Institute.

Vollmer, Rudolf J. (2000): *Long-term Care Insurance in Germany*, Berlin: German Ministry of Health.

Wagstaff, A. and Van Doorslaer, E. and Van der Burg, H. (1999): Equity in the Finance of Health Care: Some further International Comparisons, *Journal of Health Economics*, 18: pp. 263-290.

Walker, Alan (1993): *Older People in Europe: Social Integration*, Brussels: Commission of the European Communities.

Walker, Alan and Maltby, Tony (1997): *Ageing Europe*, Buckingham: Open University Press.

Warwick, Donald P. and Osherson, Samuel (1973): *Comparative Research Methods*, Englewood Cliffs (New Jersey): Prentice-Hall.

Whitehead, M. (1994): Is it fair? Evaluating the Equity Implications of the NHS Reforms, in: Robinson, R. and Le Grand, J.: *Evaluating the NHS Reforms*, London: King's Fund Institute.

Wiegele, Britta (1994): Leistungsstrukturen der ambulanten Dienste in Niederösterreich - eine Bestandsanalyse, in: Amann, Anton and Kneusel, Madeleine and Wiegele, Britta: *Anspruchs- und Effizienzanalyse der Hauskrankenpflege in Niederösterreich*, Krems: Niederösterreichische Landesregierung.

Wiener, Joshua M. and Illston, Laurel Hixon and Hanley, Raymond J. (1994): *Sharing the Burden: Strategies for Public and Private Long-term Care Insurance*, Washington (D.C.): The Brookings Institution.

Williams, E. Idris (1989): *Caring for Elderly People in the Community*, London: Chapman and Hall.

Winters, Stephan (1994): Fossil oder Vorbild? Gesetzliche Pflegeversicherung in den Niederlanden, *Arbeit und Sozialpolitik*, 48 (11, 12): pp. 10-18.

Wittenberg, Raphael and Sandhu, Becky and Knapp, Martin (2002): Funding Long-term Care: the Public and Private Options, in: Mossialos, Elias and Dixon, Anna and Figueras, Josep and Kutzin, Joe: *Funding Health Care: Options for Europe*, Buckingham: Open University Press.

Witzel, Andreas (1982): *Verfahren der qualitativen Sozialforschung: Überblick und Alternativen*, Franfurt am Main: Campus.

Yin, Robert K. (1984): *Case Study Research: Design and Methods*, London: Sage Publications.

Zuleeg, Manfred (1998): Die Einwirkungen des Europäischen Gemeinschaftsrechts auf die deutsche Pflegeversicherung, in: Sieveking, Klaus: *Soziale Sicherung bei Pflegebedürftigkeit in der Europäischen Union*, Baden-Baden: Nomos Verlagsgesellschaft.

Appendices

Appendix A Exchange rates

1 Euro =	340,75 Greek Drachma
13,7603 Austrian Schillings	0,787564 Irish Pounds
40,3399 Belgian Francs	1936,27 Italian Lira
7,4628 Danish Crowns	40,3399 Luxembourg Francs
2,20371 Dutch Guilders	200,482 Portuguese Escudos
5,94573 Finnish Marks	166,386 Spanish Pesetas
6,55957 French Francs	8,8369 Swedish Crowns
1,95583 German Marks	0,6233 British Pounds

Appendix B Experts involved in the interview procedure

Key stakeholders from France with a scientific background		
Surname, First name	**Position**	**Organisation**
Grignon, Michel	Research Director	Centre de Recherche D`Etude et de Documentation en Economie de la Sante ('CREDES`), Paris
Henrard, Jean-Claude	Professor of Epidemiologie and Health Economy	University of Paris V (René Descartes), Faculty of Medicine
Kerschen, Nicole	Lecturer and Researcher	University of Paris X (Nanterre), Institute of Juridical Research on Business and Professional Relationship, National Centre for Scientific Research
Kessler, Francis	Lecturer and Researcher	University of Paris I (Panthéon Sorbonne), AES et Droit Sociale
Martin, Claude	Senior Researcher of Social Policy, Family Policy and Welfare St.	University of Rennes I, CNRS
Key stakeholders from France with a practical background		
Surname, First name	**Position**	**Organisation**
Bastian, Emanuel	Deputy Head of Department	Départment du Bas Rhin, Conseil Généraux, Department of Income Support Services and Long-term Care Payments, Strasbourg
Beraud, Phillippe	Head of Department	Caisse Primaires d`Assurance Maladie de Hagenau, Department of Legislation and Documentation
Faessel, Alfred	Former Director	French Society of Gerontology, Paris
Lavogiez, Gerard	Director	Association Bas-Rhinoise d`Aide aux Personnes Agées ('ABRAPA`), Strasbourg
Verny, Emanuel	General Director	Union Nationale des Associations de Soins et de Services à Domicile ('UNASSAD`), Paris

Appendix B cont.

Key stakeholders from Germany with a scientific background		
Surname, First name	**Position**	**Organisation**
Brandenburg, Hermann	Professor of Gerontology and Care Sciences	Catholic University of Applied Sciences Freiburg, Faculty of Care
Busch, Susanne	Professor of Health- and Social Management	University of Applied Sciences Hamburg, Faculty of Social Education
Burk, Rainer	Professor of Health Management	University of Applied Sciences Neu-Ulm, Faculty of Health Management
Klie, Thomas	Professor of Law	Protestant University of Applied Sciences Freiburg, Faculty of Social Work
Schneider, Markus	Managing Director	Beratungsgesellschaft für Angewandte Systemforschung ('BASYS'), Augsburg
Key stakeholders from Germany with a practical background		
Surname, First name	**Position**	**Organisation**
Wetzel, Ursula	Consultant of Old People's Welfare	Caritas Bundesverband, Department of Social Affairs and Health, Freiburg
Kesselheim, Harald	Head of Department	Allgemeine Ortskrankenkasse ('AOK') Bundesverband, Department of Care, Bonn
Schmitz, Elmar	Head of Department	Arbeiterwohlfahrt ('AWO') Bundesverband, Department of Old People's Welfare and Long-term Care Insurance, Bonn
Schulz, Michael	General Manager	Verband Deutscher Alten- und Behindertenhilfe ('VDAB'), Essen
Westphal, Wilfried	Head of Department	Deutsche Angestellten Krankenkasse ('DAK') - Hauptgeschäftsstelle, Department of Care, Hamburg

Appendix B cont.

Key stakeholders from the United Kingdom with a scientific background		
Surname, First name	**Position**	**Organisation**
Davies, Bleddyn	Professor of Social Policy	University of Kent, School of Social Policy, Sociology and Social Research
Glendinning, Caroline	Senior Research Fellow in Social Policy	University of Manchester, National Primary Care Research and Development Centre
Parker, Gillian	Professor of Community Care	University of Leicester, Nuffield Community Care Studies Unit
Ungerson, Clare	Professor of Social Policy	University of Southampton, Faculty of Sociology and Social Policy
Walker, Alan	Professor of Social Policy	University of Sheffield, Department of Sociological Studies
Key stakeholders from the United Kingdom with a practical background		
Surname, First name	**Position**	**Organisation**
Eaton, Genie	General Manager	Brant Care at Home, London
Henwood, Melanie	Health and Social Care Consultant	Independent, Heathencote
Holzhausen, Emily	Public Affairs Manager	Carers National Association, London
O'Leary, Brian	Chief Community Care Commissioning Officer	Wolverhampton Council
Weeks, Simon	Policy Lead on Services for Older People	Local Government Association, Department of Social Affairs, Health and Housing, London